BUCKET
~ TO ~
GREECE

Volume 15

V.D. BUCKET

Copyright © 2022 V.D. Bucket
All rights reserved.

No part of this publication may be reproduced, distributed, or transmitted in any form or by any means, including photocopying, recording, or other electronic or mechanical methods, without the prior written permission of the publisher, except in the case of brief quotations embodied in critical reviews and certain other noncommercial uses permitted by copyright law.

All names have been changed to spare my wife embarrassment.

Editor: James Scraper
Proofreader: Alan Wood
Cover Designer: German Creative
Interior Formatting: The Book Khaleesi

Other Books in the Bucket to Greece Series

Bucket to Greece Volume 1

Bucket to Greece Volume 2

Bucket to Greece Volume 3

Bucket to Greece Volume 4

Bucket to Greece Volume 5

Bucket to Greece Volume 6

Bucket to Greece Volume 7

Bucket to Greece Volume 8

Bucket to Greece Volume 9

Bucket to Greece Volume 10

Bucket to Greece Volume 11

Bucket to Greece Volume 12

Bucket to Greece Volume 13

Bucket to Greece Volume 14

Bucket to Greece Collection Vols 1-3

Bucket to Greece Collection Vols 4-6

Bucket to Greece Collection Vols 7-9

Bucket to Greece Collection Vols 10-12

Chapter 1

The Time Warp Kafenio

Loosening my tie, I used it to mop up the beads of sweat trickling down my forehead. Even in the mountainous village of Meli, there was no respite from the scorching heat of August. Combined with the relentless humidity, the sweltering temperature created an unpleasantly sticky sensation. It was so hot that even the supine cat sprawled out by my feet appeared to be drenched in a sweaty glow.

Checking my watch, I cursed Barry for his tardiness. If he didn't show up within the next ten minutes, I would be tempted to stand him up and head home to join Marigold. I had left my wife sprawled out on the bed in a pool of perspiration, under the cooling blast of the air conditioner. Despite my many vocal reservations about installing the unit due to the risk of it harbouring germs, mould and other unhygienic nasties, I would happily eat humble pie in order to wallow at my wife's side in the artificial cold breeze.

Glancing around the *kafenio*, I felt as though I was in a time warp, the setting seemingly perfectly preserved from half-a-century ago. Large open windows gave the space a sense of airiness that was at odds with the low wooden ceiling and the drab and dingy brown linoleum floor covering; it was difficult to discern if the latter was patterned or simply exhibited a myriad of suspect stains amassed over time. A particular rusty looking red patch in one corner fired up my imagination; it wouldn't surprise me to hear that a murdered *kafenio* customer had been left to decompose there, ages ago.

A high wooden counter in one corner of the room delineated the kitchen area, dominated by an old shallow trough style sink and an obsolete double hotplate fired by an enormous cylinder of bottled gas. Tiny coffee cups, copper *brikis* and tall water glasses lined the open kitchen shelves alongside miniature bottles of *ouzo*, *tsipouro* and *raki*. Bizarrely, a battered old barber's chair occupied the opposite corner and a single camp bed made up with a blanket was shoved against the wall housing the doorway leading through to the *apothiki*. The rest of the space was given over to eight wooden tables surrounded by uncomfortable rush mat chairs, the latter spruced up with a fresh coat of traditional Greek blue paint. The stains on my slacks could personally testify that the lick of paint was exceedingly fresh.

The somewhat saggy and cat mauled rattan hinted that the seats had long ago lost a fight with felines sharpening their claws; the chairs could hardly be guaranteed to bear the weight of a well-padded posterior. The ancient cast iron *somba* in the centre of the room appeared a tad superfluous to requirements since there would be no need of the wood burner before winter. A row of small tables lined the wall outside; with no shade on offer, they appeared as redundant as the *somba*.

I reflected that it had been a stroke of genius on Spiros' part to suggest to the two warring brothers, Christos and Manolis, that they bury their differences and reopen the *kafenio* that their grandfather had established in the ground floor of the house they had gone on to jointly inherit. Both brothers had fond remembrances of the bustling *kafenio* of their childhood before they had emigrated to the States as young men in the late sixties.

Although the *kafenio* doors had been closed for more than three decades, Spiros used his powers of persuasion to convince the brothers that were they to fling the doors open once again, it would add new purpose to their days and bring in some extra cash. Keen on the idea, they had buried their differences and called a tentative truce. Whilst I had never considered Meli lacking, the village men had sorely felt the lack of a local *kafenio* and were apparently overjoyed at the prospect of their old watering hole in the village being revived.

Unfortunately, I had missed the festivities of the grand opening the day before since I had been repping on Pegasus. I was surprised to find myself the sole customer on this, only the second morning of business. Sited on a steep side road leading off from the village square, I supposed it was a little too out of the way to attract any passing trade, though word of mouth meant everyone in the village was already in the know. Since the *kafenio* offered spectacular sea views, I thought it should be a hit with any passing tourists straying away from the beaten path in their quest to discover the quintessence of Greece.

Christos and Manolis had both extended a personal invitation for me to join them, along with Barry, promising our first coffees were on the house. Significantly, the invitation had excluded our spouses, hinting that the brothers intended to stick to the dated tradition of running a male only *kafenio*. It struck me as a little short-sighted to exclude the fairer sex. If they intended to turn the business into a profitable venture, it was hardly the brightest move to potentially offend the women of the village by making it clear their custom wasn't wanted. They could kiss goodbye to any potentially lucrative tourist trade if they insisted on welcoming only men.

The screech of brakes announced the arrival of my brother-in-law. As Barry alighted from the builder's van, I was shocked to observe he appeared to have aged a good decade, his hair having turned prematurely grey in the couple of days since I had last seen him. Perchance he had been secretly applying the Grecian 2000 and had run out of supplies of the colour restoring lotion.

Bounding around to the passenger door, Barry gallantly offered Violet Burke a hand to descend. Taken aback by my mother's presence, I assumed she must have twisted Barry's arm and invited herself along on our coffee date; she did have form after all, having gate-crashed our second honeymoon. Although I am not a gambling man, I would put odds on Violet Burke making mincemeat of the two brothers if they attempted to ban her.

V.D. BUCKET

Standing up to greet my mother, I said, "I'd no idea you were joining us."

"Do I look like I've got time to be sitting around on my backside supping coffee? I'm here to see that Manolis fella. Doreen told me that he's in desperate need of my cleaning services. She reckons he's up for paying over the odds."

"It looks as though someone may have beat you to it," I said. Glancing around the *kafenio*, I was impressed by the level of cleanliness. As I spoke, Barry ran his fingers through his hair, dislodging a thick layer of plaster dust. The effect was instantaneous, Barry immediately shedding ten years by losing the grey.

"You need your eyes testing, lad. Look at all the muck that needs mopping up off this lino," Vi cackled, pointing to the layer of plaster dust now tarnishing the previously clean floor, courtesy of Barry. "Is that Manolis about?"

"I've been here for a good ten minutes and have seen neither hide nor hair of Manolis or his brother. That door at the back leads through to the *apothiki*. You might find one of them in there," I suggested.

"'Appen I'll find a mop bucket in there if nowt else," Vi said. Striding off with a determined expression on her face, she added a parting shot. "'Appen you should rub a bit of turps on your backside, lad. Fancy you being daft enough to sit in wet paint."

"You've got to admire her, taking on yet another cleaning job at her age," Barry said, the look of respect on his face indicating his words were genuine rather than a load of old flannel.

No sooner had my mother ventured through the door to the *apothiki*, than Christos emerged. Clad in an open necked shirt sporting visible sweat patches beneath his armpits, a gold medallion nestled in his chest hair; with his luscious moustache oiled and coiled, he was the picture of a sleazy Lothario. I hoped he intended to apron up before making our coffee. The last thing I wanted was a beverage topped with floating chest hairs. The short and stocky Greek had rather obviously applied a generous slather of black boot polish to his hair, clearly unfamiliar with the old adage that less is more; fortunately, it wasn't the rainy season.

Laden down with wooden boxes of *tavli* and a stack of framed photographs, our host nodded in greeting; grasping a set of nails between his teeth, he was unable to speak. Depositing the *tavli* sets and photographs on a wide window sill which served to emphasise the depth of the walls, Christos retrieved a hammer from his pocket and started banging a nail into the wall. Clumps of plaster immediately joined the plaster dust from Barry's hair.

"Do you need a hand there, Christo?" Barry offered.

"Careful, he's liable to swallow a nail if he attempts to answer you," I cautioned. I certainly didn't relish the prospect of my mother administering her own unique version of the Heimlich Maneuver on another unsuspecting victim. Although there was no love lost between Christos and myself, I wouldn't wish a set of broken ribs on the fellow; well, not unless he started making suggestive overtures towards my wife again.

Sauntering over to the stack of photographs, I leafed through the frames, fascinated to see the black and white sepia pictures depicted the *kafenio* in olden days. The original host was not only apparent since he appeared in most of the photos, but because he bore a striking resemblance to his grandsons, his moustache even more prominently luxuriant than the facial hair they boasted. One particular photograph of a strikingly handsome young man caught my eye; there was something familiar about him. "Oh, my goodness, look at this, Barry. This must have been Nikos in his youth."

Passing the photographs to Christos, he hung them from the newly hammered nails. "They add the character, yes?"

"They certainly do. These fellas look familiar,"

Barry said in a questioning tone.

"It is the four brothers," Christos replied. "They must to look the familiar because they are the father and uncles of the Spiros."

Staring at the picture, I recognised the young Leo, the only one of Spiros' uncles that had still been alive when we moved to Meli.

"You would have fitted right in, Victor. Look, they're all kitted out in ties," Barry observed.

Curious to see a picture of the man who had previously lived in my house before plunging to his death from the roof, I asked Christos, "Which one is Petros?"

The slam of a door as Christos returned to the *apothiki* was the only response.

"I don't reckon much to the service in here," Barry moaned. "At this rate, I'll have to take my coffee to go. I've left Blat on the job."

Christos returned momentarily, cradling a *bouzouki*. In no time at all the stringed instrument took pride of place, hanging crookedly from a nail on the wall.

"Do you play it?" I asked.

Tipping his head backwards, Christos clucked his tongue in the typical Greek way of saying no.

Rolling his eyes, Barry called out, "Any chance of a couple of coffees?"

Shrugging, Christos replied, "I work this

evening. Manolis is to make the coffee this morning. He is in the toilet with the old English woman."

"That would be my mother," I reminded him.

"I call him to make coffee." Striding away, Christos stopped in his tracks. "Victor, you must to bring your lovely wife next time."

"I got the impression that you were running this place as a male only establishment," I said, keen to keep some distance between Christos and Marigold.

"I will to make the exception for your beautiful wife." There was a lascivious look in Christos' eyes as he gleefully rubbed his hands together before disappearing into the *apothiki* again. Despite the evident thickness of the walls, we could hear Christos hollering for his brother to come and serve.

Looking a tad frazzled, Manolis appeared. "Victor, your mother to drive the hard bargain. She have agree to clean the *kafenio* six mornings and to do upstairs one day the week."

"So, presumably that's another woman you're prepared to welcome," Barry chortled.

"Christos and I have the dilemma." Scratching the back of his neck, Manolis sighed heavily. "We know the most of the regular clientele will be the old men who expect the traditional *kafenio* to be the place to escape their womenfolk…but we need all the custom we can get…"

BUCKET TO GREECE (VOL.15)

"It seems that tradition is rather at odds with good business sense," I posited.

"Back in my grandfather day, the woman would gather and sit on the steps across the street. They not want to join their husband. We decide that at first, we must to make the local men to think it is the men only. Once they make our *kafenio* their go-to place to relax, we can to encourage the woman," Manolis said.

"I think you should. You're hardly likely to turn a profit by humouring a bunch of misogynistic pensioners nursing one coffee for hours on end," I pointed out. I would certainly find somewhere else to drink my coffee if Marigold was made to feel uncomfortable accompanying me.

"Speaking of coffee…" Barry reminded Manolis.

Heading reluctantly over to the kitchen, Manolis banged a *briki* on the gas hob.

"Any chance of an iced coffee?" Barry called over.

Yanking the *briki* off the hob, Manolis barked, "Two the *frappé* coming up."

"Make that just one *frappé*," I said. Although Barry was addicted to the stuff, the novelty of a teaspoon of Nescafé shaken up in a beaker of cold water had long worn off. The last time we'd visited Athens, I had enjoyed an iced coffee known as a *freddo espresso*, a beverage made with real coffee rather than the instant that went in *frappé*. Alas, such sophisticated coffees had yet to reach our little corner of the Mani. Scowling, Manolis slammed the *briki* back on the hob.

"Manoli, what's with that old barber's chair in the corner? Are you offering short back and sides along with the coffee?" Barry quipped.

"The chair he is just for the nostalgia, it has always been there. When my grandfather to have the *kafenio*, the chair was always in the corner. The Adonis, the father of the Apostolos, was the regular customer and he hire the space for to give the haircut." Manolis' scowl was replaced with a wide grin as he continued to speak. "Adonis drink much the *ouzo* all the day long. By the late afternoon, only the brave would ask for the haircut. They would be lucky to escape with the ear intact."

"It makes Apostolos' lopsided necklines seem tame in comparison," I said. I had yet to suffer one of Apostolos' signature haircuts though my excuses for evading his eagerness to get snap happy with his scissors were wearing thin.

"On occasion, the barber chair would to double as the dentist chair," Manolis revealed, his expression deadpan. "My grandfather would to give the glass of *raki* before to pull out the bad tooth with the pliers."

No doubt that would explain the suspect blood stains adorning the linoleum flooring.

"Thank goodness for modern dentistry," I said, feeling a twinge of empathy for my brother-in-law as he visibly winced. Poor Barry had been afflicted with a nasty toothache of late but had refused to do anything about it, sharing Marigold's irrational fear of the dentist.

Manolis roughly deposited our coffees on the table, slopping half of my *Ellinikos kafe* into the saucer before returning to the kitchen to fill two glasses with water from the tap. Pushing my glass of cloudy water aside, I pondered the state of the pipes it had passed through. Perchance the water had been stagnating for years, if not decades. Clearly not sharing my concerns, Barry thirstily downed his glass of water in one, oblivious to the likely risk of bacteria breeding in the liquid refreshment.

Manolis' intention of sitting down to join us was scuppered when Kyrios Stavropoulos and one of his old cronies shuffled in, the pair of them ordering coffee and *ouzo*. No sooner had they taken their seats than Tina appeared, her usually pleasant smile replaced with a vinegary look. Slapping her hands on her hips, she stood over the couple of pensioners. Adopting the mantle of a deranged fishwife, she loudly berated them for their disloyalty in taking their morning coffee at the newly reopened rival establishment, instead of supping coffee outside the shop as they customarily did.

After wiping the floor with the sheepish looking duo, Tina turned her attention on me. With her usual conviviality hijacked by this almost unrecognisable shrew-like shopkeeper, it was the first time I had ever discerned any physical similarity between Tina and Despina.

"Victor, I am the much disappoint you take the coffee here instead of at the shop…"

"I had to put in an appearance. After all, Manolis is dating Marigold's best friend," I said apologetically.

"It is the disloyal of you," Tina carped.

Although Kyrios Stavropoulos and his companion couldn't understand Tina's English words, they clearly got the gist. Obviously relieved that Tina had turned her focus on someone other than them to lambast, they sniggered quietly. Annoyed to be the butt of their amusement, I determined not to be cowed by Tina. Losing my apologetic tone, I told Tina bluntly that I was free to take coffee wherever the fancy took me, adding that I had spotted the wart-faced hag, Despina, manning the till in the shop earlier.

"There are rumours going around that your mother spits in the customer's coffee," I stated. "I wasn't prepared to risk picking up something nasty from her disgusting actions."

"Who to make the rumour?" Tina demanded, scowling at Manolis as though he was the obvious culprit.

"I have no idea since most of the malicious rumours doing the rounds are generally dreamt up by Despina," I countered.

"As a matter of interest, what could you pick up from someone spitting in the coffee?" Barry asked.

"Rabies and Ebola are both transmitted in spit as is mononucleosis, sometimes referred to as the kissing disease," I enlightened him.

"It is the years since anyone to kiss my mother," Tina interrupted, slumping into a chair. Steepling her fingers under her chin, she sighed wearily, her anger visibly evaporating.

"I am sorry, Victor. It is not for me to tell you where you can to drink the coffee. I have much the worry that the *kafenio* will to steal much the business from the shop."

"Well, it's not as though the *kafenio* will be in direct competition with your main trade. They are only selling drinks, not groceries," I pointed out.

The dour expression on Tina's face indicated I hadn't convinced her. Tina's face fell as two new *kafenio* customers arrived, the local barber, Apostolos, and Litsa's garlic eating brother, Mathias.

V.D. BUCKET

The deep blue paint splattered on the back of Mathias' brown trousers hinted that he was already a regular.

Apostolos immediately zoned in on the barber's chair in the corner. Stroking the leather wistfully, he began to reminisce about picking up the trade from his father in this very spot.

Nudging me in the ribs, Barry hissed, "It looks as though Norman is heading this way, weighed down with fondant fancies."

Groaning inwardly as I spotted Norman approaching the *kafenio*, I jumped out of my chair, asking Manolis to point me in the direction of the toilet.

"Go through the *apothiki*. The toilet is in the courtyard."

Wasting no time, I rushed towards the *apothiki* before Norman could make his entrance and latch onto me. Hastening away, I didn't stop to question Manolis' bizarre demand as he called after me, "You must to flush from the bucket."

Chapter 2

An Inadequate Convenience

Bright sunlight from the open courtyard doorway flooded into the *apothiki*, highlighting the intricate thread of cobwebs suspended from the low arched ceiling and the rough stone walls. In truth, it was a fabulous space, though its potential was wasted since it served only as a storage room. Four enormous wooden barrels were shoved against one wall; I assumed they had been used for olive oil and wine, a hint of by-gone, musty grape in the air suggesting the latter.

I struggled to identify most of the rusty old

implements hanging from nails in the stonework, only recognising a fire poker and a pair of blood-smeared pliers. I recoiled at the thought they could be the very same pliers that had been used to yank out teeth, the have-a-go dentist neglecting to sterilise his instrument between victims. The rest of the space was cluttered with open cardboard boxes. Vital *kafenio* supplies spilled out; bags of sugar and Greek coffee mixed in with bottles of spirits, napkins and toothpicks.

Stepping out into the courtyard, I recognised the space from when Manolis had given me a guided tour of the property when the idea of reopening the *kafenio* had first been mooted. Like the rest of the property, the courtyard had long been neglected but I could discern visible signs of improvement since my last visit. The weeds that had forced their way through cracks in the cement had been eradicated thanks to Doreen tackling them with super-strength weedkiller. Doreen, egged on by Marigold, had highfalutin dreams of transforming the courtyard into a floral oasis stuffed with plants in ceramic pots and urns, where she could snuggle up to Manolis on a swinging garden seat. Manolis, keen to keep the budget for reopening the *kafenio* under tight control, had yet to be won over by Doreen's pleas, arguing that as the area simply served as access to the outside toilet, it wasn't worth spending the cash to improve it.

Manolis clearly underestimated the determination of the two women to implement their grand design. Ever since my wife and her sidekick turned Guzim's hovel into the pink palace of love, they have been biting at the bit to unleash their creativity whenever the opportunity arises.

Personally, I think the pair of them have watched too many episodes of 'Changing Rooms', Marigold freely admitting a bit of a fancy for the long-haired Laurence Llewelyn-Bowen. Considering the double-barrelled designer has cultivated a luxuriant moustache along with a tendency to sport open necked shirts, I would have thought he would be more Doreen's type. His taste in flamboyant clothing reminded me of some of the disastrous fashion sense displayed by the Albanian shed dweller when he paired some particularly garish and clashing cast-offs.

A low ramshackle stone wall separated the courtyard from a large square overgrown garden, full of orange and lemon trees amidst shoulder high weeds. Squinting against the brilliant sunshine, I spotted Mabel, the billy goat that Panos had gifted to Violet Burke, chowing down on the weeds. My mother had got shot of the creature by returning it to Yiota, who in turn had now hired it out to Manolis as a four-legged weed-chomper. I admired

V.D. BUCKET

Yiota's enterprising nature; attempting to make a go of her grandfather's farm, she never turned down an opportunity to turn a profit.

At the far end of the garden space, I spotted Guzim, hacking away at the weeds in a very lackadaisical way with a scythe. Since most of the building work down on the coast had come to a standstill due to the extreme August heat, I had persuaded Manolis to take him on as a temporary gardener. The garden space was just crying out to be cleared and planted with vegetables, a money saving exercise if the brothers branched out into serving meals. Although they were both keen on the idea of offering food to the customers, they were clueless when it came to creating anything more adventurous than bread and cheese. With Doreen's unique knack of turning out burnt food that was still raw in the middle, Manolis had hooked up with the wrong woman if he expected any help in the kitchen.

Ducking out of sight before Guzim could spot me, I made my way towards the outside toilet. To my dismay, I discovered the facilities were housed inside a rickety wooden structure lacking the privacy of a door, the structure resembling in size the archetypical British red telephone box. Just like the typical phone box, the tottering booth reeked with the stench of stale urine. Facing the non-existent door and in full view of anyone crossing the courtyard, an old porcelain toilet was sunk into the concrete floor. Goodness only knows what cowboy builder had been responsible for installing it since half of the toilet pedestal was sited underground; the seat area, lacking an actual seat, was crookedly set only about twelve inches above the floor.

A bucket half filled with what I hoped was water, stood in one corner. Stepping tentatively forward, I yanked the rusty chain dangling from the cistern. As I suspected, nothing flushed into the disgustingly stained toilet bowl, thus explaining Manolis' cryptic comment about flushing from a bucket. After fouling my fingers from touching the chain, I felt an urgent desire to scour my hands, thwarted alas since the tap in the cracked washbasin ran dry. Thoroughly sterilising my hands from the handy bottle of sanitiser I sensibly kept in my pocket in case of any hygiene emergencies, I couldn't believe that Manolis and Christos seriously expected their customers to put up with such a squalid and unsanitary toilet; they had, after all, both lived in the States for the duration of their adult lives.

If any public health inspector worth his salt got wind of the state of the toilet, the *kafenio* would instantly be closed down on health and safety grounds. No doubt the brothers were aware that public health inspectors were apparently thin on the ground in rural Greek mountain villages or perchance they had a brown envelope ready on the off-chance of a surprise inspection. It was no wonder they weren't too keen on encouraging the fairer sex to frequent their establishment. I couldn't imagine any woman of my acquaintance willingly using the toilet. I could well imagine the oily Christos arguing an actual door was superfluous to requirements, hoping to spy on any woman caught short enough to use the toilet out of desperation.

Stepping back in dismay, I heard my mother yelling my name. Looking up, I spotted her standing on the balcony area at the top of the outdoor stairs. Recalling the setup from when Manolis had shown me around, I remembered that like many of the older properties in the village, the two levels of the two-storey house were not internally connected. Outside stairs led up to the living quarters which were sited above the *apothiki* and the space housing the *kafenio*.

"If you need the lav, lad, I've just given the one up here a good scrubbing," Vi hollered from above. "You don't want to be going in that filthy death trap down there."

"It's certainly an inadequate convenience," I grumbled.

"That's a right fancy way of saying a mucky lav."

Since some of the concrete steps were cracked and crumbling under foot, I stepped warily as I headed up to join my mother. I may have exaggerated when I described her as yelling down from the balcony; the narrow area was nothing so glamorous, more resembling a concrete landing leading off from the top of the stairs, the shoddy wooden railing offering zero protection from plummeting to one's death in the concrete courtyard below. An overwhelming smell of bleach wafted from the outside bathroom, housed at the far end of the outdoor landing.

Relieved to see that the upstairs outside facilities actually boasted a door, I poked my head inside. Tiled with drab grey *plakakia*, the space housed an old enamel bath with a rubber shower attachment hooked to the taps, and surprisingly, a modern washbasin and toilet.

"You use the lav then I'll show you around inside," my mother directed.

"Manolis already gave me the guided tour last month."

"'Appen that Manolis must want his head testing if he reckons on seducing that Doreen in a single bed in the kitchen. She might not be what you'd call sophisticated, but I reckon even that daft mare would draw the line at that. Course, 'appen it's the other numpty what sleeps in there."

"No, it's Manolis. It was the only room in the house where Christos' cats didn't have the run of the place...Manolis is terribly allergic."

"How anyone can sleep next to a wood-fired range in this heat."

Concurring with my mother's sentiments, I recalled it had struck me as a peculiar set up when Manolis showed me around. Of course, it was not the first time I had encountered a bed in a Greek kitchen since Spiros' uncle Petros had bedded down in what was now my kitchen. The kitchen above the *kafenio* was on one side of the entrance hallway which doubled up as a dining area, the rest of the living quarters comprising a large living room with stunning sea views, and Christos' bedroom. A small room housed nothing but a couple of unopened boxes bearing labels indicating the brothers had shipped their personal belongings over from Chicago and Texas.

The dated furniture in the house, a mixture of antique and old MDF, had obviously been there for years, the two brothers seemingly not inclined to stamp their own personal touch on the place. Having seen the house before, I declined my mother's invitation to snoop whilst commending her on landing herself yet another cleaning job.

BUCKET TO GREECE (VOL.15)

"Aye, well, this one suits me nicely as they're up for me coming in nice and early. I had a free slot because I fired Norman and palmed him off on Blerta. It wasn't so much the mess he made that I minded but the way he droned on; he could bore for England, that Norman. At least Blerta can get on with it in peace, with not being able to understand him."

Having taken to Tonibler, Violet Burke had taken his mother, Blerta, under her wing, passing on any cleaning jobs that she couldn't face or that didn't fit into her schedule. Additionally, she kept an ear open for anyone that might be open to Blerta's ironing services. With Barry and Vangelis employing Blat, and Violet Burke vouching for Blerta's skill with a scrubbing brush and an iron, the young family were settling seamlessly into village life. In contrast to Guzim's myriad grumbles that as an alien Albanian he had never been truly accepted in the village, the Kosovan family had been embraced by the locals.

"I'd better be getting back to Barry," I said.

"Tell Barry to hang on till I get down. He can give me a lift to that Milton's place," Vi demanded.

"What's wrong with your bicycle?"

"It's only gone and got one of them puncture things. I reckon that manky cat of Cynthia's sabotaged my wheel by sticking a claw in it, deliberate like. The nasty thing was hanging around like a bad smell when I parked up last night."

"Perhaps next time you feel inclined to chuck Kouneli in a passing pickup, you could check with the driver and make sure he's going the distance," I suggested.

Cracking an approving grin, my mother proclaimed, "Ooh, you are a one."

Re-entering the *kafenio* through the *apothiki*, one could cut the tension with a knife. Norman, clad in a flour splattered pinny, clutched a tray displaying his latest batch of French patisserie fancies as he faced off against his estranged wife's boyfriend. Having chummed up with Christos when the two brothers had been at odds, Norman had apparently inveigled his way into persuading Christos to offer his cakes for sale along with the coffee.

Staring at the creamy concoctions with contempt, Manolis instructed Norman to take them away, telling him the customers would expect Greek snacks, not any of his foreign rubbish. Shaking a large bag of oregano crisps in Norman's face, Manolis declared, "They want the chips and the Kalamata olive."

"But your brother said..."

"Norman, are those individual Charlotte russe?" I interrupted.

"They are," Norman proudly confirmed.

"I thought so. You do realise that creamy Charlotte russe will be a veritable breeding ground for bacteria if they are left out in this heat. At the very least, they would need to be kept in a refrigerated display unit that has passed a meticulous temperature check, something this establishment is sadly lacking. If Manolis agreed to sell your cakes, he would be the one held responsible if his customers come down with a nasty dose of staphylococcal food poisoning."

Winking at me in gratitude, Manolis boomed, "What Victor say."

"And you can't just sell cakes that you've knocked up in a domestic kitchen. Your premises would need to pass a rigorous inspection first to ensure they comply with health and safety standards."

"The cleaner's been in," Norman objected. Squaring his shoulders, he dared to challenge me in my area of expertise. "I thought you were retired. You can't go round dictating rules."

"Retired I may be, but standards are standards," I retorted.

"I want to speak to Christos," Norman said huffily.

"I doubt that Christos is any sort of expert on food safety standards," I said.

V.D. BUCKET

"Christos work the night...take the cake away. I know your game, Norman. You want to poison my customer because the Doreen love me," Manolis shouted.

"You're welcome to Doreen," Norman chuntered before turning tail and flouncing off with his fancies. In his haste to retreat, he collided with my next-door neighbour, Kyria Maria, arm in arm with Kyria Kompogiannopoulou, Charlotte russe landing on the front of Maria's black widow's weeds.

Sticking her finger in the cream smeared on her bosom, Maria sucked it greedily, oblivious to the risk of bacteria. As the two women made to enter the *kafenio*, the four elderly male customers fired disapproving looks in their direction. Giving the evil eye and tutting in annoyance, they were clearly put out at the women's audacity in presuming to enter what they hoped to claim as a male only space.

Intercepting the unwelcoming looks directed their way, the two women went on the offensive. Lecturing all the men present on their need to catch up with twenty-first century mores, they told them that women had equal rights and were entitled to drink coffee wherever they chose.

Manolis was put on the spot. Clearly flustered, he had to decide whether to alienate his main customer base by welcoming the women, or risk antagonising the women by turning them away. Since Manolis had apprised me of their intention to keep women at a distance just until the regular male clientele had comfortably established a routine of taking their coffee in the *kafenio*, I decided to step in and help him out.

Playing on my knowledge of Kyria Kompogiannopoulou's hyperactive bladder and her inability to go ten minutes without needing to go, I warned her that the toilet wasn't suitable for women. "*Kyria Sofia, i toualeta edo den einai katallili gia gynaikes.*"

"*I toualeta tha einai mia chara. I Violet irthe edo gia na katharisei,*" Kyria Maria replied, saying the toilet would be fine as Violet had come over to clean.

"*Alla i toualeta den eichei porta,*" I said, telling them that the toilet had no door.

Clasping her bony hands on her bosom, Kyria Maria responded with some decidedly unladylike language, declaring the lack of a door was no doubt a deliberate ploy on Christos' part so the filthy pervert could watch them on the toilet. Considering Maria is the mother of the local papas, I was rather taken aback at the way she so readily peppered her words with choice expletives.

"*Tha valo mia porta stin toualeta poly syntoma.*" Manolis rashly promised the ladies he would put a door on the toilet very soon.

"*Loipon, den tha epistrepsoume mechri na to kanete*," Kyria Kompogiannopoulou said, assuring Manolis they wouldn't be back until he did.

As the women stormed off, their noses put out of joint, Manolis rolled his eyes dramatically. "Thank you, Victor. That was quick thinking you did to get me out of the spot."

"That outside loo of yours is a disgrace, Manoli," I told him bluntly. "You must sort it out. I'd suggest knocking the whole thing down and starting again."

"I can have a look-see and give you a quote," Barry offered.

"Vangelis look before he go on the holiday," Manolis said. "He said there is the room in the *apothiki* to wall off a space for the customer toilet."

"I remember him saying now. We'll put it at the top of our list when Vangelis gets back from his holiday," Barry said.

"He's away for another week, isn't he?" I asked.

"The perfect timing. After the week, the village men will have the routine of coming here for their coffee. Then, they will to make the grumble when the women come in but they will to put up with it." Manolis sounded pretty confident in his reasoning. I supposed that in the meantime, if any women came in, they could use the outside bathroom upstairs if they were willing to risk walking in on Christos taking a bath.

Chapter 3

Ostracised from Society

"*Ela*, Victor, Barry, *oi filoi mou*. Come to join me out here," Spiros called, claiming one of the outside tables.

"There's no shade out there," I complained.

Offering me a grubby looking tea towel, Manolis said, "Take this. It will keep the sun off your head."

Chuckling loudly, Barry said, "Careful, Manoli, or you'll get one of Victor's infamous lectures on tea towel hygiene."

Manolis shrugged as I declined the offer, instead using the tea towel to mop the sweat off his brow.

"I bet that doesn't get a good boil wash before he swipes it over the coffee cups," I hissed to Barry before calling out to Spiros to come inside in the shade.

"No, I have been all the morning with the corpse. I to need the fresh air."

"I bet he stinks of embalming fluid," Barry muttered as the two of us moved outside to join the undertaker.

"You to make the walk with me later?" Spiros asked me.

"I'm up for it if the heat hasn't killed me off, unless Marigold's roped me into something I know nothing about." Spiros was doing a sterling job of following doctor's orders by walking the medically decreed three kilometres a day. Time allowing, I occasionally joined him as did some of the other villagers. Sometimes Sherry would hitch herself to our little group; in her typical jolly-hockey-sticks manner, she had christened the walkers with the highly unoriginal name of the Meli Walking Group. Spiros' gammy leg was improving no end with the daily exercise. As an added bonus, his figure had benefited from the activity too, his rounded belly gradually deflating as though the air had been let out on slow release. The trimmer physique suited him.

"I must to ask your advice as the marry men," Spiros said.

"Problems on the home front?" Barry enquired.

"It is the Sampaguita. My fragrant Filipina flower is the upset. I hate to see her cry."

"Well, speaking from thirty-eight years' experience, you may as well apologise right off the bat. It's bound to be your fault even if you've done nothing wrong," I advised.

"I have done nothing wrong..."

"Following Victor's lead on this has worked for me," Barry concurred. "Get the apology out of the way and make it up to her with something sweet. I usually get Marigold to knock up one of her sherry trifles. Cynthia has a bit of a weakness for one of Marigold's trifles."

"I find gifting my wife some *halva* or *loukoumi* works a treat unless it's something serious. If I'm really in the dog house, I splurge on a bottle of Marigold's favourite Mastic Tears. I keep a mini-break up my sleeve as a last resort."

"I have not to upset the Sampaguita. She is the saddened because the old man she care for in the Nektar make her life the misery. He to get angry and shout at her for no reason. When he in the temper, he treat the Sampaguita like the dog..."

"That's terrible. Why doesn't she just leave? She has such an excellent reputation as a carer that she'd be snapped up immediately," I said, recalling how wonderful Sampaguita had been with Spiros' uncle Leo when he had dementia.

"And Cynthia and I never have any worries when we leave little Anastasia in Sampaguita's care. Ana absolutely adores her," Barry assured Spiros.

"The Sampaguita like very much the Ioanna, the daughter of the old man, Haralambos..."

"Ioanna as is Giannis' mother?" I asked, referencing the local bee man.

"*Nai*. The Haralambos live in the Nektar. He refuse to leave the home to move in with the Ioanna in Meli, but he need someone with him all the day now he is the nearly bedridden. They had to cut the leg off. He was, how you to say, grouty?"

"He lost a leg to gout?" I guessed.

"*Nai*, the grout. Ioanna not to want to move in with the father because she say the Giannis to need her. She spend all the time running between the father and the son, with just the Sampaguita to help," Spiros explained.

I recalled that despite being a grown man in his early thirties, Giannis had moved back in with his mother when he returned to the village from the city. Ioanna cooked and cleaned for him, in addition to washing his clothes and, no doubt, wiping his nose. Giannis may be enterprising when it comes to his honey and rabbit business ventures, not to mention his side-line in motorbike repairs, but on the domestic front, he allows Ioanna to totally pamper him. I consider it quite ironic that not only does Giannis look like a Greek god, his mother treats him as one.

"The Ioanna need the help with the old man, she cannot to manage alone," Spiros continued. "The Sampaguita not want to leave the Ioanna in the lurgies…"

"In the lurch," I corrected.

"The Sampaguita say it is too much for the Ioanna alone so she to carry on to help, even though the Haralambos make the life difficult. She make the excuse that it is the illness that to fuel his bad temper but I tell her, always he has been the bad man. Sometime he to hit the Ioanna with the crutch. I tell to Sampaguita, he lay one finger on her, I to kill him." Spiros had a murderous look in his eyes as he spoke passionately about protecting his wife. "The Haralambos used to knock the wife. No matter how many time the Haralambos put the wife in the hospital, she still to adore the husband. I to bury her the four year ago…the cancer take her."

"I find it hard to understand why a woman would stay with a man who abuses her," I said.

"She perhaps the dazzle by the good looks of the Haralambos. When he was younger, he have the much beautiful face, but it not to compensate for his bad personality."

I reflected that good looks must run in the family; certainly, Ioanna was a great beauty, as was her son.

"He is the very short." Spiros gestured with his hand, indicating Haralambos only came up to his shoulder, and Spiros isn't exactly tall. "I think the lack of the height is what to make him so the horrible, it to make him to feel the inadequate."

"Ah, a touch of the Napoleonic complex," I deduced.

"*Ti?*" My reference clearly went over Spiros' head.

"He not to allow any the person to call him the Babis or the Hari, the usual short form of the Haralambos. He think it to make him the bigger to have the big name, but he still short," Spiros said. Sighing heavily, he added, "The Haralambos shout much at the Ioanna too. It upset the Sampaguita to see the Haralambos to treat his the daughter so badly...I tell her to leave but she want to support the Ioanna. The Sampaguita has too much the good heart."

"Could Giannis perhaps have a word with his grandfather, man to man? Surely it must pain him to see his mother treated so badly," I suggested. Although I didn't know Giannis terribly well, he had always struck me as a very level-headed, polite and kind young man. He certainly always humoured Marigold when she tried to flirt with him, just as I humour the way my wife laps up the flattering attention paid to her by attractive younger men.

Of late, Giannis had been walking out with Yiota. I couldn't see Panos' granddaughter putting up with any nonsense if by any chance Giannis took after his grandfather behind closed doors. She had far too much gumption, not to mention she'd palled up with my mother. Violet Burke would never tolerate a man being free with his fists, not after that sorry business with Reginald Slack, my mother's second husband.

"It is worth the try. I will to go to speak to the Giannis after the coffee. Perhaps he not to know how badly the grandfather treat the Ioanna and Sampaguita. The Ioanna prefer to keep it the private that her the father mistreat her; she feel much the shame. Victor, you think the Marigold could to make one of her trifles to cheer the Sampaguita up?" A twinkle appeared in Spiros' eyes as he thought of a practical way to buoy up his wife's spirits.

"I'll get her to knock one up as soon as I get home," I promised. I had no qualms about volunteering Marigold for trifle making duty. She could hardly complain considering the number of times she had volunteered my services without so much as a by-your-leave. Since she is very fond of Sampaguita, I didn't consider I was taking too much of a liberty. Young Tonibler was due over later for another English lesson. I would ask Marigold to make a second trifle as a treat for the boy.

Feeling something unpleasantly moist and rough brushing against my arm which was resting along the back of the chair, I exclaimed, "What the?"

Turning around, I spotted the four-legged culprit, its long pink tongue licking away at my exposed flesh.

"It's a goat." Barry has always been the master of stating the blatantly obvious.

Shooing the goat away, I applied a liberal application of hand sanitiser to my arm. The goat's tongue may well be insanitary; goodness only knows where it had been. I was taken aback when Spiros volunteered the bizarre information that in medieval Europe, goats' tongues were used as an instrument of torture.

Assuming Spiros had fallen down the rabbit hole of another conspiracy theory, I attempted to keep a straight face as I joshed, "What? No, I never heard the like. Did they rip out the tongue to use as a lash?"

"The goat tongue he is no laughing matter, Victor," Spiros admonished me. "The torture was to tie the victim to the tree and to dip his the foot in the salt water. Then they to bring the thirsty goat to lick the foot. The goat tongue is like the sandpaper, how you to say?"

"Abrasive."

"That's it. When the goat to lick the foot, the tongue is so the abrasive it to take all the skin off to leave the bone."

"I like my tongue cooked up in a nice bowl of *patsas soupa*," Barry mused, his eyes taking on a hungry look as he spoke wistfully of the tripe soup he coveted. "I wonder if Manolis will put it on the menu here."

"There is no menu," Spiros said bluntly. "The Manolis and Christos not to know how to cook."

"And technically tongue isn't offal," I schooled Barry who had an insatiable appetite for anything tripey along with other gross bits of intestinal organs.

"So, is the goat's tongue as an instrument of torture true or did you just make it up?" Barry asked Spiros.

"It is the true," Spiros assured him.

"It's an odd thing to be up on," Barry mused.

"Many the torture method are passed down in

the undertaker network." Spiros spoke in a whisper as though he was revealing some great secret only known to those in the funeral business. I had a sudden image of a mysterious network of black suited funeral directors exchanging funny handshakes in the manner of Freemasons.

Taking another look at the goat stubbornly refusing to move on, it crossed my mind that it could be Mabel. Since the billy had grown a tad since Panos first presented it to Violet Burke, it was pretty indistinguishable to my untrained eye from other goats in the area, one goat having a tendency to look much like another.

"I hope that Guzim hasn't let Mabel out of Manolis' garden," I said, thinking it would be typical of Guzim to lose the one living creature that Yiota had entrusted to his care. He had form, after all; he was forever losing his dratted pet rabbit.

"Only if Mabel's run away to join the herd," Barry chortled, the sound of tinkling bells presaging the arrival of the rest of the trip. In no time at all, the three of us found ourselves surrounded by goats in a hue of colours, pushing against our bodies and jostling the table, the particularly pungent smell of the bucks unpleasantly exacerbated by the heat. Barry screeched in annoyance as a goat head-butted his frappé, the iced coffee instantly soaking his crotch.

A couple of goats had the audacity to venture inside the *kafenio* but were brusquely shoved out by a broom-wielding Manolis.

"*Den boreis na kratiseis tis katsikes sou ypo elencho,*" Manolis bellowed, his face contorted in scathing contempt as he demanded, "Can't you keep your goats under control?"

Turning to see who Manolis was so rudely addressing, I saw an elderly woman with short salt and pepper hair, clad in jeans and a grubby pullover with unravelled threads. Herding the goats, she leant on a worn wooden staff as she ambled towards us. Not deigning to reply, she passed the *kafenio* doorway, determinedly ignoring Manolis. As she drew level with our table, I noticed the deep wrinkles etched into her defiant face, her clear hazel eyes focused directly ahead as she stubbornly looked neither left nor right.

Hoping to make amends for Manolis' brusqueness, I offered a cheery, "*Kalimera, Kyria. Ti kaneis?*"

My words were echoed by Barry offering a similar greeting. It didn't escape my notice that Spiros, rather unusually, remained tight-lipped, studiously focusing all his attention on his coffee as he blanked the woman. Herding the stragglers together, the woman strode by, completely ignoring the friendly greeting both Barry and I had offered.

"Perhaps she's taken a vow of silence," Barry quipped.

"She's a goatherd, not a nun. I think that's the first time I've ever seen a female goatherd," I said, attempting to cover my embarrassment at being snubbed. "Odd that I've never noticed her before. She must be quite hardy to herd goats in all weathers. Is she local, Spiro?"

Finger-combing his bushy eyebrows, Spiros hesitated before rather reluctantly declaring, "She is the Sofia. She live in the shack high in the hill above Nektar. The Sofia is, how you to say, ostriched from the society."

"Ostracised," I automatically corrected. Immediately intrigued, I hoped that Spiros would spill the beans, his regular anecdotes offering rich fodder for the book that I was penning about living in Greece. Considering the huge amount of rich material on offer, I could see my book turning into an ongoing saga.

"Perhaps she keeps ostriches as well as goats," Barry posited.

"Don't be ridiculous," I scoffed. "You don't get ostriches in Greece."

"You are the wrong, Victor. The ostrich farming is taking off the big time in the *Ellada*," Spiros assured me.

"He's right," Barry said. "Cynthia was reading all about it."

"Don't tell me she wants to fill that ecological pond of yours with the things," I retorted worriedly. I had no idea if the addition of ostriches to the village would pose yet another predatory threat to my chickens. Making a mental note to do some research of my own on the subject, I considered my chickens had quite enough to contend with, living with the constant threat of being gobbled up by foxes and wild boars. It was no wonder that Guzim claimed their nerves were shot.

"No, it turns out it costs a small fortune to keep ostriches," Barry said. Turning to Spiros, he asked, "What's this about that goatherder being ostracised?"

"I to tell you, but you not to spread it," Spiros said in a solemn tone, tapping his nose to indicate his words should go no further. "The Sofia live in the Meli before she go to the prison."

"Prison. You mean she's a common criminal?" I spluttered.

"I not to know if she is the criminal because her the crime not to exist anymore. The law was to change in, I think it was the 82 or the 83."

"What crime?" I urged.

"I not to know the word in the English, in Greek it is the *moicheia*." Spiros' words left me at a loss and alas, I had neglected to bring my Greek to English pocket dictionary along. "She to make the sex with the other man who was not the husband."

"Are you pulling our legs? Are you seriously trying to tell us that she was sent to prison for committing adultery?" Barry's face was a picture of gobsmacked incredulity.

"Ah, adultery, that is the English word for the *moicheia*. I not to pull the leg. Times were the different before the government of the Andreas Papandreou make the woman the equal in the marriage. He to put the stop to the dowry and make the adultery not the crime."

"And you say these changes were only introduced in the early eighties? I can't believe that poor woman was sent to prison for playing away." I was genuinely shocked that adultery had been considered a crime worthy of doing time for in twentieth century Greece.

Despite his earlier reluctance to divulge any information, Spiros leaned in close to share the details.

"Her the husband need to catch her in the act. Suspecting the Sofia was the unfaithful to him, he to follow her. He see her to sneak into the lover's *apothiki* on the same day each week. Determine to catch her in the act, he call the friend to act as the witness and he to call the police." Spiros paused for dramatic effect, allowing me the opportunity to posit a question.

"How did he get the police to come all the way up here?" The locals had told me that for many years the nearest police station had been in town, over ninety minutes away. Perchance if this had taken place before the advent of cars in the area, it would take forever to summon a policeman on the back of a donkey.

"Back then, the village have the *agrotikos astynomikos*," Spiros replied.

"An agricultural policeman?" I queried, pretty confident in my translation.

"*Nai*, every the village to have one back then."

"Ah, interesting," I said, thinking the concept of having different branches of the police force continued to this day, with a special department given over to the sea police.

"It's the first I've heard of agricultural police. What did they do? Arrest any goat that trespassed on the neighbour's land," Barry said in a mocking tone. "Imagine having to share a cell with a goat. You'd never get a wink of sleep, worrying it might lick your feet in the night."

"Very droll, Barry," I said.

"The *agrotikos astynomikos* arrest and take to court the person who allow his the goat to eat the neighbour's lettuce," Spiros explained. "The Meli was much the poorer then and the villager need to grow the food from the necessity. They could not afford to have the food stolen, the lettuce and the cucumber were the staples. If the goat to eat the lettuce, then the police would to take the goat owner to court and the goat owner must to pay the fine to the victim. The police take to court the person who to steal the fruit from the tree and the person who to pick the neighbour's olive…"

"Never mind that, Spiro. I'd rather hear the rest of your tale about Sofia and her lover," Barry urged.

Ignoring Barry, Spiros slapped his hand against his forehead. "I was to tell you before about the Haralambos. He was the *agrotikos astynomikos* that Sofia's husband call to witness the adultery. The Haralambos was the very bad police, how you to say, corrupt. The power, it go to his head and he like to pull the gun. The story I could tell…"

"Do tell," I encouraged him.

"I tell you the story, you will not to believe, but I promise it is true. It show how the Haralambos have not the decent bone in the skeleton. One night, the Haralambos patrol the village, hoping to catch the young lovers…"

"Catch the young lovers," Barry parroted, another smattering of plaster dust falling from his hair as he scratched his head in bewilderment.

"Yes, I tell you later that story. So, in the dark

night, the Haralambos fall down the well in the Panos' field. He there all the night. The next day, the Panos in the field and he to hear the cry from down the well and discover the policeman to fall in. The Panos get the other villagers to help. They throw down the rope and haul him out. The Haralambos say to the Panos, 'You to save my life. Without your help, I would have to be dead in that deep dark hole. I will to always be in your the debt.'

"Trust Panos to have been the hero of the hour," I said.

"You will not to believe what happen next," Spiro said.

"What happened?"

"Just three the day later, the Haralambos arrest the Panos because the Panos' sheep eat the watermelon from the Haralambos' garden."

"No!" Barry and I exclaimed in unison.

"Surely not. He seriously arrested Panos after the farmer had just saved his life?" I was gobsmacked.

"What an ungrateful toerag," Barry spluttered, outraged on Panos' behalf.

"I lie you not," Spiros confirmed. "And the Panos to say…"

"I bet he said he wished he'd left the nasty ingrate down the well to peg it," Barry suggested.

"The Panos to say he would to rescue him

again." Spiros' words proved that Panos had been one in a million. "The Panos to say he could never to live with himself if he had not to pull the Haralambos out of the well. He could not to have the death of the policeman on his conscience, even if the Haralambos to arrest the Panos ten time over."

"Panos was a good 'un for sure," Barry declared.

"Manoli," Spiros called out, not bothering to shift from his chair. "Bring the three *ouzo*. We to make the toast to Panos."

Chapter 4

Secrets Brewing

After raising our glasses to Panos, Barry reminded the undertaker, "So, Spiro, what's all that about the policeman looking for young lovers? It sounds a bit of a rum deal."

"The Haralambos used to prowl at night, in the dark. He hope to catch the young lovers to make the illicit sex outside…"

"Illicit sex?" Barry queried.

"Back then, the sex would to bring the much dishonour if the couple were not the marry. Even the couple who meet to exchange the kiss and the, how you to say, the canoo must to keep the liaison secret."

"Canoodle," I volunteered.

"That's it. I like very much the canoodle with the Sampaguita," Spiros declared, sticking a superfluous Greek accent over the 'ood' bit of the word.

"You were saying that Haralambos was on the lookout for young lovers," Barry impatiently reminded Spiros.

"When he to catch them, he would to make the blackmail. He would to tell the young woman she must to make the sex with him or he would tell everyone in the village what she had been up to. If the young lovers were caught, they must to marry at that time. Some the girl so the frighten the family will find out she have the lover, she to make the sex with the Haralambos so her reputation not be ruin."

"What a shocking abuse of power," I said in disgust.

"I'll say," Barry agreed. "A blackmailing rapist hiding behind his role of policeman."

"Hold on, Spiro," I interjected. "You said this agricultural policeman was the same fellow that Sampaguita is looking after? Surely you don't want your wife going anywhere near such a vile sexual predator."

"Yes, he is the same. I would not to let the

Sampaguita help the Ioanna with her the father if the Haralambos could still to make the sex. Now his illness to make him the impotent. I to say to the Sampaguita, his the impotent must to make him much the angry."

"Sounds like he got his just desserts," Barry opined. "Come on, Spiro, you were half-way through the tale of the goatherd being arrested for adultery. Do finish it off."

"The husband, the witness, and the policeman, are in the waiting to break down the door of the lover's *apothiki* the next time the Sofia to meet the lover. They to burst in and find them without the dress. The policeman to arrest the naked lovers and take them to the police cell. He not allow them to put the dress."

"This Haralambos sounds like a real nasty pervert," I said.

"He was. Many the person the wary of him, they know he to abuse his power. As the boy, I run if I to see him," Spiros said before continuing his tale. "The next day, they go to the court and the witness and the police to swore to what they see."

"They were up in court the next day?" Having heard on many occasions just how slowly the wheels of justice turned in my adopted country, I was naturally incredulous of the speed in which a couple of adulterers were dealt with as though their illicit liaison was a high priority crime.

"*Nai*, the next day," Spiros confirmed. "They both the sentence to the eight month in the prison. When they to finish the prison, they are both the ban from ever to marry again."

This was all beginning to sound so puritanical that it was like something out of Nathaniel Hawthorne's 'The Scarlet Letter.' I was only amazed that Sofia hadn't had an A for adulteress branded on her forehead. Still struggling to get my head around the concept of people being imprisoned for adultery in the twentieth century, I asked Spiros, "When did this happen?"

"I was still the boy…I think it must be the forty year ago. Yes, it must to have been in the 60s. The Sofia was about the thirty year. She was the great beauty but too the flighty, too independent for the time. Her the husband was much the older than the Sofia; it had been the arrange marriage."

Having recognised the defiant fire of pride in her eyes, I felt a wave of sympathy for Sofia. Married off to an older man in a likely loveless marriage, she had perchance seized the chance of real love with her married lover, who may himself have been stuck in a similar loveless arranged marriage. For that, she had been sentenced to suffer a stint in prison followed by the public humiliation of disapprobation, apparently shunned by the villagers and effectively banished to some ramshackle shack in the hills.

"Who was Sofia married to?" Barry asked.

"If I to tell you, you must to promise not to talk about it," Spiros demanded in a hushed tone, swivelling his head around to ensure no one was near enough to eavesdrop.

"You can trust us to keep shtum," I recklessly promised, knowing full well that I would be filling Marigold in on all the juicy details as soon as I returned home. I would have to swear her to secrecy.

"Sofia was to marry to the Mathias…"

"No. The garlic eating pensioner? The brother of Litsa? I always got the impression he was a bachelor," I exclaimed, twisting around to look at Mathias who was drinking coffee inside the *kafenio*.

"He not like to talk about the time he was to marry…the unfaithful wife bring him much the shame and dishonour," Spiros confided.

"And who was this Sofia, Mathias' wife, carrying on with?" Barry blurted.

"You not to know him, his name was the Takis. After the prison, Takis' son to knock him for bringing much the shame to the family and for breaking the heart of his mother. The Takis to leave the village after the knock and never the return," Spiros said. "You to know the son of the Takis. He is the Kyriakos who to live with the old English man who to write the dirty book."

"You've got to feel sorry for Milton, having to contend with the outlandish rumours that he and Edna are living in some shameful menage a trois with Kyriakos," I said. "Though Milton did bring it on himself, I suppose. Baseless rumours are bound to start if one has the reputation of being the local purveyor of porn."

"So, is menage a trois one of those English words that's the same in Greek?" Barry asked, going off on one of his ridiculous tangents.

"Menage a trois is three words. And it's French, you muppet," I told him.

"So, is it the same in Greek?" Barry persisted.

"Actually, no. The Greek for menage a trois is *diacheirizomai ena trois*. Either way, whether it's in French or Greek, Kyriakos is in danger of sullying his reputation through association."

"Well, we both mix with Milton and it hasn't done any damage to our reputations, at least not that I've heard," Barry said.

"Yes, but we aren't living under the same roof as Edna and Milton," I pointed out.

"Fair point. And word has probably got round that you're a bit of a prude."

"I am not a prude," I protested.

"I thought it was general knowledge in the

village that Kyriakos is staying with Milton and Edna because he can't stand to live in the same house as his wife and his mother," Barry observed.

"The Kyriakos' mother is the much difficult woman," Spiros said.

"I've not had the pleasure…"

"It is no the pleasure, Victor," Spiros assured me. "After her the husband to make the sex with the Sofia and go to the prison, Kyriakos' mother turn cold and bitter. I think she would have to enjoy to make her the husband's life the misery but he to leave the Meli after the Kyriakos knock him. It is much the dishonour for the father to be knock by the son. To this day, the Kyriakos' mother still bear the shame of the husband go to the prison for making the sex with the Sofia. She to blame the Kyriakos, her the son, for the unfaithful Takis to leave."

"So, Kyriakos hit his father for being unfaithful to his mother…" Barry clarified.

"To protect her honour," I added. "And in turn she makes Kyriakos' life a misery because she blames him for her husband leaving."

"The Kyriakos' mother have the hard time to make the ends meet with no the husband to help," Spiros said.

I reflected that despite living in the village for three years, it was quite amazing that I had never got wind of Mathias having been married to an adulteress who had been carrying on with Kyriakos' father. I couldn't help wondering how many more dark secrets the village harboured; seemingly, in spite of the gossip that kept Meli so well-oiled, there were some things that remained unspoken, darkly closeted behind the old stone walls and shutters. There could even be new secrets brewing behind closed doors at this very moment, destined to be unspoken until decades later.

Before we could discuss the matter further, Violet Burke appeared by my side. Rocking backwards and forwards, my mother pressed her hands into her back, complaining, "My back ain't half giving me some gip."

"Well, it makes a change from your swollen feet," Barry teased.

"You cheeky 'apeth," Vi said fondly. "I've done upstairs and flicked the mop over that hideous lino down here. I reckon it will suit me right well, cleaning here."

"You to want the coffee, Violet?" Spiros offered.

"I'm late as it is for cleaning at that Milton's place...can you give me a lift in your van, Barry?"

"I didn't realise you were going round there to clean, Mother. Has Milton come into money?" Since the Hancocks were usually in a state of permanent penury, it seemed unlikely that Milton could rustle together enough cash to pay for my mother's services.

"It's that Greek fella, Kyriakos, that's paying me to go in and clean. He reckons the place is knee deep in filthy cat hairs. I always said that Edna was a lazy beggar when it comes to giving the place a good bottoming. She'd rather give the place a flick with a feather duster than get stuck in with some honest elbow grease."

"What's happened to your bike, Vi?" Barry asked.

"It's down with one of them puncture things. 'Appen Victor can fix it for me this afternoon."

Rolling his eyes, Barry scoffed, "Victor won't have a clue how to fix a puncture."

"I'm sure I'm perfectly capable of blowing up a tyre," I protested. "Even though I don't relish the thought of blowing into some grungy bicycle valve, I'm sure I'm more than capable."

"You don't fix punctures with mouth to mouth," Barry taunted. "I'll drop you off at Milton's, Vi, then pop over and sort out your bicycle tyre."

"A quick word before you to leave, Violet," Spiros said, slipping an arm around her waist. "Can you to call in on the Sampaguita? She is much the upset...I think it would to help if she have the motherly figure to listen."

"What have you gone and done to the poor lass now?" Vi snapped.

"Nothing…"

"A likely story. If I had a pound for every time some fella did something to cause upset, I'd have been able to hang up my mop by now."

"Spiros hasn't upset Sampaguita," Barry intervened. "I'll fill you in on the way over to Milton's, Vi."

"Tell the lass to come by mine this evening, Spiros. I'll chuck a Fray Bentos in the oven. Me and Sampaguita can have a proper heart to heart."

Strolling home through the village, I reflected on the secrets that Spiros had spilled. I had been genuinely taken aback to learn that people had been imprisoned for being caught out in the act of adultery; whilst the very thought of being unfaithful to Marigold would never cross my mind, I knew that not everyone had the good fortune to enjoy such a happy marriage and might be tempted to seek out affection and passion elsewhere.

It struck me that there must have been many miserable matches back in the day when arranged marriages were the norm in Greece. Giving free rein to my thoughts, I shuddered in horror at the thought of being paired off, with no say in the matter, with the likes of Doreen or Geraldine, rather than enjoying the freedom to fall in love with my own true soul mate, Marigold.

Thinking of Doreen, it occurred to me that if a more enlightened government hadn't changed the law, Marigold's sidekick could well have found herself sent to prison for carrying on with Manolis whilst still married to Norman. Of course, Doreen would have only faced prison if she'd been caught in the act by Norman bursting in with a witness and a policeman. It was a tad difficult to imagine Norman conjuring up enough of an interest in what Doreen was up to, to actually make the effort to catch her and Manolis *in flagrante*. Norman had always demonstrated considerably more interest in his tediously dull traffic cones than he had in his wife. I rather doubt that Doreen would have strayed in the first place if Norman had got his act together as a husband; as it was, she'd felt trapped in a loveless marriage, even though it hadn't been an arranged one.

In my considered opinion, whilst adultery may be immoral, it is hardly a matter that warrants criminalising the lovers and locking them up. Since discovering I was sired by the limping soap salesman, Vic, I had found myself a tad less judgemental when it came to the subject of criminality; after all, I was unfortunately spawned by a father that had served time at Her Majesty's pleasure. If it was ever to come out that I had been fathered by a common criminal, I expect that some people would be quick to judge, considering me guilty by association, even though I had never had the pleasure of actually associating with Vic.

I often wonder how our meeting would have gone if Vic had thrown open the door to Barb Foot's Macclesfield home, rather than being tucked up in a coffin in the hearse parked outside. Moreover, Vic wasn't the only blood member of my family to have served a stretch, my disreputable half-brother, Terrance, having bounced in and out of Strangeways over the years.

Thinking of Terrance, I recalled the conversation I'd had with my other half-brother, Douglas, when he'd flown over for our vow renewal service. Under duress, Douglas had visited the reprobate Terrance in prison, where the latter was serving a stretch for some sort of fraud. Although Douglas had been reluctant to go prison visiting, he had acceded to Terrance's pleas, relating to me that Terrance was planning to turn over a new leaf on his release from the big house. Terrance's claim that he intended to mend his ways was apparently inspired by discovering religion inside.

I rather suspect that Douglas was a tad gullible believing the pile of guff that Terrance came out with. Whilst I may sound cynical, I am not unfamiliar with the concept of deceitful convicts experiencing a lightbulb on the road to Damascus moment in order to con the parole board into thinking they are reformed characters, in the hope of an early release. I was sceptical about there being any truth to the yarn that Terrance had spun Douglas about being a reformed character after embracing religion, though from what Douglas had garnered, Terrance was a fickle follower, changing his God at the drop of a hat if it benefited his stomach.

It turned out that the come-to-Jesus moment that Terrance claimed he'd experienced didn't last long once he discovered he'd signed up to bat for the wrong lot. Twigging that the Muslim prison population were entitled to better prison grub than the Christians he had professed to align with, Terrance grew a beard and demanded a prayer mat in order to take advantage of the halal food that was a distinct improvement on the usual prison slop.

Pulling the wool over the authorities' eyes, Terrance convinced them that he was a genuine revert to Islam, his apparent reversion earning him a reprieve from the common prison fare comprising gristle of unidentifiable origins served up in lumpy brown gravy. His new halal diet was a vast improvement, consisting of tasty curries, turkey burgers and piri piri chicken, but it almost led to him being exposed as a fake Muslim.

When the Muslim prison population discovered, to their disgust, that a kitchen skivvy with an axe to grind had been chucking bits of ham in their halal curry, they went on the rampage. Rather than joining his new brothers in creating an affray, Terrance idled around in the kitchen, where he had been conveniently assigned work duties, eating extra portions of the hammed-up curry. It was only when he cottoned on to the compensation that he might be entitled to after being fed a pork product that was haram under his new religious convictions, that he joined in the riot by setting fire to his mattress.

The upshot was that Terrance had an additional six weeks added to his sentence as punishment for burning his bedding. On the plus side, Douglas had promised to have a word with Elaine, suggesting that on his release, Terrance could consult on some halal diet meals for her popular slimming plan.

All thoughts of my reprobate, religious con-artist, half-brother, flew from my mind as a flutter of delicate yellow butterflies oscillated in front of my path, mesmerising my attention as they flitted in and out of the gorgeous red roses growing against Athena's garden wall. Inspired by the sheer perfection of the roses and their obvious lure to the gossamer-winged butterflies, I decided I would whisk Marigold up to the garden centre on my next free day and treat her to a couple of rose bushes.

Chapter 5

A Genuine Friendship

Reaching home, my mind was still whirring with thoughts of the poor goatherder, Sofia, shunned by society for taking a lover more than four decades ago. Curious if Spiros had perchance been spinning an embellished yarn, I headed into my office to fire up my newly acquired laptop. Doreen's old touch-typing manual that had been rescued from the jumble, had proved most useful. Within the space of just over a month, through sheer perseverance, I had turned myself into a skilled touch typist, able to knock out close to thirty words a minute.

V.D. BUCKET

I had celebrated my mastery of the keyboard by replacing the clunky old desktop with a new slimline laptop on which I had almost finished typing up my edited manuscript of Bucket to Greece. Borrowing Marigold's cast iron cook book holder, I had used it to hold the printed copies of my chapters, painstakingly copying them into a new file on the laptop.

Curious to see what an internet search would throw up about adulterous liaisons in Greece, I was amazed to learn that prior to 1951, adultery was only considered a misdemeanour, before being criminalised in 1951, resulting in typical sentences of between six to twelve months in prison. Spiros' account of Sofia being caught in the act with Kyriakos' father was borne out by the information at my fingertips, confirming witnesses to the act were necessary to proceed with a successful prosecution. It transpired that Spiros had one detail slightly wrong. Rather than the couple being denied the opportunity to don their clothes before being transported to the prison cell in order to satisfy Haralambos' perversions, it was actually a state decree that the naked lovers must remain unclothed whilst being transported to their cells, no doubt to compound their indignity.

I found it quite shocking to read that as late as 1980, sixty-one men and forty-nine women were sentenced to prison for adultery; the disparity in number between the two sexes raised a few unanswered questions. It came as no surprise to read that the Orthodox Church fought hard against the reforms which were eventually enshrined into law in 1983, giving women equal marital rights and decriminalising adultery. Recalling the antics of the homosexual monks and the red panty scandal on the Island of Kithira, I tutted at the sheer hypocrisy of the church claiming the moral high ground.

My research revealed that Greece was far from being the most draconian European country when it came to such heavy-handed laws, Austria only decriminalising adultery in 1997. Moreover, my adopted homeland had been quicker off the mark than some other modern European countries, in decriminalising homosexuality back in 1951. Since Spiros insists that the Ancient Greeks invented homosexuality, it is amazing that Greece ever made it a criminal offence in the first place rather than declaring it a national sport. In contrast, it had been illegal to be gay in the United Kingdom until 1967 and until 1982 in France.

Whilst it often strikes me that Greece is behind the times in many ways, a state of affairs which I welcome rather than find frustrating, at least my adopted homeland hasn't declared it a crime to hold a salmon suspiciously as British law does, nor do the local farmers have to worry about being arrested for being drunk in charge of a cow. The bizarre English law which forbids beating a rug before 8 a.m. would make criminals of half the women of Meli who are quite fastidious in shaking their rugs over their balconies at the crack of dawn.

Closing the laptop, I headed straight to the bathroom to jump in a cool shower. Revived by the blissfully refreshing water, I wrapped a towel around my midriff and walked into the bedroom for a change of clothes.

"You'll never guess what I've just heard, Marigold. Can you believe that Mathias had a wife who was imprisoned for adultery...what the?"

I froze in my tracks, startled to see a red-faced Doreen sprawled on the bed next to Marigold, desperately trying to untangle the blade of a battery-operated hand-held fan that was stuck in her perm.

"Really, Victor. You might put some clothes on when we have visitors," Marigold chided.

"Well, you might have warned me that Doreen had infiltrated our bedroom," I countered.

"Where else do you expect me to entertain our friends? You're the one that refused to have air conditioning installed in the rest of the house. That through draft that you're always harping on about just doesn't cut it in this heat. The wall of humidity in the grand salon sapped all my energy and those useless fans just shift the hot air about," Marigold complained. "Oh, do put some clothes on, Victor. Poor Doreen doesn't know where to look."

Grabbing a pair of shorts and a short-sleeved button down, I pointed out, "I'm more covered up than I am on the beach," before beating a hasty retreat to the bathroom to dress.

Biting back my annoyance at coming home to discover Doreen had claimed my rightful place on the bed, I slipped my clothes on, grateful for my wife's sake that she was still able to enjoy the company of her sidekick. I reflected back to the time just a couple of months earlier when I had returned from a hard day's repping to discover an inconsolable Marigold freely weeping into her pillow.

Hiccupping between sobs, Marigold had declared, "Oh, Victor, such terrible news."

From the wretched look of dejection on Marigold's face, I braced myself, expecting to hear that someone had died. Since my wife appeared in no mood to elaborate, I waited pensively.

Passing Marigold a box of tissues, I took her hand, urging her, "Do spill, darling. I'm not a mind reader."

"It's Manolis... I always said he was wrong for Doreen," Marigold sniffed.

I didn't bother pointing out that Marigold had said no such thing; in fact, she had positively encouraged the blossoming relationship between Doreen and the Greek-Texan with the pornstache, her matchmaking tendencies too ingrained to ever be able resist a bit of romantic meddling. Considering my wife's obvious distress, this was hardly the moment to bring it up in some pathetic point scoring exercise.

"Has Manolis gone and done the dirty on Doreen?" I asked. It would certainly take me by surprise if Manolis had played Doreen for a fool since he had always given the impression of being totally devoted.

"No, it's worse than that, Victor. Manolis is talking about going back to Texas and taking Doreen with him. He can't take much more of having to share a house with Christos."

"So, he's not broken her heart then?"

"I wish he had, it would be easier for me to bear," Marigold cried callously. "Oh, Victor, I don't know what I'll do without Doreen. I can't bear the thought of Manolis taking her away from the village. How can he do this to me?"

I was genuinely shocked by Marigold's desolation. I had always thought that the friendship between the two women was borne out of the convenient geography of the two up-sticked Brits living in a remote mountain village surrounded by Greeks. Their friendship had always struck me as one of convenience. Since I would never have given Norman the time of day back in Manchester yet was forced to endure his company at social gatherings in the tight-knit community of Meli, I had rather assumed Marigold felt the same way about Doreen. It had been a real eye-opener to discover there was a genuine friendship at stake, a friendship that my wife clearly valued.

Fortunately, Marigold's hysteria over the potential loss of her friend abated a week later when Manolis announced he had ditched his plans to return to Texas in favour of calling a truce with his brother and re-opening the *kafenio*. Doreen was almost as relieved as Marigold at Manolis' about-turn. Although Doreen hadn't been completely sold on the idea of flitting across the pond, she was so loved up that she had been prepared to follow her heart rather than her head. It turned out that Norman was the only one to be disappointed that Doreen wasn't up-sticking to Texas after all.

My thoughts were interrupted by Marigold yelling my name. "Victor. Can you bring a wet towel in here for Fluffs? She feels awfully hot."

"Well, she is wearing a fur coat in August," I called back, hastily dampening a towel for the cat.

Returning to the bedroom, I scooped up the

kitten and wrapped her in the wet towel to cool her down. Back in June, when I had rescued the kitten from Milton's doorstep, she'd been in a terrible state; almost blind and nothing but skin and bones. Seemingly at death's door, she had tugged at my heartstrings. A tad out of character for me, I put my foot down, insisting we take her in and give her a home in the Bucket household.

Once the tiny feline was installed, Marigold had griped that she should never have allowed my mother to name the kitten Vera after Corries' own Vera Duckworth, arguing that with a Victor and a Violet already under the one roof, adding a Vera in the mix just added to the confusion. Marigold promptly renamed the kitten Fluffs, a name the kitten was growing into as her bedraggled fur started to fluff out.

"It's no use. I just can't shift this blade," Doreen fretted, her face turning increasingly red with frustration as she grappled with the hand-held fan becoming ever more tangled up in her perm.

"You must pop along to Athena's kitchen and see if she can get it out without doing too much damage," Marigold suggested.

"Have you forgotten that Athena and Vangelis have gone away on their hols?" I reminded Marigold.

"That's what we should be doing, enjoying a

nice relaxing holiday," Marigold snapped.

"In case it's escaped your notice, it's the middle of the repping season," I retorted.

"It's so unfair that you have to work in August when all the Greeks are on holiday." Thinking that Marigold enjoyed a permanent holiday since she didn't go out to work, I kept my own counsel. Since the heat appeared to have sapped all her energy, she was understandably irritated.

Sighing heavily, Marigold pulled the towel off Fluffs, using it to dab up the sweat from her cleavage.

"How you exaggerate, dear," I said. "Not all the Greeks are on holiday. Plenty of them are doing long hours and seven-day weeks, serving the tourists in bars, tavernas and shops. It's only the office workers who can take an annual break at this time of year..."

"Manolis had a terrible time getting his paperwork stamped at KEP due to everyone taking their hols at the same time," Doreen bleated.

"There's an idea, Victor. Now that you've taught yourself to touch-type, you could get an office job. You'd be entitled to take a proper Greek holiday in August..."

"Who in their right mind wants to holiday in August when everywhere is packed solid with Athenians taking their annual break? The roads and beaches will be clogged and all the tavernas heaving with sweaty bodies. Anyway, technically I'm on an extended holiday from the end of September until May."

"Isn't that when you're out of work?" Doreen piped up.

"That's one way of looking at it but no one could ever accuse me of being idle."

"If you had time off in August, we could find somewhere a bit cooler for a holiday and escape this stifling heat." Marigold's tone indicated she knew she was on a hiding to nothing. I really couldn't blame her for feeling out of sorts; the interminable heat was enough to wear anyone down to a frazzle. It was too hot to comfortably venture outdoors and the house was suffocating. "How about I make a telephone call first thing in the morning to that chap that installed the air conditioning in this room? I'll get him to put a couple of units in the grand salon and kitchen, and another one in my office."

"Oh, Victor, would you really?" Marigold simpered.

"I really will," I promised. Hygiene risks be damned; it was just too hot to hold firm to my principles.

"I bet you won't be able to get anyone out to put in air-con until the holidays are over," Doreen butted in, taking the shine off my thoughtful offer.

Grabbing a pair of scissors, I approached Doreen. "Here, let me help you get that fan out of your hair."

"I'm not sure…"

"Really, it's no bother," I said, snipping through Doreen's curls to free the battery fan from her tangles. Triumphantly holding the fan aloft, I declared, "There, all done. No one will notice that little bald spot if you comb your hair over it."

"Victor. Don't say you've…" Marigold cried.

Hurling herself from the bed and examining her hair-do in the mirror, Doreen screeched, "He has."

"Well, at least it's the right sort of weather to be out and about in a sunhat," I consoled Doreen, avoiding the withering look I just knew Marigold was firing in my direction. "Now, I'm just going to pop down to the garden to pick some salad stuff and then I'll knock up a light lunch. You'll join us, Doreen? No, don't even think of lifting a finger to help, I wouldn't hear of it."

Chapter 6

Garden Bounty

It is always such a joy to head down to the garden, knowing whatever is bountiful and most appealing will determine what I will choose to cobble together for lunch. At this time of year, the garden serves as my personal pantry, only the odd shop bought staple required to bring all the flavours together. With such a glut of glorious vegetables to hand, I was spoilt for choice. Strolling past Marigold's herb garden, the tang of fresh mint inspired my lunchtime menu. Freshly chopped mint added to thick Greek yoghurt would be a perfect accompaniment to lightly battered *tiganita kolokythakia*, fried courgettes, and make a change from the usual garlic and cucumber-based *tzatziki* as a courgette dip.

Once again, my courgette crop was a runaway success. Picking enough courgettes for lunch for three, I added some more to my basket, thinking I would give them to Tonibler later. Blerta would undoubtedly turn out some tasty *kolokythakia* dish; she might possibly have a unique Albanian take on the things to share with me.

Tonibler may well have turned up his nose at my prickly pear curry but in general he enjoys his greens. I supposed that with money being so tight in Blat's family, there had never been any need to bribe Tonibler to eat his greens; the child hadn't had the luxury of being a picky eater as so many British children tend to be. Even my brother-in-law's idea of an edible vegetable had been a potato until we moved to Greece. Only with our move had he bought into the wonders of freshly grown Mediterranean vegetables after previously sharing my mother's loathing for anything green turning up on his plate.

Lured towards the vine bending under the weight of juicy and plump ripe tomatoes, I plucked some to add to my basket, deciding to make a *horiatiki salata*, country salad, to serve alongside the fried courgettes. The other vital necessities to go in the salad, red onions, green peppers and cucumber, were all at hand in my garden pantry, just waiting to be married with a thick slice of salty *Feta*, a handful of black Kalamata olives, and a generous drizzle of extra virgin. The olives in my kitchen had been cured by Dina and, as Nikos would disparagingly say, the cheese came from the shop. I drew the line at attempting to emulate Dina's hand-made cheese.

Filling my basket with salad stuff, I was surprised to spot Guzim taking an impromptu shower under his hosepipe. Fortunately, having only removed his tee-shirt, neither Marigold nor Doreen would be subjected to the sight of the Albanian shed dweller prancing around in his underpants if they chanced to look out of the window. No doubt Guzim would justify leaving his shorts on by claiming the hosepipe doubled up as a washing machine.

Turning the hosepipe's nozzle in my direction, Guzim called out, asking if I wanted him to spray me. *"Theleis na sa psekaso?"*

"Ochi efcharisto," I declined, telling him I had just taken a shower. *"Molis ekana ena ntous."*

"Einai poly zesto," Guzim said, wearily complaining it was too hot.

When I told Guzim that I thought he was supposed to be putting in a full day in Manolis' garden rather than skiving off at midday, Guzim's response shamed me. He told me that Manolis had agreed he could take a break since Guzim was worried that my chickens would be in desperate need of fresh water. Although he had filled up their water bowls first thing, he was concerned that the water may have reached boiling point in the sun. I supposed it wouldn't do for my chickens to get dehydrated, a likely scenario considering they are covered in a winter quality, high-tog rated feather quilt, in the height of summer.

Helping Guzim to feed the length of hosepipe towards the chicken run, he asked me if I wanted some walnuts, telling me that Manolis had told him to help himself from his tree as he had plenty to spare. Although Guzim had indeed helped himself, he just didn't have the necessary teeth in his head to cope with nuts. I readily accepted Guzim's kind offer. I had been toying with the idea of experimenting with *yluka tou koutaliou karydi*, walnut spoon sweets, ever since Yiota had told me they were exotically moreish.

"*Manolis...*" Guzim began before being overcome with side-splitting laughter.

"*Ti ginetai me ton Manolis?*" I said, asking what about Manolis.

By now the Albanian shed dweller was rolling on the ground, completely overcome with a fit of the giggles. I had no idea what had set him off, but

I much preferred his uncontrollable laughter to the surly sulks he often indulges in. I will summarise the often-ludicrous exchange that followed in English. If I included all the bloopers and misunderstandings that peppered our attempts to communicate in Greek, it would take longer to pen than it would to muck out the chickens.

"Do you want to share the joke?" I asked Guzim, extending a hand to haul him up off the ground.

"The Manolis confide in me that the Christos has picked most of the walnuts already. He is going to use them to make his own batch of the hair dye," Guzim revealed.

I must confess to a slight chortle at the thought. Perchance the oily Greek had realised his overly generous application of shiny black boot polish to his hair wasn't cutting it with the ladies, a dire state of affairs since making an impression on the fairer sex seemed to be his raison d'être. Still, it struck me as a bit of a faff to create home-made hair dye when Grecian 2000 was readily available via the internet. I didn't chortle quite so much when Guzim continued.

"The men are the vain and foolish to dye the hair," he opined. "It stand out like the sign on the head when the men to dye the hair."

I didn't respond lest I dropped myself in it. The

last thing I needed was Guzim gossiping about the occasional colour touch-ups I treated my hair to. Deciding that Guzim would not dare to speak so boldly if he had cottoned on to my own subtle use of Grecian 2000, I concluded that he must be clueless to my own brush with vanity. My humble gardener would be on very thin ground if he dared to malign his employer. My own relationship with Grecian 2000 is one I prefer to keep secret, even keeping Marigold in the dark by hiding the tube of gunk at the very back of the bathroom cabinet. Fortunately, my choice of hair colour restorative is nowhere near as obvious as the popular local remedy of shoe polish.

Drawing level with the chicken run, Guzim pointed to the inhabitants. "Look. The chickens are stressed."

"What?"

"They are lying down… it mean their nerves are shot."

"What poppycock. They are simply sunbathing…"

"They are not the English chicken." Guzim must have twigged that most of the sunbathers littering the beaches and frying themselves to a frazzle in the midday sun, were from my homeland. "I tell you, they are too nervous."

Thinking the Albanian shed dweller had lost

the plot, I decided to humour him.

"How on earth can you deduce that the chickens are stressed?"

"Look, Baileys is panting and breathing too fast, it is the unnatural." Clearly unsure that I had understood his point, Guzim demonstrated by panting like an overheated dog. With his mouth open wide and his tongue lolling out, he exposed his almost toothless upper gums. "And see, Raki and Dionysus are lying down on their sides."

"Perhaps I should play the chickens some calming classical music to soothe their nerves," I suggested. "Or better yet, I could take them for a psychiatric consultation."

Guzim's scowl indicated he was not amused, my ideas going down like a lead balloon.

"My clutch live the life of Riley..."

"*Ti?*" I should have anticipated the idiom would go over Guzim's head.

"They have a carefree life," I said. "They have plenty of room to roam freely in their spacious run and they enjoy practically luxurious accommodation inside their coop."

Clucking his disapproval, Guzim muttered something about my being an amateur poulterer, merely playing at raising chickens. Before I could take exception to Guzim's critical words, he climbed up on his high horse. "It is not the joke when the chickens show the nervy behaviour. They could to keel over with a heart attack if they become overly stressed."

The shed dweller's over-the-top fussing made me wish that Panos was still alive. I could have asked the welly wearing farmer to pop round to check on my clutch and reassure me that Guzim was just spouting his usual nonsense.

"Since you are so concerned that my chickens are suffering from shot nerves, perhaps we should bundle them into boxes and drive them up to town for a consultation with the veterinarian," I said.

"Travel is very bad for the chicken nerves. Boxing them up and throwing them in the car could finish them off," Guzim warned ominously. "The chicken to get very stressed when they overheat."

"I have to concur that it is exceptionally hot today."

"I hear in the village that the Kyria Yiota lose a chicken in the night to the fox."

"Perhaps my chickens are a tad unnerved because they've picked up on the scent of a fox," I posited, finally feeling a twinge of worry for the chickens. "A fox on the loose is a serious business. I can still recall the absolute trauma of that night when a fox got into the run and viciously murdered Ouzo and Mavrodaphni, leaving a feathery and bloodied trail of destruction in its wake."

Choking back a sob at the memory, Guzim insisted, "We must to destress the chickens before the Doruntina catches their nerves."

A nervous rabbit indeed. Was there no end to Guzim's nonsense?

"Okay, smarty pants. What do you advise we do to destress the chickens since you've rejected my idea of playing them classical music and taking them to the vet? Perhaps you think I should get in there with them and start grooming their feathers with a brush or read them a soothing bed time story before they turn in at the end of the day."

For once, Guzim picked up on my sarcasm. Sticking his lower lip out, his eyes practically rotated in their sockets as he stuck his thinking cap on. It was clearly a novelty.

"We must to make some kind of shade for the chicken to stop them from the overheating." I must admit to surprise that Guzim came up with such a practical suggestion. "Can I to ask the Mrs Bucket if she have the old sheet going spare? We could rig it up as a sun canopy."

"If there's any pestering of Mrs Bucket to be done, I'll be the one to do it," I said firmly. "I will ask her if she's got any old curtains or sheets you could rig up. Will brush nylon do or will it expose the chickens to the danger of an electric shock?"

"*Ti?*" Perchance brushed nylon wasn't a thing

in Albania. It certainly seemed to have lost its popularity in my homeland these days. "You must to buy the more wire to make the chicken run more secure against the fox."

"Now that's a sensible suggestion, particularly in light of Yiota's recent loss. I'll ask Barry to sort some wire out," I agreed, hoping that Barry would volunteer to secure the perimeter of the chicken run with Guzim's help. It wasn't a job that I fancied getting hands-on with, not in the broiling heat. My brother-in-law would most likely insist on taking charge since he is forever casting aspersions on my, admittedly useless, DIY abilities.

"We must to plant the lavender around the chicken run. And we must to sprinkle some lavender in their nesting boxes; it would to help them relax." Guzim's suggestion made me revert to thinking he had lost the plot.

"Are you serious? The chickens will probably just gobble up the lavender as a tasty treat," I pointed out.

"It is okay if they eat it. It will not to kill them and it will make their poop smell sweeter. It will to help to keep the flies away from the chickens. Annoying flies can unnerve them."

It seemed there was no end to the things that could potentially stress out my chickens. They looked happy enough to me.

Wondering what sort of extravagant folly my moronic gardener would think up next, I quipped, "I suppose you think I should engage a personal aromatherapist for the chickens."

"*Ti?*" Clearly my mention of an aromatherapist had gone over his head. I supposed there probably wasn't much call for fancy aromatherapists among dirt poor rabbit farmers in rural Albania.

Piercing the air, a blood curdling scream emanated from the house. Guzim abruptly dropped the hosepipe and tore off, his flipflops kicking up a cloud of dirt in my face.

I must confess that my first thought was a tad frivolous. *How thoughtless; surely such a loud scream will upset the chickens and their nerves are already shot.* I must hasten to add, lest the reader finds my first thoughts unfeelingly callous, I had immediately determined the ear-splitting cry hadn't come from my wife. I was more than familiar with the unique pitch of Marigold's screams since she unleashes them on a regular basis, whenever she is triggered by something as terrifying as a frog, lizard or gecko slipping indoors. Even the odd snail, spider and grasshopper have been known to set her off.

Knowing that Guzim was on the case, I strolled over to the house in a leisurely fashion; there was no point in working up a sweat after so recently showering.

Chapter 7

A Near Brush with a Fox

"Ti?" Following close on Guzim's tail, I could see that he was completely flummoxed by Doreen's words as she flapped around hysterically in my doorway, ironically reminding me of a headless chicken. I instantly surmised that Doreen must have been the screamer.

"There was a fox, I tell you," Doreen screeched at the Albanian, as though raising her voice would result in Guzim miraculously making sense of her English words. "I came to the door to see what was taking Victor so long and this fox was standing there as bold as brass. It stared at me with creepy red eyes and bared its teeth. It only bolted when I screamed."

Rolling my eyes, I explained to a confused Guzim that Doreen thought she saw a fox at the door. *"Nomizei oti eide mia alepou stin porta,"*

"What are you saying, Victor?" Doreen demanded.

Ignoring her, I told Guzim, *"Mallon itan gata."*

"Victor thinks you probably mistook a cat for a fox." Appearing at Doreen's side, Marigold translated since Doreen's ability to master anything more taxing than *mou* in Greek still defeated her. Doreen had acquired quite the habit of dropping the word *mou* indiscriminately, with no context at all; it rather reminds me of the good captain's habit of dropping beautiful towels.

"It was a fox, I tell you," Doreen stubbornly insisted. "It had a very distinctive brush. The thing might have eaten me alive..."

"Oh, do get a grip, Doreen. I'm sure a fox would find my chickens a sight more of a tasty temptation than you. Anyway, foxes don't eat people," I assured her, still convinced that she had seen a cat.

"I remember reading in the paper that a fox ran off with a baby. In fact, I even saw a film about it. It had that Meryl Streep in it," Doreen said.

"I think you'll find that was a dingo, not a fox," I told her.

"And it was in Australia, not Greece," Marigold said before querying, "Can foxes even walk up steps?"

"Of course, they can," I said before regretting my words. There was no point in playing into Doreen's deluded fantasy that she'd spotted a fox lurking right on our doorstep.

"*Koita.*" Guzim, down on his hands and knees on the outside steps leading up to the door, called out to me to look. "*Yparchei kopria alepous sta skalia.*"

"What's Guzim saying?" Doreen demanded.

"He says that there is some fox poop on the steps," I translated.

"How can he tell?" Marigold asked.

"I wouldn't question Guzim's credentials when it comes to poop," I said. "He's a bit of an expert on the subject of droppings seeing as he bags up the muck and sells it to gullible Brits on the coast as top-notch fresh manure."

"So, there was a fox," Doreen declared triumphantly.

"It would appear so," I confirmed, implicitly trusting Guzim on all matters poop related.

"I don't like the thought of a fox coming up here," Marigold said, a nervous quiver creeping into her voice.

"I don't like the thought of a fox so near to my chickens," I said, worried for their safety, my words replicated in Greek by Guzim expressing the exact same sentiment.

Clearly concerned about the safety of my brood, Guzim made a selfless decision. *"Tha koimitho exo apo to kotopoula apopse gia na prosecho."*

"What's he saying now?" Doreen asked.

"He says that he'll sleep outside next to the chicken house tonight to keep watch," I translated.

"How's he going to keep watch if he's sleeping?" Marigold demanded.

"Must you pick hairs?" I snapped, before thanking Guzim for his generous offer. Sometimes the Albanian shed dweller could surprise me by going above and beyond. His gardening duties certainly didn't include sleeping in the chicken run.

"Never mind your chickens," Marigold interjected unsympathetically. "We must find a way of deterring foxes from coming up to the door. A fox could attack darling little Fluffs."

"The defenceless kitten could certainly be easy prey to any foxes bold enough to lurk on the doorstep," I agreed. Unlike Clawsome and Catastrophe, Marigold's pampered imported domestics, the newest feline addition to the Bucket household was not averse to the idea of exploring outdoors. I cringed at the very thought of poor little Fluffs being torn limb from limb by a vicious predator.

BUCKET TO GREECE (VOL.15)

With this in mind, I asked Guzim the best way to deter a fox from coming up the stairs. "*Pos tha stamatisoume mia alepou na anevainei tis skales?*"

Looking at the two women, Guzim blushed before pulling me aside and telling me that I should mark my territory. I could swear he muttered I was stupid when I asked if I should spray some of my aftershave around the door to leave my mark.

I belatedly caught his drift when Guzim's hand drifted towards my crotch area, saying I must spray something else, "*Prepei na psekasete kati allo.*"

"I think that Guzim wants you to piddle, Victor. I'm sure I read that urine acts as a fox deterrent," Marigold said.

"Surely you don't expect me to engage in such vulgar behaviour as public urination?" I spluttered.

Having clearly caught on, Guzim asked if I wanted him to do it. "*Theleis na to kano?*"

"*Ochi.*" Marigold and I shouted out 'no' in unison.

"We could put some vinegar down," I suggested, repeating the word vinegar in Greek for Guzim's benefit. "*Xydi.*"

Agreeing that vinegar might well do the trick, Guzim pointed at the bag of rubbish sitting on the doorstep, opining that it likely attracted the fox, especially if it contained any food we might be chucking out.

"Why have you left a bag of rubbish out?" I quizzed Marigold. It was something we never did since the smell could attract feral cats that may rip the bags open. We had learnt from experience that cleaning up the resultant mess was a thoroughly disgusting business.

"It stinks to high heaven in this heat. I didn't want it stinking out the kitchen," Marigold said.

"So, why didn't you take it to the bins?"

"It's much too hot to go traipsing through the village to the bins," Marigold complained. "And can you imagine how much they must reek in this heat?"

Guzim's head swivelled like a spectator at a tennis match as it followed our, incomprehensible to him, vocal rally. Tutting loudly, he grabbed the bag of rubbish and stalked off. Reflecting that he really was going above and beyond by disposing of the Bucket garbage, I decided I would slip an extra fiver in his wages at the end of the day.

Fans blasted cool air from every direction as the three of us sat down at the kitchen table to eat lunch. I tried not to stare when the rotating blast of air mussed up Doreen's perm, exposing the bald spot I had created when I'd hacked away with the scissors.

Tucking into fried courgettes and salad, Doreen

praised my culinary expertise.

"These courgettes are perfectly scrumptious, Victor."

"Victor could write a book on 101 things to do with courgettes," Marigold cooed.

"And I must say, you do cook up a good salad, Victor…"

"If you've been cooking your salads, Doreen, you've been doing something very wrong in the kitchen," I schooled her.

Remembering my promise to Spiros, I addressed Marigold. "By the way, I took the liberty of promising Spiros that you'd knock up one of your trifles for Sampaguita. She's feeling a bit low and needs cheering up."

"Really, Victor. You can't just go around promising my trifles willy-nilly to all and sundry. Have you any idea how draining it is to prepare food in this heat?"

"You do realise that I just stood over a pan of hot oil to fry that courgette you're about to consume. I can't imagine it will tax you too much to drizzle a bit of sherry over a shop bought sponge and rustle up some custard to chuck on top."

"Well, I suppose that as it's for Sampaguita..." Marigold conceded, having a soft spot for Spiros' Filipina wife.

"Any chance you can knock up a second one?"

I wheedled. "Young Tonibler is due over later for another English lesson. I bet he's never tasted trifle in his life."

"The poor little mite does need fattening up. I'll do a second trifle but leave the sherry out," Marigold volunteered, having a particular soft spot for the clever young boy. "But you can take Sampaguita's trifle over there. I'm not venturing out in this heat."

"You only need to take it downstairs. Sampaguita will be round at my mother's this evening."

"I suppose you'll be wanting me to knock up a third trifle for your mother next." Dropping the sarcasm from her tone, she hesitantly added, "Or do you think it might upset her needlessly?"

"I am yet to find anyone that has been upset by one of your trifles...not even a trifle upset," I quipped.

"It might bring back painful memories. No one loved one of my trifles more than Panos."

"I'm sure it will only bring back happy memories," I assured my wife, recalling with fondness how Vi and Panos had smuggled up on the sofa scoffing trifle in front of Coronation Street.

"Did you manage to catch up with Barry?" Marigold asked.

"Yes, indeed. We took coffee together at the

new *kafenio*. Norman was on a hiding to nothing when he turned up with a tray of his fancies and Manolis gave him his marching orders. It is perfectly absurd of Norman to think he can sell something out of his patently unhygienic kitchen in a commercial venue. He would likely provoke an outburst of food poisoning in the village."

"He's been having that Blerta to come in and clean up after him," Doreen volunteered.

"Good grief, he's getting through cleaners at the rate of knots." Ticking the names off my fingers, I listed them. "Let's see, he's had my mother…then Theo, the lapsed Jehovah's Witness. After Theo, there was that dreadful Agnesa, and now he's moved onto Blerta."

"Well, Theo just up and left Nektar when Agnesa and that strange little husband of hers…"

"Drin…"

"I don't mind if I do, Victor. A glass of wine will go down nicely with the food," Doreen simpered.

"Drin is the name of Agnesa's husband," I said, heading over to the fridge for a bottle of chilled wine. Retrieving a vintage of Lidl's finest, I looked pointedly at Doreen as I unscrewed the bottle. "Drin obviously has a drink problem."

"Really, Victor. Enjoying a glass of wine with our lunch won't turn us into a pair of raging alcoholics," Marigold tutted. Clearly the pair she referred to comprised her and Doreen; I wouldn't be indulging during the daytime since it wouldn't do for me to be tipsy in charge of a child later. "Anyway, we can water the wine down with ice cubes. Do dig some out of the freezer, Victor."

"I'm so relieved that Norman has finally replaced that dreadful Agnesa," Doreen said. "He did nothing but complain about her. He was sure she was pilfering…"

"Oh, that's terrible. What sort of things went missing?" Marigold prompted her friend.

"It was little things to start with…the sort of things that one wouldn't normally miss in the scheme of things and that one wouldn't associate with the type of things that would be tempting enough to steal."

"Such as?" I asked.

"At first it was things like cleaning materials and rubber gloves…"

"Victor would notice immediately if a dent was made in his cleaning supplies," Marigold said, suppressing a laugh. "Can you believe he keeps an itemised inventory of how many sponges he has to hand?"

"You may mock, Marigold," I said sternly. "It wouldn't do to be caught short in an emergency situation where a sponge is required."

"Then I noticed other things disappearing

whenever Agnesa had been in...handtowels and tea towels," Doreen continued. "I couldn't be certain they were missing rather than in the washing bin or out on the line...but there was no doubt in my mind when a bottle of *Metaxa* did a disappearing act. I accused Norman of turning to drink again but he swore he hadn't had a drop of the hard stuff since he started baking."

"He's certainly limited himself to just the odd glass of wine at the expat dinner parties," Marigold concurred.

"I told Norman he must sack Agnesa but he was too lily-livered to stand up to her. Agnesa kept turning up and pushing her way in, and more things kept disappearing. I was amazed when he finally grew enough of a back-bone to sack the ghastly woman."

"He didn't," I enlightened her. "He nagged me into doing it for him because he didn't know enough Greek to tell her to sling her hook."

"Well, the cowardly custard never let on that he'd persuaded you to do his dirty work for him," Doreen gasped. "Can you believe that he led me to think that he'd finally grown a pair and sacked her himself?"

"Victor, you never mentioned this to me," Marigold chided. "I do hope there won't be any repercussions. What if that horrible Agnesa woman sends that drunken oaf of a husband to sort you out?"

"It's okay, darling. The pair of them have gone now. Neither of them could find any real work in the village. I heard that a couple of Greeks gave the odd bit of charring work to Agnesa, but not at all impressed by her lax cleaning standards, they gave her the boot. Apparently, word is that a cat could give a bathroom a more thorough licking than Agnesa," I said.

"Which Greeks took her on?" Marigold asked.

"I'm not sure. I know that Litsa paid Agnesa to give her brother Mathias' place a good going over."

"I thought Litsa did all of her brother's cleaning," Marigold said in surprise.

"Usually, yes. But Litsa took a bit of a tumble and sprained her wrist. She couldn't manage for a couple of weeks. Then, of course, Kyria Maria from next door made no bones about bad-mouthing Agnesa to anyone who would listen, outraged that the Albanian cleaner had the temerity to demand the blankets off her bed. None of the locals would employ Agnesa after listening to Maria or hearing that she'd upset Dina and was trying to muscle in on Violet Burke's territory."

"But Vi can't take on all the cleaning work going...there's quite a lot of demand of late," Marigold acknowledged. It was true. My mother has established an excellent reputation as a char but she only has one pair of hands; there just aren't enough hours in the day for Violet Burke to keep up with the increasing demand for her services. Loyal to her original customers, the taverna and the shop, Sherry and the Stranges, not to mention our own Bucket household, Vi has proven herself to be indispensable, ensuring she now has her pick of any new clients. She revels in turning down anyone who irritates her or who isn't prepared to pay over the odds. Only today she had added the *kafenio* and the living quarters above it to her regular client base.

"People soon wised up to the Albanian woman's habit of acting very subservient until she had her foot in the door, then coming over all bolshie and demanding something extra on top of her wages once the job was done," I said.

"And done inadequately at that," Doreen added. "I still ended up having to wipe up Norman's mess even though he'd paid Agnesa."

"The final straw came when Spiros discovered Drin sleeping off a drunken session in the back of his hearse. He kicked his sorry backside out of town," I said, recalling Spiros' fury that the sanctity of his hearse had been violated by the inebriated Albanian. "Since neither half of the Albanian couple could snag gainful employment locally, they packed their bags and moved down to the coast. I heard on the grapevine that Agnesa has landed herself a job as a kitchen skivvy, washing up in one of the coastal tavernas."

"Good riddance, I say," Doreen applauded. "There was something about Agnesa...I don't mind admitting I took an instant dislike to her."

"I disliked her before I even had the misfortune to meet her," I revealed. "She was filling Guzim's head with all sorts of nonsense, brainwashing him into thinking he was entitled, as a poor downtrodden Albanian, to demand lots of extras on top of his wages. For a while there, he sounded as though he'd swallowed the Communist Manifesto until I talked some sense into him."

"Such a cheek considering how generous Victor has always been with Guzim," Marigold said. "There's barely a cast-off of Victor's that hasn't made it into Guzim's wardrobe."

"I did wonder where he got that awful Lycra from," Doreen said, her mouth twitching in a smile.

"That had nothing to do with Victor. Do you seriously imagine I'd let Victor out of the house in skin-tight Lycra? He'd be a laughing stock."

"It's a bit baggy on Guzim," Doreen tittered.

"As I was saying...I knew that Agnesa was going to be trouble before I even met her. She had an enormous chip on her shoulder. Anyway, with

Agnesa out of the picture, Violet Burke took Blerta under her wing, recommending her for any cleaning jobs she had neither the time nor inclination to take on herself. It was particularly satisfying to hear of Blerta's burgeoning cleaning opportunities since she had confided in me that Agnesa had looked down on Blerta as a refugee from Yugoslavia. Agnesa said some very cruel things."

"That's terrible. Blerta puts such a nice crease in your Y-fronts, dear," Marigold said.

"What really incensed me was when Agnesa made young Tonibler cry…she made derogatory remarks about his school uniform and his plastered spectacles to his face."

"Fancy picking on an innocent child," Doreen clucked.

"Victor is convinced Tonibler is some kind of prodigy," Marigold said proudly.

"Once I dispensed with Agnesa's services on Norman's behalf, my mother refused to clean up after Norman again but she sent Blerta his way."

"Blerta does a good job and I must say, I'm more comfortable having her in than your mother," Doreen reported. "I do find Mrs Burke awfully intimidating."

"She doesn't tolerate…"

Firing a scathing look in my direction, Marigold

interrupted before I could voice the word fools. "I'm happy to hear Blerta's finding extra work. I do so hate to see Tonibler with holes in his shoes."

"Yiota's taken Blerta on to clean the farmhouse once a week," I told them. "She was just too exhausted after a day of manual labour to tackle the housework. My mother had been doing it but she refused to accept a cent from Yiota. My mother told me, 'It's not right for me to take cash from Yiota, not when she's like family.'

"She takes your money and we're family," Marigold piped up.

"Well, Yiota was really embarrassed that Vi wouldn't take her money so they reached a compromise. Vi told Yiota that Blerta needed cash, so now Yiota pays Blerta to clean once a week," I explained.

I didn't feel it necessary to open a can of worms and tell Marigold that Violet Burke had said that she took my money because there would be no need to pay anyone to clean 'if that lazy wife of yours got off her backside and got stuck in with the mop. It's not as if Marigold has been digging up spuds and birthing lambs all day like Yiota does. The most strenuous thing that wife of yours does is sit around gossiping with that scatter-brained Doreen.'

Hastily changing the subject, I asked Doreen, "So, how are you surviving being separated from

Manolis now he's running the *kafenio*?"

"I think it's healthy that we're not in one another's pockets all day long." From the way Doreen's mouth turned down as she spoke, I guessed she was parroting Manolis' opinion rather than her own. "I made that mistake when Norman retired and we moved over here; there was nothing like being stuck together twenty-four seven to highlight how boring Norman is."

"You didn't notice it until then?" I quipped.

"I couldn't tolerate having Victor under my feet all day. Luckily, he always has something on the go to keep him busy and out of my hair."

"It's called work," I pointed out.

"How you exaggerate, Victor," Marigold scoffed. "It's not as though you do manual labour like Barry. Half the time, all you do is float around on a boat in the Med."

"Speaking of Barry," I said. "You won't believe what Spiros was telling us earlier. He pointed out a female goatherd who served time in prison for adultery."

"No. You can't be serious." Marigold looked meaningfully at Doreen as she continued. "You mean to say she was sent to prison for carrying on with someone who wasn't her husband?"

Doreen's eyes darted nervously around the room. Flushing profusely, she drained her glass of wine in one.

"Don't worry, Doreen," I said. "The law criminalising adultery has been obsolete since 1983."

As Doreen slowly regained her composure, Marigold started bleating on about one of her favourite subjects.

"Victor, what are you planning to cook up for the expat dinner party we're hosting next week?"

"What? That's the first I've heard of it."

"Really, Victor, sometimes I think you never listen to a word that I say. It's been in the diary for weeks."

"It was supposed to be my turn to host but things are just too awkward at home with Norman refusing to move out. Luckily, Marigold stepped in and offered to host it here," Doreen revealed, earning a withering look from Marigold for giving away that our hosting the dinner had been a spur of the moment, last minute thing. Sometimes I think that Marigold simply accuses me of not listening out of habit.

"No doubt you'll wow us all with something exotic," Doreen gushed.

"Perhaps you could turn your hand to sushi," Marigold suggested. "No one has done Japanese yet."

"You seriously think I should serve up raw fish

in this heat. I could end up sending our guests home with a parasite or a nasty case of Listeriosis or Salmonella," I warned.

"It might be safer if you cooked the fish," Doreen suggested.

"That rather defeats the object of serving sushi. I thought I'd do a light dessert of figs and yoghurt."

"That doesn't sound very Japanese," Marigold said.

"For a light dessert now, not at the dinner party," I said, busying myself with spooning thick and creamy Greek yoghurt into three bowls. Slicing fresh figs from the garden, I added them to the yoghurt, drizzling a generous amount of Giannis' excellent local honey atop the fruit. A sprig of fresh garden mint completed the delicious dessert. My efforts were rewarded with flattering words from the ladies, though my enjoyment of the dish was rather marred by the sound of Doreen slurping the yoghurt. She has the most annoying habit of sounding just like the suction pipe used to empty the septic tanks.

"Do you think we'll have to invite your mother to join us at the expat dinner party?" Marigold asked.

"It would be rude not to since she'll be staying in our spare bedroom," I pointed out.

"Why is Mrs Burke coming to stay with you

when she lives downstairs?" Doreen asked.

"She's having a friend from England over to stay and there's only one bed downstairs," I replied.

"And since this Dot is an unknown quantity until we actually meet her, we thought it would be easier if Violet stayed here rather than inviting a stranger into our guestroom," Marigold explained.

"Dot?" Doreen queried.

"She worked in the chippy with Victor's mother. We're picking her up at the airport this Sunday." Marigold oozed apprehension as she spoke. "I suppose it could be worse. The first thing that sprang to mind when Violet said she'd invited a friend to stay, was that it must be that awful Edna Billings she's always going on about."

"No danger of that, dear. My mother loathes the haddock on Friday woman."

"I know, but I wouldn't have put it past your mother to invite her anyway, just to rub her nose in her new life in Greece."

Although Marigold had never had the misfortune to meet Vi's council house neighbour back in Warrington, Edna Billings, my description of the shell-suited lout lobbing empty lager cans and lewd words had clearly left a lasting impression. I could only hope that Dot didn't come out of the same vulgar mould.

Chapter 8

Milton Drops In

After downing two glasses of Lidl white wine, Doreen came over a tad too mushy on the subject of Manolis. Rolling her eyes, Marigold attempted to hide the sarcasm in her voice when she suggested to her friend that her Greek boyfriend was probably pining for her. Emboldened by the alcohol, Doreen hiccupped that she would pop over to the new *kafenio* now in case her true love was missing her. Feeling mellow herself from the wine, Marigold kindly offered to lend Doreen a sun hat to cover the bald bit.

No sooner had Doreen skedaddled than

Marigold announced she was off for another cold shower before she got stuck into concocting trifle. Filling Fluffs' bowl with the leftover yoghurt dip that I'd rustled up to accompany the *kolokythakia*, I was pleasantly surprised to see the kitten lap it up, and I might add, a darn sight more quietly than Doreen had slurped up her fig dessert.

Sighing with irritation that I had been left with the washing up, I donned the Marigolds and immersed my hands in the suds.

"I say, old chap, the door was open, what." Milton's plummy announcement preceded his appearance. I silently cursed my habit of leaving the door ajar to encourage a through breeze. "Thought I'd just pop in on the off chance, what. You know all about embarrassing rashes…"

My steely stare stopped Milton in his tracks before he could blurt out any intimate details which I would rather not hear, the sort of details that one would be unable to unhear once heard. Pondering why Milton would assume I was some kind of expert on rashes of an icky nature, I hoped that Violet Burke hadn't opened her big mouth and blabbed about my original and exceedingly unfortunate name. The last thing I needed was my unwanted visitor getting wind of the disease-ridden connotations associated with the name V.D. Bucket.

"I just thought you might have a tube of cream lying around to alleviate the symptoms, what."

"I think you may have mistaken the Bucket household for the *farmakeio*," I retorted. Peeling my Marigold's off, I wondered if Milton was too past it to be schooled in appropriate boundaries. "The clue is in the lack of a flashing green sign outside."

"The pharmacy has already shut up shop for the day, old chap. I remembered you having a bit of an adverse reaction to rabbit fur and thought you might be able to save the day."

Recalling that I had indeed picked up an unfortunate fungal skin infection from sticking my hands into mittens knitted from loose rabbit fur, courtesy of Guzim's fluffle of dermatophytosis infected rabbits back in Albania, I realised I may have jumped the gun. I had instantly presumed Milton's rash was the type which the nylon haired Ashley would be biting at the bit to examine under his microscope. Milton had, after all, been the one to describe his condition as embarrassing.

"I thought the same stuff might work on Kyriakos, what. He's only gone and got himself a nasty rash that he's blaming on our cats." It appeared that the Hancocks' Greek lodger must have Milton wrapped around his little finger if he was sending his landlord out for rash remedies.

"If he's picked up some zoonotic itch from the

cats, why on earth is it embarrassing?"

"Well, he's afflicted in the sort of place one hardly wants to be seen scratching in polite company..."

My mind boggled as I tried not to imagine where Kyriakos was sticking the cats. Still, it struck me that Milton was being a tad prudish for someone who penned erotica. One would expect the local purveyor of porn to come right out and name the itchy body part without beating about the bush.

"One of the cats bedded down in his underpants, what. Straight off the washing line they were, but Edna went and left them on the stair lift, what."

"The cats?"

"No, Kyriakos' undies. Not that Kyriakos hasn't suggested that Edna ought to hang the cats out for a good airing. Bit over the top, what, even if he has got itchy privates. Surely there must be some sort of law against pegging cats out by their ears."

"I may have an old tube of topical cream in the bathroom cabinet. You'd be well advised to check the use-by date before applying it."

"I say, old chap, I've no intention of smearing it on. Kyriakos can do that for himself, what."

Resigning myself to Milton's uninvited appearance in my kitchen, I offered, "I think there may be an extra cuppa in the pot. Pour yourself one while I dig out the ointment."

Wading into the bathroom, I surmised that Marigold must have finished her shower and be dressing in the bedroom. My wife can be utterly exasperating at times. Leaving the door of the shower cubicle open in summer to take advantage of any breeze from the open window is a habit of hers that drives me to distraction, particularly when instead of picking up a mop, she insists that the water will soon evaporate from the floor tiles in the heat.

Rummaging through the bathroom cabinet, I wondered if Milton and Edna had any clue that word had got round in the village that they were living in some kind of shameful menage a trois with Kyriakos. Whilst I knew it was an innocent arrangement, the locals enjoyed spreading some scandal; it was all too easy to spread considering Milton had a reputation amongst the villagers as the old English man who wrote smutty books. I had of course advised him on countless occasions that he should never reveal he was Scarlett Bottom, but my advice had fallen on deaf ears.

Returning with the tube of cream, I warned Milton, "You'll need to read the leaflet to see if it's safe to apply it to sensitive areas one wouldn't scratch in public."

"Bit of a botheration, what. The leaflet's all in Greek, old chap."

"Well, that's handy, considering your lodger is Greek."

"Ah, right, with you, old chap. Easy to forget that he's a foreigner when we converse in English."

"I suppose he's no choice with your limited Greek. You might as well take the weight off your dodgy hip," I invited. "So, how are you getting on with your live-in lodger?"

"Splendidly, what, splendidly. All that business of Kyriakos refusing to move out was just an aberration. I find him rather spiffing company, truth be told. I won't deny that the fellow has some odd habits that take a bit of adjusting to, what. His not being too keen on the cats rubs Edna up the wrong way, but it's a small price to pay. The rent money has been such a boon; only wish we'd thought of it sooner, what. Edna doesn't need to scrimp on the cat food and the tea bags only get two dunkings these days."

"I'm glad to hear it's working out for you," I said with genuine relief. Wondering how I could get Milton to spill the beans about Kyriakos' strange habits without appearing nosy, I had overlooked what a blabbermouth my visitor was; he seemed keen to divulge his lodger's habits with nary a prompt from me.

"His habit of explaining how to do things can grate," Milton volunteered.

"How so?"

"Well, it's little things, little things that annoy Edna, what. He has a tendency to hover in the kitchen to explain how things ought to be done. I've noticed that about the Greeks, they like things a certain way. They're not big on putting salad cream on their salad..."

"Why would they be when we live in the land of olive oil?"

"And they eat at very peculiar hours."

"I have to agree it can take a bit of adjusting to going out to eat late at night rather than early evening."

"Even at home, Kyriakos is the same. Won't hear of Edna serving his dinner at seven o'clock."

"But that's not really a strange habit peculiar to Kyriakos, all the Greeks are the same," I pointed out. "The Greeks perceive that it is we Brits that have strange habits if we don't adapt to the Greek way of life. On the odd occasion when a Greek person has been invited along to one of the expat dinner parties, they simply can't get their heads around turning up at seven o'clock in the afternoon rather than their usual nine or ten."

"Well, it's playing havoc with the cats' mealtimes. Edna likes to wait to see if there's any leftovers before dishing up."

"You eat the cats' leftovers," I said, making no attempt to conceal my disgust.

"Of course not. I meant any human leftovers to feed to the cats." Despite Milton's unfortunate turn of phrase, I caught his drift. "The days of pretending tinned cat food is some type of edible pâté are behind us now that we've got some extra cash coming in. Boggles the mind to think of your good lady wife having taste tested the stuff for a living. We only forced it down out of desperation."

"Well, Marigold only tasted a smidgen. It wasn't as though she choked a full can of cat food down in one sitting," I clarified.

"Kyriakos is big on laying the law down, wants things done in a certain way, what. He went on for ages, lecturing Edna about the correct way to clean eggs..."

"Well, it's good that he's up on his food hygiene. No one wants to confront a mucky egg flaunting its feathers in an egg cup first thing in the morning...some of the ones that come out of my coop certainly need a good wiping down."

"He'd confused his cleaning with peeling, old chap. He had some very odd ideas about keeping eggs fresh in iced water before boiling them..."

"But that would make the shells crack..."

"And it makes them impossible to peel...and

then there's the dangerous business of eating ice cream, what. It was a bit of a luxury for us when Kyriakos treated us to a tub of the stuff but then he insisted we let it defrost for forty minutes before tucking in. Apparently, it's darned hazardous stuff that can break teeth if consumed straight from the freezer. He has myriad rules that he insists we follow to prevent us doing ourselves an injury."

"You're more likely to pick up a nasty dose of Listeria from eating defrosted ice cream. The ingredients are likely to turn in the heat," I said.

"I told Kyriakos it was all moot anyway since I have dentures. It all got rather confusing because he was clueless what dentures are. I had to demonstrate by removing my teeth before he got it."

"You really ought to apply yourself and learn some Greek. It would really help you in communicating with your lodger," I advised.

"Can't say that I trust Kyriakos on the teaching Greek front, what, not after he steered me wrong before."

"Ah, yes. I recall how you went around spouting Greek bollocks. There's nothing to stop you from learning some vocabulary from a phrase book. In fact, I have an excellent one that I can lend you," I offered, wondering where I had left the well-thumbed phrase book that Adam had gifted me prior to our move to Greece.

It had certainly served me well during our first few months in Meli, even if some of the phrases were a tad antiquated. It would surely be preferable to have Milton banging on about bagpipes and the handsomeness of the prime minister, rather than unwittingly swearing at any locals he subjected to his attempts to learn Greek. There was a risk that the locals may jump to the assumption that Milton was a mentally defective homosexual, particularly in light of the rumours that were already flying around about the threesome in the Hancock household, but I expected Milton would simply take it in his stride. Being very thick-sickened, he wasn't one to easily take offence.

"Jolly good of you to offer your phrase book, old chap, though I could be short of time to apply myself to getting to grips with the old Greek lingo what. I really need to buckle down to my writing..."

"More porn?"

"Erotica, old chap, erotica, but actually no. Since writing as Scarlett Bottom hasn't proved very lucrative, Kyriakos suggested I should pen a book about moving to Greece..."

I tuned out as Milton droned on. Marigold would have a fit if she got wind of Kyriakos' suggestion; even if Milton's book wasn't competition for my own musings on the subject, Milton couldn't be trusted not to give away our secret mountain location. I realised I must talk up Milton's erotica and dissuade him from penning anything to do with up-sticking.

"Whilst that sort of book can be quite popular, I don't think you have enough material, Milton," I advised. "Despite moving over here yonks ago, you haven't really integrated into village life…"

"We've integrated with the local Brits, what," Milton argued.

"Yes, but the people that buy that sort of book want to read about local culture, not about a bunch of boring expats. Let's face it, Milton, apart from your stays in a Greek hospital, you haven't really ventured out much beyond the village…"

"That's down to having no car and no money, old chap…and it's a bit difficult to get out and about with a dodgy hip…"

"I think you should give the erotica another go," I said, hardly able to believe I was actively encouraging the old fool to churn out yet more dire smut. "Best to write about something you have an actual interest in."

"I expect you're right, old chap, you usually are. Can't say you've steered me wrong yet," Milton admitted.

Her Titian locks still damp from the shower,

Marigold breezed into the kitchen, attempting to conceal her dismay at discovering Milton cluttering up the place.

"I didn't realise you had company, Victor," she said. "Don't mind me, I just came in to make a start on the trifle."

"I always say to Edna, there's nothing like one of Marigold's trifles, what," Milton said with more than a hint in his voice.

"I can send you home with the recipe," Marigold volunteered, her steely glare indicating there would be no free puddings heading Milton's way today.

"Milton was just saying that Kyriakos is trying to persuade him to write a book about moving to Greece," I volunteered.

"Oh, no, you don't want to do that," Marigold opined in horror at the thought. "No one is interested in that sort of thing. You should stick to your erotica. After all, you've made quite a name for yourself as Scarlett Bottom."

"You think…" Milton practically preened under Marigold's false flattery.

"Have you ever thought of spicing it up with the addition of lots of exclamation marks?"

Chapter 9

Unnaturally Swollen

The sound of the *apothiki* door slamming below our feet alerted us to Violet Burke's return from her afternoon cleaning job, the slam serving as Marigold's cue to pop downstairs with the decadently delicious trifle she had knocked up for Sampaguita. Since Marigold had allowed me to lick the spoon, I knew that the creamy dessert was particularly scrumptious, so tempting that I toyed with the idea of perhaps calling in on my mother later in the hope of being offered a helping.

"Victor. Victor."

V.D. BUCKET

There was nothing dulcet about my wife's voice as she screeched up at me from the street; it was most unlike Marigold to carry on like a vulgar fishwife. There was an urgency to her tone that sent me scampering down to the *apothiki* posthaste, worried that something must be very amiss.

Joining her on the pavement, I panted, "Don't tell me there's another fox."

"No, it's your mother's ankles. The way they've swollen up is completely unnatural," Marigold said, her tone suffused with worry as she clutched my arm and pulled me into Vi's living room, hissing, "I really think you should bung her in the Punto pronto and whisk her down to the clinic. Just ignore her if she protests."

"That's easier said than done," I commented. My mother could be nothing if not stubborn.

Slumped on the sofa, Violet Burke struggled to remove her shoes; they appeared to be welded to her feet.

"Will you stop your fussing, lass. You know I'm prone to swollen feet," Vi said, dismissing Marigold's vocal concern. I could only stare in the general direction of where I would expect my mother's ankles to be since they had apparently completely disappeared. The lower half of her legs were swollen to twice their normal size, resembling solid tree trunks shoved into her serviceable lace-ups.

"That doesn't look good," I opined, sharing my wife's unease.

Rolling her eyes, Vi quipped, "'Appen my ankles will explode before my feet."

"I really don't like the look of them," I reiterated.

"I might have had a right pair of shapely pins when I was younger but don't forget these feet of mine have been carrying me around for eighty years now," Vi said, bizarrely adding, "At least I've still got my own hair."

"Well, you've still got your own feet..." I pointed out before realising how ludicrous I sounded.

"Of course, they're still Vi's feet. She's hardly likely to be walking around on someone else's," Marigold interrupted.

"Are your ankles painful, Mother? They certainly look it." Having finally managed to prise the first shoe loose, Vi lobbed it towards the open front door. The shoe was met with a pained meow that sounded as though it came from a scalded cat.

"That'll teach that dratted moggy of Cynthia's to keep its distance instead of hanging around for scraps," Vi said, sighing with satisfaction. "My feet have been giving me gip all day but it's hardly nowt new..."

V.D. BUCKET

"I think Marigold's right, Mother. We should get your ankles checked out by a doctor...they certainly weren't all puffed up like that this morning."

"Fine, have it your own way. If you can get me an appointment, I'll see a doctor. 'Appen it will shut the two of you up from your nagging."

"There's no need to make an appointment, Vi. The clinic is open now. Victor will drive you down," Marigold said, volunteering my services without bothering to consult me.

"Well, 'appen it would be more convenient to go now rather than have to cancel one of my mucky clients tomorrow." Picking up her other discarded shoe, Vi's face turned a strange shade of puce as she attempted to ram it back on her foot. "It's no good. It won't go back on. You'd best fetch my slippers out of the bedroom, Marigold."

"And I'll just pop upstairs and get my English to Greek dictionary in case the medics on call aren't familiar with swollen ankles."

"They'd have to be blind not to notice them..." Vi joshed.

By the time I returned with the dictionary, Vi was ready for the off, a pair of gaudy red furry slippers gracing her feet; fortunately the slippers were backless. Marigold and I assisted Vi to the Punto, supporting her bulbous form between us.

BUCKET TO GREECE (VOL.15)

Adjusting the passenger seat, I moved it back to allow a little extra wiggle room for my mother to cram her feet in.

"I've just remembered Tonibler is due over for an English lesson..."

"Don't worry about that, Victor. I don't mind staying here to keep the boy entertained. I've a trifle in the fridge with his name on it," Marigold assured me. She made no attempt to hide her relief that the imminent arrival of the child provided her with the perfect excuse to swerve coming along to the clinic to offer her mother-in-law moral support. Marigold has never been too keen on sterile environments or places where needles are routinely flashed around.

As we approached the taverna in the Punto, Violet Burke instructed me to stop the car, demanding that I rush inside to make her excuses to Dina. "I won't be able to do the spuds if I'm at the clinic, will I now? I hate to let Dina down."

Luckily Dina had made an early start in the kitchen so I was able to bring her up to speed on my mother's medical emergency.

"*Pairno ti mitera mou stin kliniki me tous prismenous astragalous tis*," I said, telling Dina that I was taking my mother to the clinic with her swollen ankles. Admittedly my phrasing was a tad clumsy; it wasn't as though my mother could very well leave her swollen ankles behind.

"Ennoeis ta podia?" Dina replied, asking me if I meant feet. Dina was clearly accustomed to my mother's ceaseless complaints about her swollen feet.

"Ochi, einai oi astragoloi tis," I said, confirming it was her ankles.

Wiping her hands on a tea towel, Dina rushed out to the car, opening the passenger door to get a good look at Violet Burke's ankles.

Raising clenched fists to her mouth, Dina's eyes grew as big as saucers as she declared, *"Fainontai frikta."*

"What's she saying?" Vi demanded.

"She said they look horrible," I translated.

Fussing over my mother, Dina told her not to worry about missing her shift, repeatedly exhorting her to get well soon, *"Perastika."* Violet Burke appeared to get her drift without demanding I translate every word. Amazingly, Dina didn't suggest that I step into my mother's shoes to help with the peeling though I wouldn't be at all surprised to receive a call from Nikos later asking if I was up for a bit of woman's work, as he disparagingly phrased it.

Continuing on our way, I glimpsed in the rear-view mirror, spotting Dina standing in the road, waving us off. It was a given that as soon as the taverna opened for business, my mother's ankles would have swollen to such ginormous proportions that they would be likened to an elephant's legs. Anything medical has a tendency to be exaggerated in the extreme as soon as it hits the lips of the local gossips.

Driving down to the coast, my mother prattled on endlessly about the arrival of her friend, Dot, this coming Sunday. "She's never been to Greece before but it's not like she's a virgin where abroad is concerned. Her and Wilf used to go regular like to Torremolinos, before the daft beggar went and pegged it."

"Does that mean this is Dot's first time travelling abroad alone?"

"Oh, she won't be coming on her own, lad." Vi's words took me by surprise. She hadn't mentioned that Dot would be bringing a companion to stay with her in the *apothiki* while my mother bedded down in our guest room. Surely Vi had mentioned there was only one bed. "She never goes anywhere without Wilf's ashes."

"She's bringing her dead husband's ashes to Greece?"

"Aye, she's been after somewhere nice to scatter him. There's nowt but a grimy square of slabs between her terrace house and the ginnel. The local park is knee-deep in dog muck and she worried someone might scrape him up along with the dog's doings. It would hardly be a fitting end if Wilf ended up in the bin in a bag full of..."

"It doesn't sound as though much scraping up goes on if the place is knee-deep in the stuff," I said. "She can think again if she gets any bright ideas about scattering him in my garden. I won't have my chickens exposed to human remains...I would imagine it would put them right off their laying."

"Dot reckons it would be right romantic to empty Wilf's urn on a beach, 'appen at sunset..."

"Let's hope that we are spared a sea breeze." I could just imagine the horror of a clump of Wilf's ashes drifting into a tourist's sundowner, or a late afternoon swimmer showering away what they thought was sand from their body, clueless they were washing away gritty specks of Dot's dearly departed husband.

"I'm that looking forward to seeing Dot again. We must have racked up ten years together in the chippy before they went and demolished it."

"Did she manage to get another job after the chip shop closed?" I asked.

"Nay, lad, she hung up her chip shovel and makes do on her pension. She still had a bit of cash left over from Wilf's life insurance even after she'd shelled out to cremate him..." Her words were replaced with a heartfelt groan. "'Appen I should have got that wife of yours to fill up your washing up bowl so I could have given my poor feet a bit of a soak."

"The water would have slopped everywhere on these bends," I pointed out, making a mental count of how many of my washing up bowls had been rendered unusable by my mother soaking her swollen feet in them. Considering she shares my interest in kitchen hygiene, she never demonstrated the least compunction about polluting my bowls. "We'll be there in a jiffy. Hopefully the doctor can give you something to reduce the swelling."

"I'm not one for swallowing pills, lad, but I do want my feet right before Dot lands. We plan to be out and about in the afternoons; I've jiggled my shifts around so that I'm just doing mornings next week."

"Hmm," I huffed in a non-committal way, wondering if my mother planned to rope me into service as her personal chauffeur to show Dot the sights on the days that I was free from repping. "I'll give Captain Vasos a ring and see if you and Dot can smuggle yourselves onboard when I do the lazy day cruise next week."

"Aye, she'd like that, lad. It doesn't get much better than swanning around in a yacht with that old charmer, Vasos. If I was twenty years younger, I'd have snapped him up. 'Appen Blerta can cover my shift at the *kafenio* if you can sort it out for coming on the yacht with my old mucker, Vasos."

"Consider it done," I promised, not bothering to correct her persistent delusion that the tourist boat was a yacht. Having a day out on Pegasus with her friend would make Violet Burke a happy camper; the perpetually embarrassed state it would likely leave me in whilst on repping duty was a small price to pay for my mother's happiness. "Just as long as the doctor gives your ankles the all-clear."

Slowing down at the sight of a couple of Lycra-clad cyclists pedalling uphill in tandem, I silently cursed them for hogging the road, making it impossible for me to safely overtake. Showing no restraint, Vi stuck her head out of the passenger window, yelling at the top of her voice, "Stick to the side, you pair of numpties."

The two cyclists frantically shifted to one side, their bicycles wobbling precariously as they lost their concentration. "I can't be doing with bicyclists on these narrow roads," Vi spluttered, cackling gleefully as the first cyclist came a cropper, losing his balance and landing on his backside in the field.

"That's rich coming from you. You cycle to all your cleaning jobs in Meli," I said.

"It's hardly the same. I'm not some wet-behind-the-ear tourist who knows nowt about Greek roads. Anyhow, I can hardly be expected to plod about on these feet of mine. I hope that Barry has fixed my flat tyre…"

"You can depend on Barry."

"Aye, he's a right good lad, that Barry. 'Appen he can bring the nipper round later for a bit of Marigold's trifle. She did Sampaguita proud by the looks of it. I just hope she didn't hold back on the sherry."

"I hope she did if you're planning on feeding it to Anastasia."

The only response my mother made was a snore. I was relieved that despite the obvious discomfort from her swollen appendages, she was able to catch forty winks.

Chapter 10

A Lovely Whiff of Bleach

T his is a bit of all right. There's a lovely whiff of bleach about the place. It's a sight cleaner than the doctor's surgery back in Warrington. On a bad day, it was knee-deep in common riff-raff coughing up their germs," Vi pronounced as we entered the light and airy clinic. "Half of them had never heard of hankies."

"Of course, this is your first time at the clinic," I acknowledged.

"I'll have you know that I'm not one of them hypochondriacs."

Arriving at the reception desk, the receptionist

greeted us by asking what she could do for us. *"Ti boro na kano gia sena?"*

"I mitera mou echei prisomenous astragalous," I responded, saying my mother had swollen ankles.

"Kathise." Gesturing towards the plastic chairs lining the corridor outside the consulting rooms, the receptionist told us to take a seat. I was relieved to see that Vi was the only patient waiting to be seen, making it unlikely we would be in for a long wait. I had it on good authority that the place was generally heaving first thing, but that it rarely resembled the crowded scrum battling to get seen at the hospital.

The last time I had been to the clinic was on the occasion when Panos' guard dog took a bite out of Guzim's buttock. I hoped my earlier visit wasn't remembered; it wouldn't do to get a reputation for delivering embarrassing patients to the medics. I decided to share the details of my previous visit to the clinic with my mother, thinking it might cheer her up.

"The last time I was here, Panos and I brought Guzim down in the tractor after Apollo bit him."

"Apollo bit Panos? Stuff and nonsense. That dog doted on Panos."

"No, Apollo bit Guzim," I clarified.

"I hope he got a rabies shot..."

"Guzim?"

"No, the dog you idiot. Of course, I meant Guzim. That mutt used to be a right terror but I have to say Yiota has a right way with him. He's more likely to lick you to death these days than tear a piece out of your backside."

"Apollo won't be much use as a guard dog if Yiota is spoiling him," I said. "Anyway, when the three of us turned up here before, Guzim was wearing Papas Andreas' trousers and they stunk of *ouzo*, so the doctor pegged Guzim as a sloppy drunk. Panos insisted the doctor examined the dog before Guzim; in fact, Panos and I got in a bit of a barney when I let slip that Marigold had run into his dog with the Punto and we'd stashed what we thought was the dead canine in Guzim's shed."

"How did the dog bite Guzim if it was dead?"

"It wasn't dead." Since my mother appeared confused, I wondered if a possible side effect of her swollen ankles was a swelling of the brain.

"You can't half ruin a good yarn, lad. Panos told that story better than you and he hardly had what you'd call a good grasp of English…"

"Charming, I'm sure. I thought the amusing anecdote might take your mind off your feet." Folding my arms, I surveyed the corridor for any sign of a medic, my irritation with Violet Burke fading when I caught another glimpse of her by-now hideously swollen ankles, looking even more painfully bloated than they had earlier.

"Ah, here's the doctor now," I said, recognising the white-coated youngster strolling down the corridor as the same fellow who had stitched up Guzim's buttock. Despite his evident youth, I was relieved it was the same doctor that I had met before since I recalled he spoke excellent English. Relying on my Greek language skills, even with the assistance of my trusty dictionary, could well mean taking risks with my mother's health. Since I could hardly claim to be an expert in Greek medical terminology, one mistaken wrongly placed word might result in them whipping out Violet Burke's appendix. There again, looking at my mother's ankles, they rather spoke for themselves.

"Come," the doctor said in English, indicating we should follow him into the consulting room. Either he remembered me from my previous visit or something about us gave us away as British. Recalling the same young chap had invited me in to watch his needlework on Guzim, an invitation I had happily declined, I didn't hesitate in accompanying my mother inside. Just because the doctor spoke English didn't mean he would be able to make head or tail of Violet Burke's colloquial version of the language.

"My mother's ankles are abnormally swollen," I told the doctor.

V.D. BUCKET

"Much swollen," he observed, peering at her bloated bits with a remarkably passive expression before telling Vi to hop up on the examination table. The door swung open and a middle-aged female nurse joined us. As she assisted me with helping my mother onto the table, she smiled reassuringly.

"Eisai aneta?"

"The nurse asked if you are comfortable," I translated.

"Has she seen the state of my feet?" Vi mithered.

"Ta podia tis." Saying 'her feet' for the nurse's benefit, I marvelled at the woman's professionalism in not instantly recoiling at the revolting sight of Violet Burke's swollen appendages. With her feet still stuck in the red furry slippers, it was hard to tell where the slippers ended and her ankles began since Vi's ankles had taken on the exact same scarlet hue. Heat practically radiated from her ankles. I presumed that the short dark hairs on her shins were standing up to attention as a result of the air conditioning blasting in the examination room. Considering it was the height of summer, one would have presumed she could have made the effort to take a razor to the nasty, stubby hairs.

Watching the doctor scrub his hands thoroughly before slipping them into a pair of Latex gloves, I felt confident that my mother was in capable hands. I always interpret it as a good sign when medics adhere to strict hygiene guidelines. My confidence wavered just for a second when I recalled this was the same doctor who had insisted on wheeling a gurney out for Panos' filthy guard dog. I could only presume it had been thoroughly disinfected before being wheeled out again for humans.

"I will to touch…" the doctor declared before thoroughly poking the swollen flesh on my mother's shins, ankles and feet, a look of intense concentration on his face. I couldn't help but notice the indentations he made in her flesh remained even after he removed his hands.

"How long has the swell been there?" the doctor enquired.

"Well, I've suffered with swollen feet for yonks, lad, but nowt as bad as this."

"Yonks?" the doctor queried.

"She means for ages," I translated, helpfully adding, "But she can usually get her shoes on."

"Is worse in the hot, yes?" the doctor asked.

"Aye, the heat can be a right beggar."

"Yes, much worse in this heat," I added, seeing the flummoxed look on the doctor's face. Violet Burke speak didn't translate well at all.

"I see this much in the older patient…"

"Less of the old, you cheeky apeth. I'll have you

know that I'm nowt but a spring chicken…"

"My mother is eighty," I said, pre-empting another confused expression.

Shooting a grateful look in my direction, the doctor continued, jokingly saying, "I think we can to rule out the pregnant as the cause."

"I still had a neat pair of pins even when I was up the spout with Victor here," Vi chuckled.

Even though the doctor looked somewhat confused, I didn't bother to translate.

"Too much the sit can to make it the more swell…"

"I'm not one of them lazy apeths what's got time to be sitting around on my backside all day. I'll have you know that I'm out cleaning every day…"

"She's on her feet most of the day…" I clarified. It seemed my English to Greek dictionary was superfluous to requirements. If I hadn't accompanied my mother to the clinic, the doctor would have needed an English to vernacular English dictionary to make any sense of Vi's words.

"Too much on the feet can to make the swell…you must to sit down more," the doctor advised.

"I haven't got time to be sitting around on my fundament. There's folks relying on me to yank the hair out of their mucky plugholes, bleach their lavs and put a shine on their knick-knacks," Vi snapped.

"Her cleaning job keeps her on her feet."

"You to have the pitted heat oedema," the doctor diagnosed after some more poking. "It is the much common in the hot temperature."

"So 'appen it won't be fatal if it's right common?" Vi cackled.

"Not fatal," the doctor confirmed, an amused twinkle in his eye which I put down to the stoicism of his patient. "I write you some water pill to reduce the swell…"

"Aren't they diuretics?" I asked.

"Die-you-what?" Vi chuntered.

"They'll flush the excess fluid out of your ankles," I explained.

"Well, they'd better not have me running to the lav every two minutes like Sofia." I was pleasantly surprised to hear my mother was on first name terms with Kyria Kompogiannopoulou; then again, I supposed she would never get her mouth around Sofia's tongue twister of a surname. "Even after a good bleaching, I don't want to be using that outside lav at the *kafenio*."

"The one upstairs was perfectly fine…a bit dated but perfectly clean after you'd finished scouring it," I reassured her.

"Aye, if you're happy to have that smarmy Christos walking in on you. There's no lock on the door, lad. I'm not having that Christos perving on me."

"I'll ask Barry to fix a lock as a priority." There was no way I was risking Christos walking in on Marigold in the bathroom if she happened to pop over to the *kafenio* with Doreen.

"There are the other things you must do to make the swell reduce," the doctor said as the nurse battled to try and shove the slippers back onto Violet Burke's feet. "You must to lose the much weight..."

"Are you trying to say that I'm fat, lad?" my mother spluttered even though she'd clearly had to shoehorn her stout frame into the outfit she wore for charring.

"I've been telling her that for ages but she doesn't listen," I said. "She practically lives on chips and pies."

"You must to eat the healthy Greek diet; salad, oil, vegetables, the fish..."

"And he doesn't mean battered," I interjected.

"You must to cut out the salt..." My mother's mouth turned downward at this instruction; she loved nothing more than a salty chip. "And you must drink much the water..."

"Does the water in my PG Tips count?"

"My mother drinks lots of tea," I translated.

"The *tsai tou vounou* is very good," the doctor said with a smile, referencing Greek mountain tea.

"I can't be doing with that muck with them twigs floating round in it," Vi spat.

"She's not very keen on the local brew," I explained.

As an aside, I pointed out to my mother, "Maria lives on the stuff and she hasn't got an ounce of fat on her bones."

"Nothing to protect her likely brittle bones...'appen they'll be the death of her," Vi scoffed.

"You must to drink the eight glasses of water and put the legs up when you sleep...put them on the...what is the English word for the *maxilari*?"

"A pillow. Don't worry, doctor, I will ensure that my mother follows your instructions to the letter." Shooting me down with a daggers drawn look, my mother muttered something about interfering nuisances under her breath. Deliberately ignoring her, I asked the doctor, "Is there anything else that would help the swelling to go down?"

"Try to avoid climbing the stairs," the doctor advised.

"I don't have any to avoid," Vi said triumphantly, seemingly forgetting she would need to traipse up the stairs in the houses she cleaned.

"And you must to wear the *kaltses sympiesis*..."

"Compression socks?" I hazarded.

"In this heat," my mother practically

thundered.

"Only in the day. You can remove them in the shower and the bed," the doctor clarified.

"We'll pick some up now at the pharmacy along with your prescription for water pills," I told my mother who was still huffing under her breath.

Thanking the doctor and nurse profusely, I steered my mother out of the clinic, suggesting that we grab a cool beverage whilst we waited for the pharmacy local to the clinic to open. "I know a good little *kafenio* by the harbour. Panos and I went there whilst we waited for the doctor to stitch Guzim up."

"Do they do a good plate of chips?"

"Really, Mother, didn't you listen to a word that the doctor just said? You have to lose weight. From now on, chips will just be a distant memory. You're going on a strict diet and I intend to police you to make sure you keep to it."

For once in her life, Violet Burke was completely lost for words.

To ease the pressure on my mother's feet, I drove along the harbour, dropping her off at the *kafenio* whilst I went off to park the Punto. Needing a break from her constant mithering, I strolled back along the harbour front at a leisurely pace, appreciating the picturesque sight of the moored fishing boats, a colourful display against the pristine blue backdrop of the sea.

Stopping to drink in the glorious view, I realised that I would have my work cut out persuading my mother to follow doctor's orders; nevertheless, I resolved to persuade her, even if it meant barging into her kitchen and binning the salt along with any Fray Bentos pies that I could lay my hands on. I would also confiscate her mucky fat smeared toastie maker.

I was sure that Marigold would be more than happy to keep an eye on my mother's diet when I wasn't around; okay, perhaps happy was pushing it a bit. I felt confident that Marigold would make the effort to monitor her mother-in-law's diet since it was having an adverse effect on her health. Luckily, I was in the fortunate position of being able to hold Dot's imminent visit over Violet Burke's head as a bargaining chip; I would simply point out that the two of them wouldn't get any gadding done unless my mother could squeeze her enormously enlarged feet into her shoes.

Continuing on my way, I weathered the stern glances of the local fishermen frequenting the quaint harbourside *kafenio* where I had deposited my mother. A combination of uncomfortable seats and the unwelcoming steely looks from the local clientele acted as a tourist deterrent, outsiders generally feeling embarrassed to muscle in on what seemed to be a strictly for locals' hangout that appeared to be none-too friendly. Accustomed to the Greek way, I knew the fishermen would grunt approvingly and return their attention to their games of *tavli* once they heard me place our order in Greek.

Sliding into the seat across from Violet Burke, I noticed her furtive expression as she drained what appeared to be a glass of brandy.

"Is that *Metaxa*?" I demanded.

"What if it is?" Vi retorted defensively. "The doctor had nowt to say about having a drink. I reckoned I might as well have a crafty tipple since I won't be doing the taverna spuds this evening."

"It's not a good idea to mix alcohol with pills," I pointed out in exasperation.

"But I haven't had a pill yet," Vi argued.

"You are supposed to be drinking lots of water…"

My scolding was interrupted by the *kafenio* owner arriving to take my order. Before I could get the words out to request a coffee, Violet Burke defiantly barked her demand for another brandy. Interjecting, I cancelled her order and asked for a coffee along with a large bottle of water. As expected, the frowning fisherman tutted approvingly at my mastery of their language.

"Who do you think you are? The drink police.

You're turning into a right nag," my mother accused. "It's not often that I get to take the weight off and enjoy a drink by the sea..."

"You should be elevating your feet and drinking your own body weight in water," I snapped back. Pulling out a chair, I tipped the cat off that had been dozing on the seat. "Stick your feet up on that. You can hardly expect to enjoy your week with Dot if you haven't got the use of your feet."

"Aye, 'appen," she reluctantly conceded, planting her feet on the chair. "I've just thought...how am I supposed to stay at yours when the doctor told me to avoid the stairs? 'Appen I'd better stay put in my own place and let Dot have your spare bed."

Agreeing with my mother's logic, I inwardly groaned at the thought of Marigold's reaction when I announced she would need to host a complete stranger for a week. I took a deep breath before fibbing, "We'll be delighted to have her."

"'Appen that wife of yours won't like being put out..."

"She'll be fine," I fibbed again. The lion's share of any hosting would inevitably fall on Marigold's shoulders since I would be off repping on three of the days we'd be stuck with Dot.

"I told you that you should have got one of

them fancy stairlifts like that drippy Milton has."

"It would completely ruin the character of our house."

The *kafenio* owner returned bearing a tray with our drinks. Winking at Violet Burke, he placed a snifter of brandy in front of her. Gesturing towards an elderly customer, he said, "*Apo ton Yiorgo.*" Before I had time to tell him to take it away, Violet Burke had raised her glass and glugged the contents, acknowledging the stranger who had sent the drink over with the sort of hideous grin that would send all but the bravest of men running for the hills.

"Please don't encourage him, Mother. You need to concentrate on drinking plenty of water."

"There's not many can say they've still got it at my age." A lewd wink accompanied Vi's hearty chuckle. "Swollen ankles and all."

Chapter 11

The Meli Walking Club

Marigold raised her eyebrows as I walked into the kitchen laden down with Violet Burke's mucky fat polluted toastie maker and her stash of Fray Bentos.

Marigold immediately quizzed me. "Were her ankles as bad as they looked? What did the doctor say?"

"She'll live. The doctor didn't envisage any imminent explosions. He diagnosed my mother with a case of pitted heat oedema." Marigold's nose twitched tellingly, indicating her alarm. I hastily assured her, "Don't worry, it's not contagious. The doctor insisted that she must lose some weight, cut out the salt and drink plenty of water. I've taken the precaution of confiscating her pies for the foreseeable."

"Well, don't think that you can go tucking into them without my noticing," Marigold warned. "We are both reaping the benefits of following a healthy Greek diet."

"Indeed, we are, my love. I rarely get the urge for a Fray Bentos these days. The doctor advised my mother to eat Greek but it's going to be an uphill battle to expect her to change her ways at her advanced age. The language she came out with when I forced her into the medically recommended compression socks was vulgar in the extreme."

"Can you blame her? Imagine having to wear some ghastly nylon mix in this heat. The itching will probably feel like a plague of ants running wild up her legs," Marigold sympathised.

"Well, I've already handed over the itch relief cream to Milton."

"At least the sight of your mother in compression socks might stop Milton mooning over her like a lovesick puppy," Marigold chortled. "So, how do you intend to keep Vi on the straight and narrow? We both know how stubborn she can be."

"That's an understatement. Mother has the incentive of Dot's arrival on Sunday. I pointed out that she won't be able to go gadding about with her friend if she can't shove her feet into her shoes. Speaking of Dot, there's been a slight change of plan..."

Folding her arms in front of her chest, Marigold's face fell. "You may as well spit it out, Victor. It's a bit of a giveaway from your expression that I'm not going to like whatever you're about to tell me."

"The doctor told my mother to avoid stairs, so she's going to have to stay put in the *apothiki* next week..."

"But there's only one bed..."

"Which is why we will be hosting mother's friend, Dot, in our spare bedroom."

I was amazed that Marigold accepted the news so calmly, taking it completely in her stride. Shrugging in a resigned fashion, she said, "Well, it can't be helped, I suppose. And Dot may pleasantly surprise us. She may not be half as bad as your mother."

"I do hope you're right," I said. Crossing my fingers behind my back, I secretly expected the worst.

"This Dot may turn out to be perfectly normal," Marigold reasoned. "Just think, both Moira Strange and Sampaguita genuinely like your mother and consider her a real friend; and there's nothing strange about either of them…"

"Nothing strange about them at all apart from Moira's strange surname…"

"That little quip of yours is getting awfully stale, Victor," Marigold said, failing to raise a smile at my rather jaded pun.

"What happened to young Tonibler?" I asked. "Didn't he turn up for his English lesson?"

"He did but he's just popped next door to Maria's house. I took Tonibler down to the garden because he wanted to see the chickens. Maria spotted him and invited him over to see her tortoise."

"Maria…"

"Yes, Maria. I just said so. How many next-door neighbour's do we have with that name?"

"I was referencing Maria's tortoise. She named it Maria too. And you didn't go to Kyria Maria's with Tonibler?"

"Clearly not as I'm here. Tonibler went over the garden wall. It would have been most undignified of me to clamber over."

"But Blerta left him in your care," I pointed out.

"I doubt he'll come to any harm next door. Anyway, he won't be long. He's very excited at the prospect of sampling my trifle. Ah, that sounds like him now," Marigold said. The way she cocked her head at the sound of feet scampering up the stairs put me in mind of Waffles. "I'll just dish up his trifle."

"Sorry about our English lesson," I said to Tonibler as Marigold plonked a bowl of trifle in front of him.

"That's okay. I saw your chickens and Maria the tortoise. The old witch next door..."

"Marigold," I remonstrated. "You must watch what you say in front of young ears. Now, Tonibler, you were saying something about the sweet old lady next door..."

Marigold emitted an involuntary choking sound at my description of Kyria Maria as sweet.

"She let me hold the tortoise and pet it," Tonibler said.

Snatching the bowl away from the child, I instructed him, "Don't touch that trifle until you have thoroughly scoured your hands. Maria is probably riddled with Salmonella..."

"Really, Victor, I think that's going too far," Marigold interjected. "I know she can be a bit annoying at times. Whilst Maria's personal habits can sometimes be questionable, she always keeps a clean house..."

"Maria the tortoise," I clarified. "Tortoises are renowned as carriers of Salmonella. It's not worth taking any chances with young Tonibler's health."

After scrubbing his hands with a strong

carbolic, Tonibler tucked into his trifle, a look approaching ecstasy on his face.

"I'm surprised you've any room left for trifle," I observed. "Whenever I've been next door to Kyria Maria's, she insists on force feeding me meatballs or *loukoumades*," I said.

"Kyria Maria said she hadn't cooked yet today. She made me drink a cup of *horta* tea. She said it was good for my bowels." I gathered from his grimace that he'd found the tea to be perfectly disgusting. "It was horrible. I tipped it in the flowers when the Kyria turned her back."

"*Horta* tea is a bitter brew indeed," I confirmed, wincing at the memory of forcing a cup of Maria's vile concoction down. She swore it was a general cure-all but my stomach felt decidedly dodgy by the time I'd downed the murky green liquid extracted from boiling weeds; roiling as my mother would put it.

"Victor."

Hearing the familiar voice of Spiros bellowing up from the street, I stepped out onto the balcony to see what he wanted.

"Victor. You are the walking? Come join me."

"Just give me a tick," I called back, my voice almost drowned out by Spiros yelling at the neighbouring house for Papas Andreas to join us for an early evening walk.

BUCKET TO GREECE (VOL.15)

Marigold looked at me as though I'd lost my marbles when I asked if she would be joining the Meli Walking Group. "In this heat. The only time it is cool enough to walk is first thing in the morning…"

"But you are always sleeping then," I said. "We haven't enjoyed a walk together for days. You're going to have to cut back on the *halva* and *loukoumi*, not to mention the Mastic Tears, if you aren't getting any healthy exercise."

Marigold's hand involuntarily strayed to her stomach. Sucking her breath in, her fingers traced the slight round mound accentuated by her fitted frock.

"I suppose you're right, dear, but I just can't face going outdoors in these temperatures. I will set the alarm so that I can be up with the lark tomorrow and join you for an early morning route march before it really heats up. You're always saying it's lovely and cool at first light."

The sceptical look on my face must have spoken for itself; the idea of Marigold being up with the lark, patently absurd.

"I will, Victor, I promise," Marigold insisted. "It's very important that we keep fit. I really don't want to start piling on the kilos."

"Well, I will join Spiros now. Come along, Tonibler. We'll walk you home," I said, grabbing a bottle of water to keep hydrated and gathering the bagful of fresh garden vegetables I'd set aside for Blerta earlier.

As Tonibler and I joined the undertaker, Spiros ruffled the boy's hair in a welcoming fashion, asking him if he was sure he could keep pace with the grown-ups. The look on Tonibler's face indicated he thought the adults would have trouble keeping up with him; he was, after all, a bundle of excited energy.

"I just need to drop Tonibler off at home before we get our three kilometres in," I told Spiros.

After filling my friend in on my emergency trip to the clinic with my mother and bringing him up to date on the doctor's diagnosis and instructions, Spiros whipped out his mobile.

"I tell the Sampaguita to take the healthy meal to Violet this evening."

"Marigold's done one of her trifles for your wife. Tell Sampaguita to make sure Vi doesn't indulge."

"I tell the Sampaguita to bring the trifle home. I can to help her eat it," Spiros said, a dreamy look coming over his face at the thought of tucking into one of my wife's delectable sherry trifles. Since Spiros was engaging in daily walks, a portion of the custardy dessert wouldn't add a bulge to his rapidly deflating stomach.

BUCKET TO GREECE (VOL.15)

The three of us were joined by Papas Andreas, the local cleric looking overheated before we'd even set off. I could only imagine how he must suffer the heat with a full beard, not to mention his long clerical vestments. As a single concession to the humidity, Andreas had replaced his clerical hat, a *kamilavkion*, with a more practical baseball cap emblazoned with the word *Hellas* along with the Greek flag.

As the four of us set off through the village at a pace befitting the stultifying temperature, Tonibler was aquiver with curiosity, asking endless questions in English. I felt a tad inadequate when I wasn't able to furnish him with the name of a very tall, thin green cactus resembling a telephone pole, nor another small cactus sprouting yellow flowers, only redeeming myself when I trotted out prickly pear for the familiar cactus plant that had inspired the disastrous curry.

"There certainly seems to be many varieties of cacti flourishing in the area but I'm not familiar with their names. Mrs Bucket is the budding botanist in the Bucket household. You must direct all your questions about cacti to her next time you pop over," I told Tonibler.

The ceaseless singing of the cicadas prompted the child to ask, "Mr Bucket, what is the English word for *tzitziki*?"

"Cicadas."

Pointing into the distance, Tonibler asked, "And what is the English word for that tree?"

"Which one?" I asked, squinting in the general direction of the hill Tonibler was pointing to.

"The very tall one…"

"Ah, the one that looks as though its branches are hugging the trunk. That is a cypress tree…"

"In Greek, he is the *kyparissi*," Spiros volunteered. I mentally added the word to my list of ever-expanding Greek vocabulary.

I couldn't resist a chuckle when Papas Andreas paused to mop his sweaty brow with the hem of his long black robe, revealing a pair of what appeared to be pyjama shorts beneath it. Twigging that Tonibler was keen to expand his English, Andreas addressed the boy in faltering English.

"In the Greek mythology, the god Apollo love the handsome boy name the Kyparissos. The boy he to have the pet, how to say…"

"A cat," Tonibler eagerly interrupted.

"*Ena elafi*," Andreas continued.

"The Kyparissos have the deer," Spiros translated. "He love the deer the very much but he to kill it by the accident."

"How can one accidentally kill a deer?" I posited, not being particularly up on this gem of Greek mythology.

"The deer was sleeping in the woods and the boy throw the, how to say, *ena dory*?" Andreas said.

"A spear," Spiros translated.

"The Kyparissos was the heart broke when he to kill the deer; he to say his tears will to flow forever. So, the Apollo, he to turn the Kyparissos into the Cypress tree," Andreas continued.

"Did the boy's hair turn green?" Tonibler asked. The child's question surprised me since I had assumed his mind was too logical to buy into such fables.

"Yes, the hair turn the green," Andreas confirmed. "And the sap from the tree look like the tears…"

"Like the tears from the mastic tree," Spiros added.

Whilst it was all very well and good filling Tonibler's head with tales from Greek mythology, I preferred to impart some practical wisdom relating to hygiene since the child had recently developed a strong interest in the subject.

"Tonibler, did you know that cypress trees can live for up to seven hundred years?" I asked. "Back in the old days before modern medicine, the cones and seeds of the cypress tree were collected and made into a tea as a cure for dysentery."

"Mr Bucket, what is dysentery?" Tonibler asked.

"It's like a really nasty stomach ache," I explained.

"I had one of those after Mrs Burke made me a toastie."

"I expect she stuck it in that lethal sandwich maker of hers that is coated in layers of rancid mucky fat…"

"Mucky fat?" I bit my lip to hide my amusement at hearing the confused words come out of the Papas' mouth.

"Lard," I explained before offering Tonibler a few additional facts to satisfy his craving for knowledge. "Dysentery is a tad more serious than your run-of-the-mill upset tummy. It strikes when a person consumes water or food contaminated by bacteria or a parasite."

"I love bacteria," Tonibler enthused just as we reached his home.

Waving the boy goodbye, Spiros chortled. "Victor, I think the Tonibler will to turn into the miniature you. He will to grow up to be the germ inspector."

"Well, if he has aspirations to follow in my footsteps as a public health inspector, it is a more practical ambition than the one that Blat has in mind for his son. I fear that all Blat's talk about Tony Blair and the Mayor of London, is filling Tonibler's head with unrealistic nonsense. Health inspecting could well be an illustrious career for the boy."

"The Blat can give the family the good life in the *Ellada*. Why he the so obsess to think he must to move to the England?"

"I think it's a case of the grass is always greener..."

"For you, the grass was the more green in Greece," Spiros said as we followed the turning leading to Panos' farmhouse, now Yiota's home.

Since the farm kept Yiota so busy, I was surprised that the young woman elected to join us; one would assume the physical labour she engaged in on the farm would count as enough exercise for anyone. Falling into our rank of three, Yiota explained that she had hoped to catch up with me as she was concerned about the way Violet Burke's ankles were swelling up. I was touched as always by Yiota's genuine concern for my mother who she regarded as a surrogate *yiayia*. Once I had assured her that Vi had been checked out by a doctor, I extracted a promise from Yiota that she would ensure nothing but salad would pass Vi's lips when the two of them got together for their regular knees-ups. It was a relief to know that I wouldn't be the only one playing the grinch and nagging my mother about her diet. Our conversation turned to other topics as we fell into step together behind Spiros and Andreas.

"Do tell me how you are getting along with Giannis," I pried. "Marigold is such a meddling matchmaker that she will have my guts if I don't report back on any progress in the romance department."

Blushing, Yiota gazed into the distance, winding a loose strand of hair around her fingers. Lost in thought, she appeared oblivious to the magnificent view in front of her, the sea visible on the horizon through the olive groves. "I like Giannis very much. He is good company and very handsome."

"So Marigold tells me. I believe 'smouldering good looks' is the phrase she uses…"

"He is very sexy," Yiota admitted, blushing furiously and avoiding my eye. Sighing deeply, she turned to address me directly. "But Giannis is a total disaster on the domestic front."

"How so?" I asked. In truth, my question was a tad superfluous since I had a pretty good idea that Yiota was about to divulge that Giannis suffered from the typical male Greek god complex that left him leaving everything on the domestic front to the women in his life. I assumed he was firm in the belief that cooking and cleaning were women's work; or as Nikos puts it whenever he wants me to lend a hand in the taverna kitchen, 'the woman's work.'

"When I invite Giannis over to eat with me, he doesn't lift a finger to help even though we've both been working all day; he just assumes it is my place as a woman to cater to his every need." I imagined that the defiant look on Yiota's face was a tad more defiant as she regaled her worries to me, than it was when she was with Giannis. "It's very exasperating. I don't want to tie myself down with a man who expects me to wait on him hand and foot. We're not in the 1990s anymore."

"That will be down to Ioanna cosseting her son to such an extent that Giannis doesn't understand that times have moved on. Perhaps if you told him how you feel…"

Suppressing a snort, Yiota asked, "Can you see him wearing an apron and cooking a meal?"

"Perchance he just needs encouraging. It's not as though he's incapable. Even Norman has learnt to find his way around a kitchen and he's been set in his ways for forty years."

Even though I recalled that Giannis' last girlfriend, Poppy, had been as clueless on the domestic front as Giannis, the pair of them relying on Ioanna, Giannis' long-suffering mother, to do everything for them, I chose not to mention it to Yiota. I doubted she would appreciate my rubbing her nose in her boyfriend's past relationship. Moreover, the two young women were very different. Poppy's parents had gone out of their way to break the mould for their daughter, encouraging her to focus on her education rather than learning how to cook or run a home: whilst equally independent, Yiota was much more practically minded and could turn her hand to the domestic tasks that Poppy eschewed.

"I doubt Giannis even knows how to make his own bed though he's patently capable of learning how," I said. "Some of these Greek mothers don't realise they are making a rod for the back of any future daughter-in-law. Dina was just the same with Kostis. When he married Eleni, he left all the housework and childcare to his wife whilst he went off carousing. Kostis only changed his ways when Eleni upped and left him."

Lowering her voice to a whisper, Yiota said, "Sampaguita does everything in the house for Spiros."

"The difference is she enjoys doing it whilst you, quite rightly, want to share the domestic burden."

"Well, it's early days with Giannis yet. His mother is always dropping hints that she'd like to see us married; she's told me that Giannis is keen to settle down. And, of course, Violet tells me that my *pappous* was keen on the match." Yiota's face lit up, her hazel eyes sparkling as she spoke of her late grandfather. "I think Giannis could be a good match...we have many interests in common..."

If Yiota hoped to find a life-partner to settle down with in Meli, Giannis was the only available red-blooded man under sixty in the village. Throwing her net wider was difficult when her work on the farm took up most of her waking hours.

"But, if and when I marry, I want an equal partner, not a boy-child incapable of pulling his weight around the house."

"It sounds to me as though Giannis needs to mend his ways and join the twenty-first century. My advice to you would be to raise the matter bluntly and let him know where you stand. If you let Giannis get away with being bone idle around the house while the two of you are courting, I fear he will think it is an acceptable way to behave. You must consider that if you don't let him know what's on your mind, once the first flush of romance wears off, you will end up resenting Giannis for his Neanderthal attitude."

"I think you are right, Victor. I must take the cow by the horns..."

As Yiota hesitated, thrown off course by botching the English idiom, I finished her sentence for her.

"And let Giannis know that he must man up

and don a pinny."

"I will," Yiota promised with a dazzling smile.

"Just don't tell Marigold that I said anything about any of this. She wouldn't approve of my meddling in your love life. Meddling is Marigold's department."

Chapter 12

Dragged out of Bed

Marigold, determined to wake up with the lark so that she could join me on a vigorous walk around the village in the relatively cool early hours of first light, suggested an early night.

"What time should I set the alarm for, dear?" she asked.

"It depends if you want coffee before the off. First light at this time of year is about 6.30 a.m."

"I'll set it for six then. I don't want to be caught out and about with my hair looking as though I've just been dragged out of bed."

"I doubt there will be anyone else about at such

an hour to see your mussed up bed hair," I assured her. Sensing the withering look about to be directed my way, I hastily back tracked, saving the situation with a dollop of flattery. "I always think your hair looks lovely and natural when you wake up. Not many women can carry off mussed with such panache."

The way that Marigold preened at my compliment convinced me that I had prevented a marital crisis by the skin of my teeth.

Even though it was my regular habit to be up well before dawn, my body clock waking me naturally, I let Marigold set the alarm. It might take more than me to rouse her at what she generally referred to as such an unspeakable hour. I would much prefer her to vent her inevitable irritation at the bleeping clock, rather than me.

Even though I hate to admit Marigold was right to insist on having air conditioning installed in the bedroom, it was a lifesaver in these temperatures. We were able to drift off easily under the cooling blast. Without it, we would have tossed and turned for hours on sheets revoltingly soggy from sweat. Although I missed having the windows flung open as we slept, I knew it would defeat the object of running the unit; besides, the air on the other side of the windows was hot enough to cut with a knife.

The two of us were not the only ones to benefit

from the air-con as Clawsome, Catastrophe, and Fluff, all joined us in the bedroom. Demanding their share of our bed, they sprawled out lazily. Catastrophe insisted on sharing my pillow, a thoroughly unpleasant experience when she stuck her wet tongue in my ear. Pickles, being the spawn of Cynthia's vile cat, Kouneli, was of hardier stock, preferring to roam the dark recesses of Meli during the night rather than bedding down with his human companions.

It was pitch black outside when I woke with a start, disorientated, rudely disturbed from my slumbers by the persistent ringing of the telephone. Padding through to the grand salon, I barked into the phone, demanding to know what blithering idiot was telephoning in the middle of the night.

Identifying himself as the blithering idiot, Spiros responded, "*Ela*, Victor, you must to come at once. *Fotia. Fotia.*"

"Fire," I parroted, the urgency in Spiros' tone finally seeping into my still sleep befuddled brain. "Is the fire in Meli?"

"No, he is much distance away but you know the drill," Spiros said.

"Is this a practice drill Spiro, or the real thing?"

"He is the real. You know what to do, yes? *Ela, grigora.*" Telling me to come quickly, Spiros hung up.

V.D. BUCKET

Alarm coursed through my body, the adrenaline instantly banishing any lingering traces of sleepiness. Rushing through to the bedroom, I pulled a pair of slacks on over my pyjama bottoms, grabbing a short-sleeved button down to button up en route; there was no time to lose. Dashing back to the telephone, I mentally ran through the checklist that Spiros had drummed into me when I was encouraged to join Meli's fire-watching team.

Wild fires are a constant worry in the scorching heat of summer, literally spreading like wildfire if they catch hold, causing untold destruction to the landscape. In our area of the Mani, the village is not serviced by a regular fire brigade but by a volunteer corps of fire-fighters that are trained by the state. Nationally, the volunteer corps was founded in 1991, its members an invaluable asset in remote areas such as Meli.

Whilst I wasn't an actual signed-up member of the voluntary fire brigade, I had been press-ganged into joining the group of village men who did their bit by standing watch if any fires broke out in the wider area, thus giving advance warning to the actual fire-fighting volunteers of the direction the fire was heading. A fire burning well in the distance could change course on a turn of the wind and needed to be monitored to determine if it was heading our way.

BUCKET TO GREECE (VOL.15)

I had suggested that the other expat men in the village could also be roped into service, a suggestion that had resulted in vociferous arguments amongst the local Greek volunteers; they considered non-Greek speaking Brits might prove to be more of a hindrance than a help. It wasn't just the Brits that some of the local Greek men objected to. Yiota, keen to join the actual volunteer firefighters, was initially poo-pooed as a mere woman; clearly made of stern stuff, Yiota stood her ground and refused to back down. With solid support from the respected voices of Spiros, Vangelis and Giannis, who considered she would be a valuable asset, Yiota was accepted into the ranks of volunteer firefighters and had duly participated in some strenuous training.

My own duties in the event of a fire didn't involve anything so dangerous as actually getting close to the flames. I was merely a humble cog in the line of fire-watchers that would raise the alarm if any fires that broke out in the distance appeared to be heading in the direction of Meli, a particular worry if the wind picked up. In the event of a fire breaking out in the village, I was under orders to rouse my neighbours and evacuate my family urgently. Once again, the voices of Spiros, Vangelis and Giannis proved the voice of reason, arguing that the extra man power was much needed and that the non-Greek speaking Brits could be utilised as volunteer fire-watchers if they were teamed up with English-speaking Greeks.

Now that I had received the call, I recollected the drill that Spiros had drummed into me. My first order of business was to rouse my fellow expats; just the fellas that is. Once I had summoned them from their beds, they were expected to congregate at a pre-arranged spot in the village square. Once there, we would receive further instructions from Spiros, who since retiring from the volunteer fire brigade due to his gammy leg, served as the coordinator in charge of the village fire-watchers. Mentally running through the list of names, I knew that I had four urgent telephone calls to make; to Barry, Gordon Strange, Norman, and John Macey. Due to his age and his inability to move at a quick pace with his dodgy hip, Milton was exempt from the call to duty.

Barry and Gordon hopped to it at once with barely a grumble, whilst to my chagrin, John Macey had turned off his phone, thus leaving our group of expats one man down. Calling Norman, Doreen answered the phone, barely allowing me to get a word in edgeways when I identified myself as the blithering idiot disturbing her in the middle of the night. After ascertaining that Marigold hadn't suffered some dreadful accident, Doreen's attitude switched from concern to crossness, complaining that waking up Norman would mean she would have to venture into the spare bedroom where her estranged husband kipped down with his collection of traffic cones.

"Victor, it really wouldn't be seemly for me to barge into Norman's bedroom in the middle of the night. It could convey entirely the wrong impression…"

"Doreen, just go and wake Norman up now. We have an emergency situation on our hands," I shouted.

"There's really no need to take that tone…"

"Just wake Norman up and tell him he's needed on fire-watching duty…"

"Fire. Why didn't you say so at once? My darling Manolis could be in danger. He's in the volunteer fire brigade…"

"Can you just stop twittering on, woman, and tell Norman to get himself over to the pre-arranged meeting spot," I demanded, hanging up in frustration at Doreen's mithering.

Since Spiros had assured me that Meli wasn't in imminent danger of going up in flames, I had no intention of waking Marigold and alarming her unnecessarily. Grabbing the emergency bag I kept on hand for such an eventuality, I crept out of the house and hot-footed it down to the garden.

Banging on the door of Guzim's shed, I cursed the useless Albanian for being so difficult to wake.

"*Guzim. Siko tora,*" I thundered, demanding that he get up now.

I nearly jumped out of my skin when a quiet voice behind me muttered in guttural Greek, "*Kratiste chamila ton thoryvo. Tha xypniseis ta kotopoula.*" I could hardly believe that Guzim had just told me to keep the noise down in case I woke the chickens.

Stating the obvious, I said to Guzim, 'You aren't in your shed.' "*Den eisai sto ypostego sou.*"

"*Koimomoun sto kotopoulo.*" Guzim reminded me that he was sleeping in the chicken run.

My demand that Guzim come quickly to join the ranks of the village men serving as fire-watchers, was met with a blunt refusal, the Albanian shed dweller stubbornly refusing to abandon the chickens and his pet rabbit. When Guzim pointed out that someone must be on hand to rescue our pets if the fire took hold in the village, I dropped my demand that he left them to their own devices. The very thought of my chickens going up in flames was enough to bring me out in nervous palpitations. Leaving Guzim to take the precaution of filling up every bucket the Bucket household possessed with water, I hurried away to the meeting spot.

BUCKET TO GREECE (VOL.15)

The call to duty had been answered by most of the able-bodied village men, clustered in the village square around Spiros. Despite turning out in his pyjama bottoms paired with a grubby vest, in his role of coordinator, Spiros was all business, telling everyone that the local fire engine was en route to Meli from its station further down the coast. The volunteer fire-fighters representing Meli comprised Giannis, Papas Andreas, Yiota, and Manolis, the foursome joining the trained members from other villages that were responding to the call. In their heavy high vis jackets and trousers, sturdy boots and helmets, the four of them stood out. I barely recognised Andreas; it was the first time I had ever seen him dressed in anything other than his clerical uniform. I have to say that ditching his usual formal dress took years off him. It was a good job that Geraldine wasn't staying with us. The sight of Andreas in a fireman's uniform would have turned her head.

Putting Giannis in charge of the volunteer firefighters that would make their own way by pickup to the area engulfed in fire, Spiros speedily dispatched them, telling Manolis to wait and jump in the fire engine when it came through the village. The rest of us sent them on their way with a resounding cheer.

I was taken aback when Nikos vented his anger

that he had been replaced on the fire engine by Manolis. Nikos ranted that he was an indispensable member of the fire-fighting team, his years of experience and knowledge of tackling a blaze, vital when it came to quenching the flames. He nearly came to blows with Spiros when the undertaker had the temerity to remind him that he'd been retired off at the end of the previous fire season, deemed too old in his late seventies to still be an active member of the volunteer fire brigade. Spiros pointed out that Manolis had undergone a lot of training in tackling fires for his job running a Texan gas station and that Nikos' experience could still be put to good use, even if he had been demoted to the lowly position of fire-watcher along with the totally green Brits.

Returning to the task in hand, Spiros ignored the fulminating taverna owner, concentrating on pairing off the fire-watchers. Spiros began directing them to various locations above and around the village, saving some spots for the stragglers yet to arrive.

"Where is the fire?" I asked.

"You can to see," Spiros told me, pointing to an area high up in the hills above Nektar. The night sky was illuminated with an orange glow, the visible flames eerily red against the midnight black backdrop of the mountain; it was easy to imagine the flames greedily devouring anything in their way, the heat of the scorching night intensified by the fire.

Although it was difficult to gauge the distance, Spiros announced it was at least twenty kilometres away, fortunately in an uninhabited area. Nevertheless, the risk of the fire spreading in the direction of Meli was very real if the wind picked up. The fire could prove disastrous if it wasn't contained at once; it would burn its way through the trees and fauna, in addition to being a threat to any wildlife.

I recalled Giannis choking with emotion when he'd told me of a fellow apiarist in a distant village who had lost his entire collection of bee boxes to fire several years earlier. The bee keeper had been too distraught to replace the lost bees, unable to face the trauma of perchance losing a second lot. The same wildfire that had taken out the bee boxes had also burnt its way through acres of olive groves, leaving nothing but charred destruction in its wake, the acrid stench of smoke lingering in the air for weeks, the ground coated in a thick layer of ash. Driving through the area a couple of weeks after the fire, with the maudlin interest of a rubbernecker, I had been struck by the complete silence, not a bird nor an insect making a sound; the desolation palpable.

As Spiros fired out directions, I sidled over to

join my brother-in-law. Barry lamented the fact that Vangelis was away on his holidays since the builder was a key member of the volunteer fire brigade.

"I think I should sign up for training," Barry mused.

"I can't see that going down well with Cynthia," I replied, nudging Barry as Norman finally deigned to show his face. Still in his pyjamas, Norman was struggling under the weight of a pile of traffic cones. Quite what use he imagined they would be in a fire situation, was beyond me.

"I couldn't get hold of John Macey," I told Barry. "I thought he intended to be fully integrated member of the village, yet at the first sign of trouble he makes himself unavailable."

"He's not moved into his house here yet," Barry told me.

"He's delayed it again," I queried.

"He wants to wait until every last piddling item on the snagging list is ticked off."

"That's a bit precious," I snorted, recalling how Marigold and I had moved into our home mid-renovation work, living without a kitchen in our first days in Meli. Barry's own refurbishment had left him and Cynthia without a toilet whilst the bathroom suite was replaced. It was okay for Barry as he simply polluted Cynthia's ecological pond when his wife wasn't looking, but Cynthia was forever dashing over to make use of the Bucket loo. When Barry discovered to his horror that Cynthia had been bathing in the ecological pond until the new shower had been installed in the bathroom, he didn't dare confess he had been using it as a temporary toilet.

"I reckon it's just an excuse. Macey is dragging his feet about moving in so he can delay settling what he owes," Barry griped. "He's a right penny-pincher."

"An apt choice of words considering that he's been staying as a guest with that Penny woman, the one with the dog, Percy," I said. "It saves him the cost of a hotel. Perchance he's got his feet well under the table…"

"Barry," Spiros loudly interrupted. "You to partner up with Kyrios Stavropoulos." That made sense, Barry having enough Greek to communicate with the curmudgeonly, communistic pensioner.

With Barry matched up and on the move, I waited all agog to hear who my partner would be. Spiros sent Norman and Christos off together, then Gordon with Dimitris. Watching the other British men making tracks with their Greek partners, I was left standing around like a spare part. Glancing around, I noticed the only remaining villagers were Apostolos, Mathias and Nikos. I hoped I wouldn't be paired up with the scissor-happy local barber.

Horrible memories of being on tenterhooks as I waited to be picked for a football side back in junior school, flooded my mind. I recalled desperately hoping that the bullying Derek Little wouldn't make me his pick; being on his team would give him plenty of opportunity to more easily torment me.

I was pleasantly surprised when Spiros announced he was pairing me with Nikos, directing the two of us to a high point about four kilometres above the Stranges' house.

Still indignant that he had been tossed aside in favour of a younger man in his sixties, Nikos instructed me to hop up behind him on the back of his moped. Reluctant though I was to ride pillion in the dark on his tatty and frankly, unroadworthy moped, Nikos was in no mood to be argued with. Nor, in the face of Nikos' smouldering anger, did I dare to voice my worry that I would be breaking the law by riding without a helmet.

Tentatively climbing on behind Nikos, I thrust my arms around his waist, holding on for dear life as the machine puttered off through the village.

"Slow down," I hollered as the moped scraped through a pothole.

Turning around to face me, Nikos bellowed in my face. "I should have to know you would to ride like the woman."

Chapter 13

The Hero of the Hour

"What do we do now?" I asked, my legs trembling as I scrambled down from the moped. I had come close to coming a cropper when the fire engine summoned from down on the coast had whizzed past the moped at speed and I had momentarily lost my firm grasp on Nikos.

"We walk," Nikos grunted, pointing to higher ground, the stony route clearly unsuitable for his tatty contraption. "We to watch from the summit and put out the call if the fire to change his direction."

I was relieved to see that Nikos had calmed down, his terrible temper of earlier replaced with amusement as he poked fun at me, telling me that Dina rode side saddle on his moped and he was yet to take a passenger that clung on to him as tightly as I had.

"If I not to know better, Victor, I would to think from the way you to hold me, that you were to make the *romantikos* move on me."

"What do you expect when you tore off through the village with no regard for safety measures? I could have been fined if a policeman spotted me without a helmet; it's illegal, you know. As a retired public health inspector, I take safety standards seriously. Not to mention going helmetless is reckless and dangerous."

"Better to feel the wind in the hair on the hot night," Nikos chortled, dismissing my concerns, his usual good mood now restored.

Nikos took the lead uphill, impressing me with his agility. In comparison, I found the almost vertical trek a challenge despite my relative youth. Discovering my torch was out of battery, I cursed; such an amateur mistake may well cost me an ankle if I tripped over in the dark.

"How much further do we have to traipse uphill?" I panted, short of breath.

"Just to there. You see?"

BUCKET TO GREECE (VOL.15)

All I could discern in the still pitch dark was a scrubby outcrop of rocks. Apparently, it was our dedicated fire-watching spot. Reaching the rocks with a last push, the pair of us threw ourselves down on the stony ground. I immediately found myself irresistible fodder for pesky mossies.

"You have the, how to say, goggles?"

"Goggles? You mean night vision goggles? I don't. Spiros never mentioned they were necessary. I just have a pair of plain old binoculars."

"That what I mean. You must to survey the landscape with the binocular to see if the fire come closer. If he come this way, we must to telephone the next watch spot to make the alert."

Groping around in my emergency bag for the binoculars, I saw that Marigold had thoughtfully bunged a jar of Marmite inside. After smearing the stuff on my exposed bits, I scanned the mountain through the binoculars for any new evidence of fire. To my untrained eye, it appeared that although the flames were still blazing, the fire hadn't spread. I desperately hoped that the volunteer fire brigade would be able to contain it. If necessary, firefighting, water bombing planes would be deployed in daylight to scoop up huge quantities of water from the sea to dump on the fire. The Canadair water bombing planes were a regular sight during the summer, the drone of them flying overhead a common sound.

"It is the lucky there is no village in that area," Nikos said. "It would be the terrible for the people to fear their home to burn."

"How do you suppose the fire started in such a remote spot?"

"The Turk," Nikos dryly replied.

"The Turk? What Turk?" I had certainly never come across any Turkish people in the area.

"The Turk from *Tourkia*," Nikos spat contemptuously. "The *Tourkia* send many the spy here to spy on the great *Ellada*. I think the Turk must to have start the fire to destabilise our country. Always the Turk, he want to make war. The Ottoman was the yoke around the Greek neck and then in the war that start in 1919, the Turk to banish the Greek from their home in Asia Minor."

I hid my amusement as Nikos spouted the ludicrous conspiracy theory that was a popular topic amongst the villagers in the taverna. Spiros wasn't the only one to revel in a good conspiracy theory and Nikos wasn't the only one who loved nothing more than a spot of sabre rattling towards Greece's neighbour.

Naturally, I was aware that relations between the two countries were on a constant knife-edge. Hostility fuelled by mutual animosity was only exacerbated by the two governments constantly exchanging public jibes and disputing ownership of the islands in the Aegean Sea. Nevertheless, Nikos' theory of a Turkish spy committing a deliberate act of arson in the middle of nowhere, struck me as a tad far-fetched, the chosen spot hardly representing some area of high importance in the geographical political sphere.

Marigold and I had ventured uphill in the general vicinity of the inhospitable area where the fire had taken hold, the Punto struggling on the poorly maintained road, barely more than a dirt track in places. Whilst the area provided magnificent views over the Mani region, it was primarily rocky with mostly barren scrubland.

Noting my scepticism, Nikos changed tack. "If not the Turk, it could be the developer that start the fire. He may to want to build the houses or hotel up there."

I was familiar with the local opinion that developers were responsible for many of the fires that blight Greece each summer, and the theory behind it. Forested land that appeared attractive to developers, but wasn't classified as land to be built on, could be reclassified as suitable building land in the wake of the area being devastated by fire. Trees and forests that went up in flames would be replaced by more profitable luxury villas and hotels. It was certainly a credible theory; still, it didn't strike me as a likely scenario in this instance.

"Any developer would have to out of his mind to think that plonking a fancy hotel down in the middle of nowhere would turn into a profitable venture. It's not exactly coveted high-value real estate up there," I argued. "Tourists are drawn to the beaches and classical Greek sites, not to the top of some rocky scrubland with inaccessible roads. Now, I could understand your reasoning if the Orthodox Church was scouting for somewhere remote and difficult to access as the site for a new monastery."

Mulling the wisdom of my words, Nikos changed tack, admitting, "It could to be the electrical pole came down and ignite the fire."

"Or a random person recklessly disposing of a cigarette out of a car window, rather than a deliberate act of arson," I suggested.

"The random is still the arson," Nikos pontificated.

"You don't think the fire will spread to Meli?"

"I think not. In the case where the fire to start near to the Meli, we have already taken the precaution. We not to burn in the summer, we to cut the brush to stop the fire to easily take hold, and we to water the ground with the hose..."

Nikos' words were interrupted by the ringing of his mobile, prompting him to leap up. Scrambling to a craggy spot to one side, he muttered under his breath about the dodgy mobile signal. Finally settling on a spot where he was able to hear the caller, he listened intently before returning to join me.

"The Giannis report the fire look to be under the control before the morning. He will to keep us update. Luckily, there is no the wind tonight."

"It's lucky indeed," I agreed, mentally pummelling myself for being selfish enough to wish for a breeze to bring some relief from the stifling humidity.

"You to have any food in the bag?" Nikos asked me.

"Just a jar of Marmite," I replied, proffering the iconic British savoury spread.

"The Greek food, not the foreign from the shop," Nikos groused, refusing the jar.

Rummaging around in the bag, I found a packet of *halva*. Quite why Marigold had thought I would want *halva* in an emergency situation was beyond me. She knew full well how much I detested the sweet confection that she was addicted to, since it always stuck in my teeth. In the heat of the night, the *halva* was semi-melted, nothing more than a sticky mess. Passing it to Nikos, he chewed away at the tahini-based treat in silence, every now and again raising his binoculars to survey the terrain.

Keeping watch through the night, we observed with relief how the fire in the distance diminished, the orange glow on the horizon gradually abating, an observation that was confirmed by the regular updates Nikos received from the Meli based firefighters. As the night wore on in endless tedium, I welcomed the drop in temperature to bearable. By the time Nikos received word that the fire was out, I was shivering, our hilltop perch having turned decidedly chilly. I made a mental note to throw a pullover in the emergency bag in case I was ever called upon for a repeat performance of the night's events.

"*Ela*. We all to meet now at the *kafenio*," Nikos announced.

Our path downhill back to the moped was less precarious to tackle in the early morning twilight. As we made our way down, the blackness of the night gradually lifted, grey filtering through the black until the skyline was awash with a palette of magnificent colours and the air alive with the sound of birds chirping.

Taking a moment to stand still and appreciate the sheer beauty, I asked Nikos his opinion on the *kafenio*, presuming he may share Tina's attitude that the recently established business represented competition. Nikos assured me that he wished the brothers well, stressing that he kept the taverna open for company more than anything else. It was true that money wasn't his motivation. In the three years we have lived in Meli, Nikos had never once raised his prices from ridiculously cheap.

Approaching the *kafenio* at first light, I sighed in annoyance, noticing that the hems of my slacks were now smeared with Marmite applied in the dark. It would take more than a good boil wash to remove the stains along with the paint.

When we strode into the *kafenio*, it was bustling with fire-watchers that had made it through the night. The harsh fluorescent lights illuminated the motley collection of volunteers, more than one or two still in their pyjamas; I amused myself with the thought that they looked as though they were prepared for an early morning trolley dash round Tesco.

Christos busied himself preparing Greek coffees all round, served with a morning shot of *raki*. A spontaneous roar of applause broke out when the volunteer firefighters from Meli joined us, the quartet looking sweaty and exhausted, soot smeared across their faces.

Throwing his arm around Yiota's shoulder, Giannis made an announcement in Greek, provoking hearty cheers from the locals.

"What's he saying?" Gordon Strange asked.

"He to say the Yiota is the hero of the hour,"

Spiros proclaimed. Beaming with elation, Yiota's face flushed beneath the thick layer of soot. For the benefit of the non-Greek speaking expat Brits that had answered the call of the duty, Spiros continued to translate Giannis' words. "The firefighters bravely fight the fire together but through the roar of the flame, the Yiota listen a different noise. She to hear the distress bray of the donkey. She to follow the manic bray and to find the donkey going the crazy. He was the tether to the tree with the flame approaching. The Yiota cut the donkey free and lead him to the safety."

"*Bravo, Yiota,*" I called over. "You are a true heroine, saving the life of the tethered donkey."

"It was terrible, Victor. I thought I would not be able to reach the donkey before the flames consumed him. The poor creature was frantic with nerves. On the way back, we passed a poor incinerated cow that had its legs hobbled together. Unfortunately, it had no chance to escape."

"But you save the donkey, Yiota," Andreas reminded her. "And no the people or the houses were hurt."

Giannis burst into another indecipherable Greek speech, Spiros immediately translating his words for the benefit of the Brits.

"The Giannis he say that most of the people here said the fire brigade was no place for the woman, but Yiota fought the fire with the same bravery as the men."

Tellingly, the locals that had indeed objected to Yiota being accepted in the volunteer brigade, avoided the eyes of Giannis and Yiota, shifting uncomfortably. Only Kyrios Stavropoulos had the grace to admit they had been wrong. "*Kaname lathos. I Yiota ekane kalo se ena koritsi.*"

"What's he saying," Norman asked.

"He said, 'We were wrong. Yiota did good for a girl."

"*Perissoteri raki gia olous. Pana mou einai,*" Kyrios Stavropoulos declared, saying 'More *raki* for everyone. It's on me.'

Unaccustomed to indulging in *raki* before the day had even begun, I must confess that I was a tad unsteady on my feet as I weaved my way home. Falling into bed beside Marigold, I slipped into the sleep of the exhausted. I had barely closed my eyes and managed forty winks before the piercing sound of the alarm clock penetrated my brain. Covering my head with a pillow, I ignored it, only to find myself being rudely shaken awake by my wife demanding that I get up so we could enjoy an early morning stroll together through the village.

Groaning, I marvelled at how contrary Marigold could be; this was probably the first time in years that she'd been up and about at first light. It struck me that it was sod's law that Marigold was so perky and persistent on getting me up on the very day that my body was crying out for a much-deserved lie in.

Chapter 14

Confiscating Vi's Contraband

Prior to departing for the airport to collect Violet Burke's friend, Dot, I popped downstairs to check up on my mother's ankles. Violet Burke's extreme reluctance to admit me to the *apothiki* indicated that she had secreted away a stash of forbidden food she wished to keep hidden from my prying eyes. Barging my way in, I made a beeline for the kitchen where the smell of fried chips lingered.

"I'll take this upstairs so you won't be tempted," I said, grabbing the chip pan before rifling through the cupboards in search of edible contraband. Discovering the hidden horror of six tins of Spam, I lined them up next to the chip pan, chiding, "Really, Mother, you ought to know better at your age."

"There's nowt unhealthy about Spam, lad."

"There is when you insist on deep frying it." My mother deliberately avoided my eyes. "You know what the doctor said about sticking to a strict diet."

"Rome wasn't built in a day, lad...you can't expect me to change the habits of a lifetime overnight."

"It's for your own good..."

"Well, that wife of yours is forever nagging you to cut back on your cholesterol but you don't take a blind bit of notice even though it's for your own good."

"There's nothing wrong with my cholesterol levels. Marigold just likes to parrot some article she read about potential health problems in middle-age."

"'Appen you must have inherited it from me..."

"Inherited what, Mother?" If Violet Burke suffered from high cholesterol, she'd kept it under her hat.

"Not taking a blind bit of notice."

Changing the subject, I asked, "How are your

ankles, today?"

"Well, as you know, I'm not one to grumble. They're not as bad as they were. Much as you may mock, I have been following doctor's orders."

It sounded as though Violet Burke had renounced her usual stubbornness and done as she was told for once.

"Mindful of what that young foreign doctor had to say about stairs, I had Blerta do a couple of my regulars that have stairs while I sat on my backside with my feet propped up higher than my head."

"Perchance you're not a lost cause after all, Mother," I said.

"I watched young Tonibler for Blerta while she did a couple of my shifts. He's a good lad and right obliging about fetching me bottles of water from the fridge, though it has to be said that he's a bit odd. The way he comes out with some right grandiose words for such a young 'un puts me in mind of you."

I preened just a tad at the thought that my influence might be rubbing off on Tonibler. Certainly, his understanding of germs was coming along at quite the pace and he was developing a genuine interest in foodborne bacteria.

"Will you be okay for money if you've cut back on your shifts?" I asked.

"Aye, lad, not to worry. I'll muddle by. I only had Blerta do a couple. It's right easy doing the cleaning for that Kyriakos because of Milton's stairlift."

"There's no point dropping hints. I am not installing a stairlift and that's my final word on the matter."

"'Appen you should think about re-jigging that bucket on a rope then."

"What?"

"If you swapped out that bucket for a right big basket, you could haul me upstairs in it."

"It would take a hydraulic winch to get you up there…"

"I'm just pulling your leg, lad," Vi cackled. "Anyhow, I slept with my feet in the air last night, like, so I'm hoping they don't give me too much gip on the way to the airport."

"Coming to the airport is out of the question until the swelling goes down some more," I insisted. "You can hardly keep them elevated in the Punto for four hours. And why haven't you got your compression socks on? You're supposed to wear them all day."

"You sound like the stocking police," Vi sneered. "If you must know, they're on the washing line. They were getting a bit whiffy…"

"I will pick another pair up from the pharmacy

for you so you'll be able to don fresh ones as soon as you get up in the mornings," I promised. From the look of dismay on my mother's face, I surmised she considered my promise to be more of a threat. I can't say I blamed her for loathing having to wear the constrictive things in the heat but I was determined to keep her on the straight and narrow. Softening my tone, I reminded her, "You'll thank me for nagging you when you're able to enjoy a few afternoons out with Dot."

"Aye, 'appen," Vi reluctantly conceded.

"I'd better make tracks if we don't want to keep your friend Dot waiting. Now, how will I recognise her?"

"Well, I can't rightly say. 'Appen she might have changed her hair colour since the last time I was over in Warrington. She did mention that she'd lost a shedload of weight since finishing at the chippy."

"I need something more than that to go on," I pressed, reluctant to follow Barry's example of holding up a piece of cardboard with a name scrawled on it. I had no desire to be mistaken for a chauffeur.

"You'll be right, lad. I told Dot that if I couldn't make it up there with my feet, she's to look out for a tall, handsome fella in a sunbonnet…"

"A sunbonnet!" I exclaimed.

"Aye. I'll give you a lend of my straw one, you know the one. You remember how I livened it up by sticking some of your chicken feathers on it."

"You seriously expect me to stand around in the airport wearing that ridiculous sunbonnet of yours?"

"Well, it won't be the first time," Vi cackled. "You were glad enough of a borrow that time we went up to town to fix my toastie maker and your forehead went all red and started peeling."

Reluctantly accepting Vi's sunbonnet, I resolved to simply hold it aloft in the airport to attract Dot's attention, rather than plonk it on my head.

As I gathered all Violet Burke's contraband together to take upstairs out of temptations way, she stopped me, adding another item to the pile.

"Here, lad, I've dug out that electric blanket that Marigold got me when I first moved over. Take it upstairs with you. I couldn't be doing with it but I reckon Dot will be that grateful to have it. She's not one to worry about the risk of being electrocuted in her sleep. Get that wife of yours to stick it on the guest bed for her, make it nice and cosy."

"It may have escaped your notice, Mother, but it's August. No one needs an electric blanket in these excessive temperatures."

"That's all you know. I'm still quite partial to a hot water bottle even if it is summer. 'Appen you'll get what I'm saying when you get on a bit."

"But you told me that Dot is sixty-four. That's hardly getting on." Being just on the wrong side of sixty myself, I discounted the preposterous notion that sixty-four was getting on.

"Well, you'd better keep Dot's age to yourself, lad. She likes to pass herself off for forty-nine. She's not aged a year in the last two decades."

"Surely that would make her sixty-nine."

"You'd best not go spreading rumours like that. If she wants to delude herself that she's still in her forties rather than sixty-four, it's got nowt to do with anyone else. Anyhow, I thought you'd been brought up too proper to go questioning a woman's age. It's not considered polite, you know."

"Surely you don't intend to go to the airport in that?"

I sighed in irritation at the inevitable delay that would transpire whilst Marigold changed her outfit. There are times when my wife can be completely exasperating. Although she knew full well what time we needed to set off, she still wasn't ready. As lovely as Marigold looked in a turquoise swimming costume and matching silk sarong, it was hardly appropriate attire for wandering around the airport arrivals lounge. I just knew she would take an age to change and I do so hate to be tardy.

"Of course, I don't. People would think I'm a tourist..."

"Well, you'll need to change pretty sharpish or this Dot woman will end up hanging around the airport like a spare part...Vi said it's the first time she's travelled abroad on her own since her husband passed."

"I'm too exhausted to face that drive up to the airport in this heat." Looking as fresh as a daisy, Marigold's appearance belied her words.

"But you've only been up for two hours and you enjoyed the luxury of breakfast in bed." Thinking that perchance I could guilt my wife into changing her mind, I added, "I know that for a fact since I was the one that rustled it up."

"You've no idea how draining it was making up the bed in the guest room..."

"I helped you to do it..."

"Really, Victor, must you try and point score?" Deliberately avoiding my eyes, Marigold protested, "Besides, I've far too much to do here, dear."

"Such as?" I had no intention of accepting any of Marigold's feeble excuses. She would need to convince me that she had a good reason for abandoning the idea of accompanying me to the airport. I had been looking forward to the pleasure of her company on the long drive.

"I simply must tone my arms..."

"Tone your arms. There's nothing wrong with your arms," I argued.

"I couldn't help but notice that Doreen's upper arms have a definite touch of the bat wings. I'm determined to eradicate any wobbly arm bits before they take hold."

"Nonsense, there's no wobble on any of your bits," I flattered sincerely.

"You are biased, darling. Your mother made no bones about telling me I was developing a bit of jiggly flesh. After my initial shock, I was actually grateful that she was so blunt. Once it gets hold, it will be almost impossible to get rid of."

"So, does this mean you'll be joining an exercise class?"

"No, I'll just stay here and lift some weights to tone up my arms."

"Weights? We don't have any weights."

"I'll improvise with some cans of vine leaves until we can get up to town to buy some proper weights."

"The tins of vine leaves aren't very heavy," I pointed out. "Lifting 400 grams won't give you much of a workout."

"It will be 800 with a tin in each hand. Anyway,

I don't want to overdo it at first..."

"Just don't go turning yourself into a female version of Arnold Schwarzenegger. I'm not a big fan of muscly women. I prefer something soft to get hold of," I said. Turning on the charm, I wheedled, "Why not come with me, darling? Instead of staying at home to lift tins of vine leaves, you could tone up your body by taking a dip with me in the sea in town. We can stop on the way back for a swim and a late lunch at that swanky hotel on the seafront that you like so much. You always enjoy it when we do that. I've already put my swim shorts on under my shorts. Just throw a frock on over your cossie and we can be on our way."

"It's out of the question, Victor. I've far too much to do here. I still need to add a few personal touches to the spare room to make our guest feel at home," Marigold argued. Her stubborn reluctance to be persuaded put me in mind of my mother. I sincerely hoped Violet Burke's influence wasn't beginning to rub off on my wife.

"But Dot won't be at home. She'll be cluttering up our home."

"Must you be so churlish, Victor." Despite reprimanding me, Marigold clearly agreed with me since she wasted no time in adding, "Hopefully Dot will spend most of her time downstairs with your mother."

"Let's hope." Our imminent houseguest remained an unknown quantity, the titbits I'd gleaned from my mother doing little to reassure me that this Dot woman might turn out to be anywhere near normal.

"You can't expect me to meet this Dot person on my lonesome, Marigold," I wheedled. Thinking I could influence Marigold by sparking her jealousy, I posited, "What if she's some kind of voracious man-eater?"

"I'm sure you'll cope, darling," Marigold said in a blasé fashion, demonstrating not a hint of the green-eyed monster. "Anyway, I invited your mother to eat here this evening with Dot and the two of us, so I'll have to prepare a meal…"

"You mean you don't expect me to do it when I get back from the airport?" Instead of responding, Marigold simply pouted her disapproval of my sarcasm. "Well, don't forget that mother is on a strict diet."

"I'll do a salad," Marigold said, drifting towards the front door. She really did look quite lovely in her cossie.

"It's a tad early to be picking the salad ingredients now," I said as Marigold headed down to the garden.

"I know that, Victor. I thought I'd get a spot of sunbathing in first. I doubt I'll get a moment to myself once you bring this Dot person home with you."

"I'll be off then," I called after her, hoping the note of desolation in my voice as I grabbed the car keys would change Marigold's mind.

"Victor, you couldn't just move the sunbed into the shade…"

Dragging the sunbed towards Marigold's preferred spot, I grumbled, "You're going to make me late, Marigold."

After jumping to Marigold's demand that I pop back upstairs to grab her current paperback about a pair of Brits up-sticking to Italy, along with a glass of freshly squeezed orange juice so she'd stay hydrated in the heat, the sense of disappointment I had harboured since Marigold announced she couldn't be bothered to accompany me to the airport was replaced with a feeling of relief. At least alone in the Punto, I would be free of demands. I reflected that some peace and quiet on the drive was just what I needed.

Annoyed to discover a pigeon had left an unsightly deposit on the rear window of the Punto, I set to removing it with a bottle of spray glass cleaner and a cloth. As I concentrated on ensuring a smearless job, I was accosted by Milton's lodger, Kyriakos. Rapping me on the arm with one of the crutches he was still reliant on for getting around, after making a dramatic flight from his balcony resulting in two broken legs, he made a request.

"Victor. Can I to ask you for the help?"

"I already give the itch relief cream to Milton a few days ago," I replied.

"No, it is not the rash. I need the help to carry some the things from my house to the Milton's house. I cannot to manage with the crutch and the Milton..."

"Is a bit too much of big girl's blouse to be of any use," I said, finishing Kyriakos' sentence for him. "Sorry, Kyriako. I've no time now. I need to make haste to the airport to collect someone flying in from England."

"Later then?" Kyriakos pressed.

Having no wish to be roped into carting possibly heavy belongings about, I ran a list of plausible excuses through my mind, hoping to fob the Greek man off.

"It would to help me the much if you can to come with me to my house," Kyriakos continued. "I think the wife and the mother would be the too embarrass to make the, how you to say, the scream match, in front of the foreign."

A sudden thought occurred to me. If I acquiesced to Kyriakos' request, I could get a first-hand look at his mother, the woman whose husband was sent to prison for carrying on with the goatherd, Sofia, who had been married to Mathias at the time. Having never heard a good word said about Kyriakos' mother, my curiosity was certainly piqued.

"Shall I pop over and meet you at Milton's later, after I've returned from the airport?" I suggested.

"Yes, but make it the late afternoon…"

I interpreted that as evening.

"My mother will to blow the gas…"

"I think you mean gasket."

"If we to wake her from the afternoon sleep."

"I'll stop by later," I promised.

No sooner had I set off in the Punto, than I spotted two familiar figures walking through the village. Pulling over to greet Blat and his son, Tonibler, I had to chuckle at Blat's choice of tee-shirt, emblazoned with a life-size image of Tony Blair's head.

"You like the dress?" Blat enquired as I grimaced at the sight of Tony Blair's messianic smile. "The Mr Barry get it for me. You and the Mr Barry are the best boss I ever have."

"Mr Barry has always enjoyed making a gift of novelty tee-shirts," I diplomatically replied, thinking of some of the horrors that Barry had surprised me with over several decades of Christmases. Fortunately, Barry had spared young Tonibler from an equally tasteless tee-shirt. I was pleased to notice that for once, the boy wasn't wearing his school uniform, instead sporting a pair of shorts that ended just above his ankles and a tee-shirt that nearly came down to his knees. I supposed with cash being short, his clothes had been carefully selected to allow for any growth spurts over the coming years.

"Are you two off anywhere nice?"

"We go to the renovation of you and Mr Barry."

"You're working on a Sunday?"

"Yes. The Mr Barry want we get on to finish."

"And you're taking Tonibler along?"

"I must. The Blerta is to clean at the English man house. The Mr Norman tell her it is not professional to bring the child to work so I must to take Tonibler with me."

"The boy's a sight safer with Blerta in Norman's kitchen than he would be on a building site," I opined, annoyed that Norman could be so petty. Knowing Tonibler as I do, I imagined he wouldn't get underfoot; he was more than capable of finding a shady spot in Norman's garden to settle down with a book. Thinking that our renovation project was no place for a child, I rashly invited young Tonibler to come along with me to the airport, explaining to Blat that I would enjoy his son's company.

"Please can I go with Mr Bucket, *Baba*? We can

practice our conversational English and talk about fascinate germs," Tonibler enthused.

"Fascinating," I corrected before proposing, "We can stop for an ice cream on the seafront."

"Can I watch the aeroplanes landing?" Bouncing up and down on his toes, Tonibler was more excited than I'd ever seen him.

"He'll be perfectly safe in my capable hands," I assured Blat.

"I know. I to see you with the Mr Barry baby," Blat said. "The Tonibler not be in your way?"

"Not at all. He will save me from the boredom of driving up there alone. Mrs Bucket had too much to do at home to come with me."

Since Tonibler's evident excitement was hard to say no to, Blat agreed that the child could come along with me. Compared to giving the odd lift to the likes of Milton, at least I would have the pleasure of some intelligent company.

Chapter 15

Soaking up the Sun

"Keep a firm grip on my hand," I instructed Tonibler, thinking it would be terribly remiss of me to lose the child in the crowds that would be spilling into the airport arrivals area at any moment.

"Mr Bucket, why are you holding a lady's hat?" I noticed Tonibler's impeccable English was beginning to develop just a trace of a northern accent.

"It belongs to Mrs Burke. Since her friend that is arriving doesn't know what I look like, Mrs Burke insisted I bring it along so her friend could easily identify me."

"And you are holding it because you would look silly wearing it on your head?" Tonibler openly giggled at the thought.

"Got it in one. There's no need to go out of my way to look like a complete prat," I said. "Quite why Mrs Burke couldn't have stuck with the proverbial rolled up copy of the Times or a pink carnation in my buttonhole, eludes me."

"What is the proverbial?"

Explaining its meaning, I reminded myself to bear in mind that a six-year-old child might not have a full grasp of English vocabulary, particularly when they are learning it as a third language. Nevertheless, I was impressed by Tonibler's keen and enquiring mind.

"The tour operators are beginning to descend to collect their charges," I said, watching as the reps began to arrive, straightening their polyester and slapping on fake smiles. "They need to herd the package tourists onto the coaches. Oh, good grief. What utter moron gave Smug Bessie a job?"

Explaining what a rhetorical question was to Tonibler, I jammed Violet Burke's sunbonnet firmly on my head in an attempt to disguise my appearance and prevent Smug Bessie from recognising me. Luckily the hat had a very wide brim; the chicken feathers dangling over my face providing additional camouflage.

Unfortunately, the addition of the hat only served to make me more conspicuous. A couple of the younger reps started tittering behind their hands in the most juvenile fashion; really, anyone would think they had never seen a man wearing a woman's sunbonnet before. Fortunately, the appalling Bessie was far too busy smugly bossing the other reps to notice me. I was quite gratified to see the tittering directed at me replaced with lots of eye rolls behind Bessie's back; clearly her colleagues shared my opinion that the know-it-all woman was quite insufferable.

Thankfully, I realised that Cynthia hadn't caved in and given Bessie a job since the dreadful woman was wearing the uniform of a rival company. I felt a touch of smugness myself when I realised her shirt was fashioned out of nasty cheap nylon, a most uncomfortable fabric to suffer in the heat. Watching as Bessie marched out to harangue a coach driver, I overheard her fellow reps clad in the same unfortunate uniform talking about Bessie behind her back.

"Are you sure that Bessie is only doing airport runs, Julie?"

"Yes, I'm sure. Imagine if we had to put up with her on the meet and greets, or other excursions. I don't know who she thinks she is bossing us around like that. I'm going to put a formal complaint in when we get back."

With Bessie safely laying into some poor coach driver outside, I removed the ridiculous hat just as the new arrivals began to flock in. Since the plane had landed promptly, there were lots of smiling faces, happy tourists eager to get to their resorts and commence their holidays. The crowds washed around us, finally parting to reveal a woman with faded blonde hair peering at me intently through a pair of enormous, heart-shaped sunglasses with a tortoiseshell frame. Waving frantically, she called out. "Cooee. Victor Bucket? It's me, Dot, Vi's pal."

There was something rather familiar about the short, slight woman before me; it was the hairdo. Her perm immediately put me in mind of Doreen's dyed mop but the resemblance ended with the hair, Doreen always dressing in sensible blouses as befits a middle-aged woman. In contrast, I could spot leopard print legs sticking out from the bottom of Dot's lightweight beige mac, the raincoat nearly drowning her. Stripping off her coat and slinging it in my direction as though I was one of those portable clothes hangers on wheels that one finds in hotels, I saw that Dot was done up in some frumpy, drab, grey shapeless top from neck to waist, her lower half encased in somewhat saggy leopard print leggings.

BUCKET TO GREECE (VOL.15)

It could have been worse; in my mind I'd expected her to turn up in a shiny nylon shell suit like the one sported by Edna Billings. The leggings part of Dot's outfit was bunched up around her middle, drawing attention to her rotund stomach. Apart from her protruding belly, Dot was stick thin. If it wasn't obvious that she was very much on the wrong side of sixty, I may have hazarded a guess that she was pregnant.

"Hello, Dot. I hope you had a good flight…"

Ignoring my question, Dot carried on as though I hadn't spoken.

"I'd have known you anywhere, Victor Bucket. You look just like that photo of you that Vi had on her mantelpiece over the chippy." Barely stopping to draw breath, she gushed, "And who's this little nipper? It must be your grandson. Benjamin's little lad, is it? Hang on, your Benjamin's gay. Vi never said he'd turned straight and had a kiddy."

"This is Tonibler, a young friend of mine who lives in the village."

"Tony Blair. Aye, I remember Vi mentioning the lad, now." Bending down to converse with the boy on his own level, Dot cooed, "I've heard you're a right little clever clogs. Vi's that fond of you."

Dot looked rather taken aback when Tonibler displayed impeccable manners, extending his hand and saying, "Pleased to make your acquaintance."

"Ooh, aren't you just the cutest thing," Dot gushed. Ignoring his outstretched hand, she smothered him in a full-on hug. Watching the child squirm uncomfortably, I was glad I'd brought him along. Without the child on hand to receive her smothering embrace, I may well have ended up being the one on the receiving end. "Vi did suggest I try and find a newt to bring over for you, Tony, but I can't be doing with anything reptilian. Never mind, I've got some Warrington eggs in my case. You're in for a right treat."

"You'll have to keep those eggs away from my mother," I warned. "She's under strict doctor's orders to lose some weight to relieve the swelling on her ankles."

"Aye, she reckoned she might not be able to make it to the airport on account of her ankles. She didn't reckon you'd want her sticking her feet up on your dashboard."

"So, you've spoken to Vi since she saw the doctor?"

"Aye, that wife of yours lets her use your telephone for long distance when you're not there to grumble about the bill." I would be having stern words with Marigold once I got home. "Vi says you can be right pernickety when it comes to where folks stick their feet. Always moaning about your washing up bowls, I hear. Where's that wife of yours then? Marigold? Her name always puts me in mind of them yellow rubber gloves...course I wouldn't have recognised her, not with her having no head in Vi's photo. Lovely blouse she had on though, Marks and Sparks, according to Vi. Right posh."

"Marigold couldn't make it. She was busy preparing the guest room for you."

"Oh, I wouldn't have wanted to put the lass to any bother on my account, not with her being so delicate, like."

"Delicate?"

"Well, Vi says she does all your cleaning so I reckoned your Marigold must be out of sap. Enfeebled like. I can muddle along without any fuss, lad, don't you worry. Just because I'm on my holidays doesn't mean I won't be mucking in to keep the place spick and span. Take the pressure off Vi's ankles like."

"Marigold's the picture of health," I assured her, wondering just what Violet Burke had been saying about the Buckets. The phrase 'letting her gob run away from her' sprang to mind.

"I have to say it's right decent of the pair of you to invite me to stop at yours." The warm smile she sent my way emphasised the myriad of fine lines around her mouth. How she could possibly think she could pass for forty-nine was beyond me. She certainly seemed to be a good-natured soul even if it could prove to be a tad difficult to get a word in edgeways. Remembering she would be spending most of her time with my mother, I returned her smile.

Realising that Dot wasn't burdened down with suitcases, I asked where her luggage was. Her handbag didn't look large enough to hold a sizeable stash of Warrington eggs nor an urn full of her late husband's ashes. Perchance the late Wilf had travelled in the hold.

"It's going round on that concertina thing in there," Dot replied, pointing to the area set aside for passengers to retrieve their cases.

"You mean the conveyor belt…"

"Aye, that'll be it. They were flying around too fast for me to grab them."

"Well, let's make a grab for them now. Come along and point out your cases to me."

Since there were only two suitcases left making the rounds, it didn't prove too onerous to identify them.

"Let's get these in the Punto and head back," I said, practically giving myself a hernia as I negotiated my way through the airport with Dot's cases. From the weight of the things, I hazarded a guess that she'd flown half a ton of Fray Bentos over to Greece.

BUCKET TO GREECE (VOL.15)

The second we got outside, Dot advised me to put her suitcases down and take a quick breather. Thinking it was thoughtful of her to worry I might strain myself, I expressed concern when she plonked herself wearily down on top of one of the cases, using it as a makeshift seat.

"Are you okay, Dot?" I asked solicitously.

"Aye, lad. Nothing that a crafty fag won't fix. Can you believe it was no smoking on the plane? I did think of lighting up in the lav like but there wasn't half a right queue." Winking at me, she stuck a cigarette in her mouth and lit up. Blowing a plume of smoke in my face, Dot, hissed, "Any chance of stopping off at the pub on the way back? I could do with a quick snifter. My nerves are shot from all that flying. Unnatural it is."

"You have something in common with my chickens," I quipped, wondering if perchance she had been hitting the bottle on the flight.

"You'd think they'd be used to it. What with having wings and all..."

"Used to it?"

"Flying, lad."

"No, you misunderstood. Their nerves are apparently shot because of the heat," I explained.

"Ooh, I like a bit of heat myself. Can you believe it was piddling down in Warrington when I set off for the airport? Mind you, it was grey and drizzly in Manchester too. I've been that looking forward to getting horizontal on a beach. You don't get much of a tan by the Ship Canal."

"Did Vi mention that we don't actually have a beach, with living up in the mountains?"

"I can't say that she'd need to since it's right obvious there'd be no beach in the mountains, what with them not being at sea level. She said where you live, it's mainly fields, olive trees and hills, but she reckons you have right lovely views. The view at home is nowt but a row of grimy terraces and overflowing bins. The binmen don't take half as much pride in their job as they ought, the mucky beggars."

I agreed that we could stop at a beach bar for coffee and an ice cream for Tonibler. It would do the young boy good to have the chance to let his hair down on the beach. Indeed, a swim might well be in order; I was after all prepared, having driven to the airport with my swim shorts on under my shorts.

Piling into the car, I advised Dot that the Punto was a strictly no-smoking zone, as was our home in Meli. Dot chuntered on without taking a breath as I negotiated the busy traffic from the airport to town. The seafront was packed with cars and motorbikes illegally parked on the pavement. Fortunately, I was familiar with a small car park opposite the beach; after driving around in circles for ten minutes, I was able to grab a space being vacated.

Taking our life in our hands, we crossed the busy road. I directed my charges towards a rather plush hotel that welcomed non-residents to use their sun terrace and the beach that fronted their property, as long as drinks were purchased.

"Let's enjoy a coffee before we go on the beach," I suggested, grabbing a table on the scenic terrace, conveniently sited next to a wooden changing booth.

"This is a bit of all right. Right posh it is." Sinking into the well-cushioned rattan two-seat sofa offering a direct view of the beach and the sea, Dot sighed in contentment as Tonibler settled down next to her. Taking the chair at one side, I marvelled at the sheer number of people on the beach, sprawled out in the sun on sunbeds under sun umbrellas, the women strolling along the beach impeccably turned out in bikinis with matching sarongs and accessories.

The more energetic beachgoers engaged in vigorous games of bat and ball. No doubt many of the people enjoying the beach were locals taking advantage of their weekend break, along with holidaymakers from Athens making the most of the August holiday. There were unlikely to be many Brits in the mix since none of the tour companies sold package holidays in town, focusing their attention on the smaller resorts.

I was delighted I'd chosen this particular venue since the sea directly in front of the hotel wasn't nearly as packed as it was further along where the beach was public.

"What's the local tipple then, Vic?" Dot asked.

"It's Victor," I corrected.

"Fancy them Greeks naming a drink after you…"

"Mr Bucket does not like to be called Vic," Tonibler piped up.

"The local drink is *ouzo*," I told Dot, just as the waitress arrived to take our order.

"I'll try your local *ouzo*, lass. Make it a double, love," Dot requested, leaving me to order a bottle of water and an ice cream for Tonibler and a coffee for myself.

When the drinks arrived, Dot protested as I poured a generous measure of water into her *ouzo*. "Here, lad, don't go diluting my drink."

"It's the custom to dilute *ouzo*," I assured her. "See, the addition of water turns the clear drink milky."

Tasting the drink, Dot broke out in a fit of coughing. As the coughing fit abated, she stuck another cigarette in her mouth before declaring, "This *ouzo* stuff will put hairs on my chest. It's got a right kick to it."

"This is delicious," Tonibler enthused, digging into his tub of two scoops of ice cream, chocolate and strawberry. "Mr Bucket, is scrumptious a synonym of delicious?"

"Indeed, it is." I was most impressed that the child had remembered the chat we'd had in the car about synonyms, his vocabulary extremely advanced for someone of his tender years. Thinking his brain was nothing short of a sponge, I pondered the possibility of having his IQ tested. It wouldn't surprise me if his score was high enough to qualify for Mensa. "Other synonyms include delectable and ambrosial." A feeling of pride engulfed me as Tonibler sounded out the new words with a serious expression.

Looking out to sea, the water was extremely tempting, barely a ripple disturbing the smooth blue surface. The idea of a swim before heading back was extremely tempting.

"Who fancies a swim before the drive back?" I asked.

"If it's all the same to you, lad, I'm happy to just relax here in the sun, but don't let me stop the two of you from going in. Truth be told, I never got the hang of anything more adventurous than a paddle. I'll stop here and watch the pair of you," Dot said.

Tonibler's mouth gaped open in wonder. "You

really can't swim?"

"That I can't."

"I thought all grown-ups could swim," Tonibler said before confiding, "I can't swim."

"Well, if you'd like to learn, we can go and buy you some armbands and I'll teach you to swim" I offered. It was a skill I has successfully taught Benjamin when he was just a tad younger than Tonibler.

"Really?" The initial excitement in Tonibler's tone tapered off. Flushing with shame, his lower lip trembled. His voice barely above a whisper, he confided, "I don't have anything to swim in."

"You don't want to let that bother you, lad," Dot butted in. "Just go in the sea in your underkecks."

"She means your underpants," I explained.

Looking extremely uncomfortable, Tonibler hissed, "I can't. They're full of holes."

"Then we must rectify that at once," I said. "I'm sure one of the shops on the seafront will sell swimming shorts along with armbands. We'll head over there now. Are you sure you'll be okay here on your own, Dot?"

"Don't worry about me, lad. I'm having the time of my life just soaking up a bit of sun. 'Appen it'll bleach out my roots. Now, just remind me what this drink was called again, just in case I fancy another."

We were in luck, one of the beachfront shops having boys' swim shorts and armbands in stock. Kitting out the child in bathing attire of an appropriate size, I steered Tonibler back to the hotel where I directed him into the changing booth whilst I settled down next to Dot to blow up the armbands. It was no easy feat; no matter how much air I expelled from my lungs, the armbands remained stubbornly deflated.

"Ere, give them to me." Grabbing the armbands, Dot blew them up as though she was a professional, quite an accomplishment for a heavy smoker. "I'll put them on for him," she offered as Tonibler emerged from the cubicle. I felt a lump in my throat at the sight of the boy; it was the first time I'd ever seen Tonibler wearing an item of clothing that actually fitted him.

Walking across the hot sand together towards the water, I asked Tonibler if he'd been in the sea before.

"Not in the sea," he told me. "But we had a school trip to the beach."

"Where did you go?" I asked, chuckling to myself when the child revealed that the trip had been to the beach in the same village as the school. He revealed that none of the children had been in the sea but they had played a game of football on the beach.

Despite it being Tonibler's first time in the sea, he exhibited no sign of nervousness as he ventured in. Allowing him time to get comfortable in the water before starting the swimming lesson, I delighted in the boy's sheer enjoyment. Because the child is such an egghead, it is easy to forget that he is a mere six-years-old. When it came time to teach him a few moves, he picked it up quickly, kicking water into my eyes as I supported him with my arm beneath his chest until he got the hang of it. Confident he had mastered the art of floating without sinking, I removed my arm.

"Look, I'm swimming," Tonibler shouted joyously.

The drive home was uneventful, my two passengers sleeping soundly. Tonibler, worn out from sheer excitement, slept with his head on Dot's lap while Dot snored softly, half-sozzled from her introduction to the national drink of *ouzo*.

Chapter 16

Old Friends Reunite

Dropping Tonibler off with Blerta before returning home with Vi's visitor, the Kosovan woman was moved to tears when her son recounted that not only had I treated him to a pair of swim shorts and armbands, I had given him his first swimming lesson.

"I can swim, Mama," he declared, bouncing up and down on the spot with excitement.

"Just don't think about going in without your armbands until you've had some more practise," I said.

"I won't," he promised.

"Tonibler took to it like a duck to water," I said to Blerta.

"That's an idiom," Tonibler proudly announced.

Embracing her son, Blerta dropped kisses on the top of his head. As she thanked me profusely for taking Tonibler out for the afternoon, I couldn't help commenting on how much her English had come along since we first met.

"Tonibler is teach me," Blerta revealed.

Not only was Tonibler my star pupil, he was exhibiting excellent skills as a language teacher.

"He must come along with us next time we go to the beach," I invited. "Tonibler is delightful company."

"I feel bad. It is the school holiday but Blat and I must work."

"Terrible bad form of Norman not welcoming the boy while you clean. I will have words next time I see him," I promised, before driving away.

Pulling up at the house, I rapped on the door to the *apothiki*, Dot squirming with excitement beside me at the prospect of being reunited with her dear old friend.

"That's odd, my mother isn't answering yet her bicycle is here."

"'Appen Vi's having one of them afternoon *siesta* things. I remember her saying that wife of yours is quite partial to them."

BUCKET TO GREECE (VOL.15)

"It's the Greek way," I said, not wanting Dot to get the ridiculous idea that Marigold was lazy.

"Dot. Up here."

Doing her best fishwife impression, Violet Burke screeched down from my upstairs balcony, solving the conundrum of where she had got to. So much for the sanctity of siesta time.

"Vi. I'm here, Vi," Dot yelled back.

Leaving me to struggle upstairs with her luggage, Dot practically skipped ahead, colliding with my mother at the top of the stairs. I have to say, for someone with enormously bloated ankles, Vi had made quick work of the distance from the balcony to the door. Considering my mother isn't one to be demonstrably affectionate as a rule, I was surprised to see the two women locked in a firm embrace, Dot almost engulfed by the much larger figure of Violet Burke.

"Vi, it's been forever."

"Dot, it's that good to see you."

As the two women reunited, Marigold dragged me through to the kitchen, complaining I was late back.

"I expected you back ages ago, Victor. I've been stuck here for hours with your mother. Once she'd climbed the stairs, she didn't think her feet would make it back down again."

"I told you that you should have come to the

airport with me." I couldn't resist the opportunity to rub it in. "I took young Tonibler along in the end. We've had a lovely afternoon. We stopped at that swanky hotel you like on the beach on the way back for a coffee and a swim."

"So, you've been off enjoying yourself whilst I've been left to police your mother. I didn't dare turn my back in case she discovered where you'd hidden her stash of pies…"

"I won't be having any pies, lass," Vi interrupted, having caught the tail end of our conversation as she plodded into the kitchen, arm in arm with Dot. "I'm following doctor's orders to the letter so I can get out and about to show Dot the sights. It's her first time in Greece."

Raising her eyebrows, Marigold said sceptically, "Following doctor's orders. Since when?"

"I might have had the odd wobble, lass, but 'appen that doctor was right. Like Dot says, if I don't shift the lard, my feet could be the death of me. Dot's lost a shedload of weight…"

"What's your secret, Dot," Marigold asked, no doubt still fretting over the possibility that unattractive bat wings might spring up on her arms overnight.

"Grief."

"Ah, yes, sorry. Vi did mention you lost your husband," I said.

"I've not been grieving Wilf. He pegged it back in 2003."

I was confused. Since Violet Burke had told me that Dot carried Wilf's ashes around with her everywhere in case she chanced upon a suitable spot to scatter him, I'd got the impression that his death was quite recent. "Grief over the chippy closing. Going out to work was about as much of a social life as I got."

"Aye, lass. I miss it too. If my Victor hadn't wanted me to move over here to live under him, I'd have gone stark staring bonkers stuck in that council flat next to that motley Billings' clan. It's no fun getting older without family around. Now, sit yourself down, lass, and Marigold can make herself useful for once and stick the kettle on. You must be right parched with having to listen to Victor going on in the car. He doesn't half love the sound of his own voice."

"Nay, lass, he was no bother. I slept all the way back from the beach. I reckon it must be that jet lag."

"Nothing to do with all the *ouzo* she knocked back," I muttered to Marigold.

"Did you manage to get my PG Tips past them nosy jobsworths at customs control?"

"Aye. They're in my case," Dot said.

"Victor, go and grab Dot's cases," Vi instructed. "You've nowt but Yorkshire tea bags up here."

"Nonsense, we have a wide selection of tea; Earl Grey, Lapsang souchong, green, vanilla, and your favourite twig stuff," I teased before dragging Dot's suitcases through to the kitchen.

"Did I mention my Victor's a bit of tea snob? He can't produce a decent mug of builder's brew though," Vi hooted.

Rummaging around in one of her suitcases, Dot triumphantly cried, "Got them. Here, Marigold, stick some proper PG in the pot." Further rummaging revealed a plastic container. "Get your gnashers stuck into these, Vi. I made them special to bring over."

"Warrington eggs. Not on my watch," I said, making a grab for the container. "My mother is not allowed to eat them whilst she's on a strict diet."

"All the more for you then, Victor."

"Absolutely not. They'll play havoc with Victor's cholesterol levels," Marigold snapped. My wife has never taken to the Warrington delicacy, dismissing them as a heart attack on a plate.

"Put them to one side for Maria next door," Vi told Marigold. "She's right partial to a Warrington egg though I reckon a dozen might be a bit much for her. 'Appen Manolis might be glad of any that Maria can't manage. He was saying that he's keen to offer some traditional snacks along with the drinks. He's hardly going to turn a profit from them old geezers sitting around and making a Greek coffee last all day."

"In what world are Warrington eggs a traditional snack?" I snorted.

"In Warrington, you daft apeth," Dot chortled.

"'Appen if Manolis offered them in his new place, it'd be like English pubs offering pickled eggs," Vi argued. "Anyhow, anything is an improvement on them horrible snacks what Doreen knocked up."

"Oh, good grief. Don't say that Manolis has given Doreen a free hand in the *kafenio* kitchen?" I scoffed.

"Aye, she was making a right pig's ear of things yesterday morning when I was over there mopping. You'd hardly credit that a woman of her age could be so useless in the kitchen," Vi sniggered.

"It could hardly have come as a surprise to you, Mother. I believe you've sat through more than one of Doreen's excruciating expat dinner parties."

"Aye, and gone home with a rumbling stomach to a Fray Bentos every time, lad." Noticing that Dot was only listening with half an ear as she rummaged around in the suitcase for something, Vi asked, "Did you forget to pack something vital, lass?"

"It's all right, I've found him," Dot declared triumphantly, plonking an oversized, tacky orange urn down next to the teapot. "This is my Wilf, well, what's left of him anyway."

"You were taking a bit of a chance carting him over in your hold luggage," Vi said. "You'd have been in bits if they'd gone and lost your case."

"You certainly chose a vibrant colour," Marigold observed, tactfully not pointing out that the urn bore a remarkable resemblance to an ornamental pineapple.

"Aye, well, I did that deliberate like. I reckoned something bright would stand out. And I had them put him in fibreglass; that way, if I dropped him like, he wouldn't smash."

"You did right, lass. Imagine if you were forever dropping him and he spilled out over the carpet. He'd be hoovered up before you know it."

"Ooh, my giddy aunt." Dot had finally caught sight of Violet Burke's ankles. Openly gaping, her face took on a serious expression. "Them ankles of yours have swelled up more than that Billings' tart's knockers when she went and had them surgically enhanced with plastic…"

"Billings' tart," I spluttered.

"That would be Edna Billings' daughter, Flora. Right aptly named she is, what with her always spreading it about," Vi cackled. "My ankles are nowt now to what they were about four days ago when Victor took me to see the doctor. You should have seen the state of them then. They look worse than they are now because of these blasted surgical socks. They're a right bugger in this heat."

"Well, I'm here now, lass. We'll soon get you right," Dot said, still mesmerised by my mother's ankles. "I'll come along with you to your cleaning jobs. 'Appen you can take it a bit easy like, Vi, and I'll get stuck into the grunt work for you."

"But you've come over for your holidays," Marigold interjected.

"The only reason I flew out all this way was to spend the week with my old mucker, Violet. I ain't half missed her since the chippy shut down. It'll help her feet mend faster if I muck in and cut the workload in half."

"My clients will be getting two chars for the price of one this week, eh Dot," Vi quipped.

"You could just take the week off, Mother," I suggested. "I'm sure your clients would be understanding in the circumstances. Rest your ankles up and enjoy a break with Dot."

"Have you met that lazy lot of entitled Brits that I char for? If I hang up my mop for a week, the likes of that scheming Agnesa will be sniffing around, undercutting my rates and trying to do me out of a job," Vi countered. "You should know me well enough by now, son, to know that I'm not one of them bone-idle malingerers."

"Your work ethic is admirable, Mother."

As Marigold topped up our cuppas with more PG Tips, Dot stood up to stretch, taking a moment to have a good nosy around the grand salon.

"Ooh, I say, you have done well for yourself, Victor. Look at this place. Ooh, you've got one of them balcony things. Is it safe to step onto it, like? I'd hate for it to collapse under my weight and send me soaring to an early grave." By the way Dot was carrying on, anyone would think that they'd never heard of balconies in Warrington.

"There's nowt of you, lass," Vi shouted over. "Just watch where you're stepping, you don't want to go tripping over a cat. Marigold is cat mad. I did warn you that the house is knee-deep in the things."

"I've nowt against cats as long as they haven't got fleas," Dot said, stepping out on the balcony. Her words prompted Marigold to roll her eyes at the very suggestion her imported pedigrees would be common enough to attract fleas.

"Ooh, would you look at this view, it's right grand. That's the sea down there." Stepping back into the grand salon, Dot's exuberant praise for her week's lodgings continued as she gushed over the décor, her enthusiasm only waning when she finally noticed the tiled floor.

"Ooh, did you run out of cash before you had the chance to get some proper carpets down? I reckon you should have saved the money you wasted on all these decorative knick-knacks..." Dot held one of Marigold's ornate scented candles aloft to make her point, "and put something over these tile things. A nice bit of shag-pile would be right welcome. You must freeze your feet off in winter or is it hot like this all the year?"

"Come and get your cuppa before it goes cold, Dot," Marigold invited, clearly not wanting Dot to get hands on with any more of the decorative touches she'd squandered our money on instead of investing in a decent shag-pile carpet.

As Dot re-joined us at the kitchen table, the ugly topic of the Billings' clan raised its head again. It turned out that Vi's old nemesis of haddock on a Friday wasn't the only Billings on Dot's radar.

"I don't know how you're going to take this, Vi, but our Kevin has only gone and got that right little slapper, Chardonnay Billings, up the duff." Dot's words conjured a vivid image in my mind of a pyjama clad young woman, a rusty stud suppurating in her pierced tongue, littering the aisle of Tesco with a snotty brat in tow.

"Your Kevin. Last time I saw him he had too much acne to be pulling the girls. He looked like something had erupted on his face," Vi snorted. "Mind you, none of them Billings' lot have ever been what you'd call choosy about where they put it about."

"And Kevin is?" I asked.

"Kevin's my lad. He's just had his twentieth." I did the maths in my head. I supposed it was doable for a sixty-four-year-old passing herself off as forty-nine.

"Kevin was her menopause baby," Vi revealed.

"Aye, I was forty-four when I had him," Dot said. Since Vi had made such a point of telling me that Dot blatantly lied about her age, I assumed the copious amounts of *ouzo* she'd downed had loosened her tongue like a truth serum.

"There's nowt for it but to let that Chardonnay and her Tyrone move in with us," Dot said with a heavy sigh. "I'm not having our Kevin moving in with that Billings' riff-raff; likely he'd pick up a load of bad habits. I don't want to see him going the way of that lot."

"Strangeways," I ventured.

"Aye, that's where half them Billings' lot spend half of their time," Vi sneered.

"Our Kevin's gone and got himself a right good job," Dot said.

"Aye, well, he had the example of your Wilf to follow. What job's he got himself, then?" Vi asked.

"He's in packing at the factory…"

"Nice and steady with a regular wage packet coming in?" Vi checked.

"Aye, not to mention the chance of promotion if he keeps his nose clean," Di said proudly.

"'Appen that Chardonnay's not as bad as the rest of them Billings' lot. 'Appen if you let her move in, you could steer her right," Vi said. "Teach her some manners and how to dress proper so she doesn't look like a common trollop."

I could barely conceal my laughter at the thought of Dot giving clothing advice to a girl barely out of her teens. There again, the only clothes I'd ever seen Chardonnay in were night clothes, most inappropriate attire for wheeling her trolley around Tesco.

"That Tyrone's a right little tyke, mind…" Dot admitted.

'Appen your Kevin will be a good influence on the brat. It'll be right nice for you to have a little one around. It warms the cockles of my heart when little Ana calls me Granny…"

"So, your Benjamin did go straight after all?"

"Don't be daft. Anastasia is Barry's nipper, my Victor's niece."

"Aye, I remember now. It's going to be right good to finally put some faces to all these names," Dot said. Turning to Marigold, Dot turned on the flattery, saying, "It's a crying shame that you were headless in that picture of you over the chippy. Now that I'm seeing you in the flesh, I don't mind saying you're a right stunner, lass."

As Marigold preened under Dot's flattery, I chuckled. "Marigold has been promoted these days. She has her head firmly on her shoulders in the family photo that graces Vi's mantlepiece in the *apothiki*."

Yawning widely, Dot referenced her delusional jet lag again.

"Perhaps you'd like to take a little nap before dinner," Marigold suggested. "You must be exhausted after the flight, not to mention the drive back from the airport. Come along, Dot, I'll show you to the guestroom."

As Marigold and Dot left the room, I hissed at my mother, "Your friend isn't jetlagged, she's been on the *ouzo*. You might have warned me she's a secret tippler."

"What Dot? Never. Dot was never owt but sober when we were at the chippy together. 'Appen she might have found solace in drink since Wilf pegged it, but more likely she just wanted to calm her nerves after flying. It's not natural, not to mention it's a right song and dance if you need the onboard lav."

"Victor. Can you bring Dot's cases through?" Marigold called.

Dragging Dot's suitcases through to the guest room, I delighted in witnessing our visitor's response to the room. I can honestly say that out of all the people that have had the good fortune to spend a night in the Bucket guest bedroom, none had been more gushingly grateful than Dot.

"Ooh, you haven't half got good taste, Marigold. It's done out that nice. It's like something out of one of them glossy magazines." Despite Dot's praise being just a tad over the top, Marigold was lapping it up.

"I do like to think I have quite the eye for décor. I chose the colours for Violet's place downstairs too, and I'll be advising Victor and Barry on the décor of the old house they're converting…"

"You're too modest, darling," I interrupted. "You forgot to mention how you transformed that old shed at the bottom of the garden into the pink palace of love."

"Well, I reckon this is just lovely," Dot reiterated. Moving over to the window, she gushed again, this time raving about the view of the garden.

"Ooh, I never. Did you know there's a flasher out there? The cheeky bugger's stripping right down to his underkecks."

"It sounds as though Guzim must be cooling off under the hosepipe after a hard day's toil," I said.

"Guzim. Aye, I remember now. He's that toothless fella that lives in the shed. Vi warned me he was partial to flashing his bits."

"It's nothing more revealing than anything you saw on the beach this afternoon." Remembering how Guzim had so gallantly volunteered to sleep in the chicken run, I felt duty-bound to defend him.

"Why don't you enjoy a nice nap before dinner, Dot," Marigold suggested again.

"Don't you mean sleep it off?" I muttered under my breath.

"Now, I didn't bother making a meal for this evening," Marigold continued, ignoring my comment. "I thought it would be nice for the four of us to dine at the local taverna."

"Are you quite mad, Marigold?" I said, questioning my wife's sanity. "You know that we have to keep my mother away from the chips, not go out of our way to put temptation in front of her. I suppose as you haven't bothered cooking, I'd better make something."

"Nay, lad, we can go along to the taverna together like Marigold said," Vi piped up. "Cross my heart, I won't eat a single chip. I'll force one of them oily salads down and get Nikos to chuck a nice bit of skinless chicken on the outside grill. I can't wait to introduce Dot to Dina and Nikos. The pair of them have been right good to me, giving me time off over this feet business."

Chapter 17

Argy-Bargy from Morning till Night

Remembering that I had promised Kyriakos that I would give him a hand shifting some of his belongings from his house to his temporary lodgings at Milton's place, I steeled myself to break the news to Marigold that I was popping out, leaving her to police Violet Burke yet again, whilst Dot slept it off.

When I explained where I was off to, Marigold took the news surprisingly well, sticking the kettle on to make another cuppa for herself and my mother. Violet Burke's reaction was another matter.

"Cor, if you're going over to that Kyriakos'

house, 'appen you'd better have a lend of my bicycle helmet, lad," Vi said. Her forehead wrinkling in a frown, my mother subjected me to a steely stare over the top of the spectacles which had slipped down to the tip of her nose. I couldn't help noticing she bore a marked resemblance to a pensive owl.

"What on earth do you mean?" I asked.

"'Appen you'll need to protect your head from flying missiles being hurled about. From what I hear, there's nowt but trouble at that Kyriakos' house...argy-bargy going on non-stop from morning to night."

"Where on earth did you hear that?" I asked before recalling that Kyriakos had been paying my mother to rid Milton's place of an excess of cat hair. "I suppose that Kyriakos must have been confiding in you about his home life whilst you've been charring."

"He hasn't, lad. He's right tight-lipped on the subject, though I reckon that's because that Edna is always hovering. She has a horrible habit of sticking her beak in where it's not welcome. Peck, peck, peck, she is, trying to get the fella to open up," Vi disclosed. "Someone else with a big mouth must have blabbed Kyriakos' secrets; I hear all sorts, lad, when I'm out cleaning. Dina likes to fill me in on any gossip when we do the spuds...if I can't make out what she's on about, we get Nikos in to translate. There's nowt Nikos loves more than a bit of tittle-tattle; he can be a right old woman."

The irony of Vi accusing Nikos of being a gossiping old woman appeared to go over my mother's head. Suppressing a chuckle, I realised she still had more to say on the matter.

"Then, of course, Tina lets her mouth run away with her when I'm mopping the shop. Maria, from next door, hears all sorts too. I reckon that son of hers, you know the one in the dress, isn't backward about coming forward when it comes to repeating what he hears in the confessional."

"Papas Andreas isn't a Catholic priest," I schooled my mother. "The Greek Orthodox lot aren't into confessionals…"

"Well, some of the stuff he tells Maria would make your toes curl, lad."

"You've kept this very close to your chest, Vi," Marigold complained. "You might have thought to share the odd bit of gossip you've picked up."

"Perish the thought." Marigold rolled her eyes dramatically at hearing what she dubbed a Victorism emanating from the mouth of her mother-in-law. "I'm not one of them gasbags, repeating what I've been told in confidence, lass."

"You're quite loose-lipped when it comes to repeating all the goings on over at Sherry's,"

Marigold reminded her.

"And it appears you were happy enough to go revealing things about what transpires in the Bucket household to your visitor. Dot had plenty to say about the pair of us," I carped.

"Aye, but you're family, lad. I don't need to listen in on the gossip about the two of you. I can see what goes on right under my nose with my own two eyes. And before you go getting nowty with me, Dot knows nowt about that bucket business."

"Well, it wouldn't reflect well on you, would it?" I pointed out rhetorically. Wondering how Violet Burke had explained away the advent of the long-lost son she had abandoned in a bucket to Dot, I decided to save my question for another day. "I'm not at all happy that you gave Dot the impression that Marigold is some kind of consumptive invalid, too enfeebled to do her own cleaning…"

"Well, if the hat fits, or in your case, the sunbonnet," Vi cackled. "Anyhow, I said nowt about Marigold being enfeebled. I just 'appened to mention that she's not one for getting her hands mucky…"

"Really, Vi. You forget that I'm part of the beautifying the cemetery group. I'm on my hands and knees in the dirt pulling out weeds…" Marigold protested.

"You can't deny that you're not one for getting

stuck into a good bottoming. Your idea of a good spring clean is nowt more than a tickle with a feather duster," Vi accused.

"Victor, I told you we should have invested in a Roomba," Marigold grumbled. "At least it wouldn't have gone about gabbing about our business and casting aspersions."

"You can't expect one of them robotic vacuums to be getting into the corners proper like," Vi spat contemptuously. "'Appen if you had one of them posh Roombas, them daft cats of yours would spend their days trying to mate with it."

"Clawsome and Catastrophe aren't in the least promiscuous," Marigold objected, appalled at the very suggestion her precious cats would be attracted to a mobile robotic vacuum cleaner.

"Can we stop all this petty squabbling, please?" I begged, attempting to restore domestic harmony. "Mother, you still haven't told me why I may need the protection of your bicycle helmet over at Kyriakos' house."

"Well, word is that his mother is a bit cracked in the head…"

"From having missiles hurled at it…"

"No, from all that business about her husband being sent to prison for cheating on her…I heard it turned her into a right mardy cow. I hear tell that she hasn't left the house in thirty years." It really was news to me that Kyriakos' mother was a recluse.

About to demand how on earth my mother had heard about the adulterous affair that ended in a prison sentence, I bit my tongue. Although I'd only just heard the decades old news about Kyriakos' father carrying on adulterously with Mathias' wife, I was slowly coming to realise that Violet Burke apparently had the inside scoop when it came to matters of local gossip. Without another word, I flounced off to Milton's house. Strolling through the village, I couldn't help but wonder if the arguments between Kyriakos' mother and his wife had started off in a similar fashion to the spat currently underway in the Bucket household.

Opening the door just a crack, Edna peered out at me suspiciously. Dispensing with the usual pleasantries, her tone was accusatory. "I hope you haven't got your mother with you."

"No, I'm alone," I stated, wondering if Edna had been getting her knickers in a twist about Milton's decades long infatuation with Violet Burke again. "I've called round to collect Kyriakos. He needs me to give him a hand carrying some of his personal belongings over from his house."

Edna visibly relaxed. "Well, don't be bringing all his furniture. We've little enough room as it is, making room for a lodger on top of the cats."

"Do I look like a furniture removal man?" I snapped, hoping that Kyriakos hadn't got any ideas about shifting any heavy and possibly hernia inducing items. Considering that Barry used to make a living from furniture removals, I kicked myself for not sending Kyriakos in my brother-in-law's direction instead of making myself available. "I believe that Kyriakos just wants a hand with some personal belongings, most likely clothes and such. He can't manage to balance his bags with his crutches."

Finally opening the door more than a crack, Edna beckoned for me to follow her inside, affecting an artificially posh voice as she yelled up the stairs to summon Kyriakos. Careful to avoid tripping over a member of Edna's clowder, I waited around impatiently as the painfully slow stairlift transported Kyriakos downstairs. The strong whiff of air freshener and furniture polish made a change from the usual overpowering smell of cats, indicating my mother hadn't let her swollen ankles allow her to slack off on the charring front.

"I am the happy you can to make it, Victor." Shifting from the stairlift to solid ground, Kyriakos adjusted the crutches to take his weight, careful to keep hold of a bunch of flowers that I guessed he had purloined from the cemetery.

"Kyriakos, what time will you be back for dinner?" Edna asked. "I'm planning to dish it up in half-an-hour."

"It is still the afternoon," Kyriakos declared petulantly.

"It's gone seven already," Edna argued, fidgeting nervously.

"The seven is the afternoon," Kyriakos snapped, slowly making his way down the garden path.

Gripping my shirt sleeve, Edna wheedled. "Can't you have a word with him, Victor? He likes to eat at very strange hours."

"He's on Greek time," I pointed out, not wishing to involve myself in the domestic timetable of the Hancocks.

"The Edna cannot to cook the good Greek food," Kyriakos complained as we ambled through the village at a suitable pace to accommodate his use of crutches. "She always to cook the soft, tasteless food she can to share with the cat."

"It was Milton who generally turned up for my Greek cookery classes," I told him. Despite having attended quite a few of my classes, Milton had confessed that he was of the firm belief that the kitchen was Edna's domain. He tended to view my classes as a social occasion with the added bonus of leftovers thrown in, rather than a practical guide to getting hands on in the kitchen.

"I miss the Voula's cooking," Kyriakos sighed.

"Voula?"

"My wife. I bring her the flower."

Nearing Kyriakos' house, I surveyed the balcony from which he had hurled himself whilst under the drug-induced delusion he could fly. Considering his flight path had been over a rough looking piece of cement rather than a grassy knoll which may have broken his fall, it was easy to see how he'd managed to shatter the bones in both of his legs. He was lucky that he hadn't ended up completely splattered like Spiros' uncle when he fell off my roof terrace.

"This is my home," Kyriakos announced.

I noticed his house was similar in style to my own, though desperately dilapidated and in dire need of a makeover. The *apothiki* was shuttered up; the wood rotting in its frames, indicating it wasn't being used for anything but storage. Taking in my surroundings, I surveyed the unkempt garden. I reflected that Guzim would have a fit if he spotted the rundown condition of the henhouse the chickens were expected to put up with. Considering the state of the miserable looking, scrawny chickens pecking around in the dirt with a desolate air, I was inclined to finally accept that Guzim had a point when he insisted that some chickens were prone to stress.

"I was the born in this house. I live here all the life until the fight between the mama and the wife get too the much," Kyriakos said, leading the way up the outdoor stairs. His nimble gait made me suspect that he was no longer quite so reliant on his crutches as he made out and had only used them as a prop to drag me along for moral support.

"I imagine having your wife and mother under one roof could well put a strain on your marriage," I commented, thanking my lucky stars that I'd had the foresight to renovate the *apothiki* and park Violet Burke off downstairs.

Entering Kyriakos' house was like stepping back in time. With the shutters firmly closed against the sun, the interior was gloomy to say the least, an unshaded electric lightbulb of dubiously dull wattage precariously dangling from the ceiling, casting a shadowy light on the dated brown and orange linoleum floor covering. The front door opened directly into a dining area, the plastic cloth adorning the table apparently chosen to match the dreary lino. Dismal religious icons were strategically placed along the shelves, presumably best placed to keep a beady eye on the diners. As Kyriakos opened the door to what I presumed was the kitchen, the sound of stertorous snoring filtered out.

BUCKET TO GREECE (VOL.15)

Kyriakos shouted, "My mother has gone too far. She has to move her bed into the kitchen. She must to have done it from the spite to enrage the Voula."

As if on cue, Voula put in an appearance, but I have to say she looked far more browbeaten than enraged. To my surprise, I recognised Kyriakos' wife: she had been a regular customer during my stint standing in for Tina as the manager of the village store. A mousy shy woman, always drably dressed in some shapeless number, she'd had little to say for herself when she paid for her groceries, failing to make an impression on me at the time.

"Give me the minute," Kyriakos said to me, taking Voula's arm and pulling her to one side. As he presented her with the rather forlorn bunch of flowers, Voula noticeably blushed.

Casting a sidelong glance as the couple conversed in Greek, I observed that Voula had made a bit of an effort appearance wise. Presumably apprised that her husband would be popping over, she was nicely turned out in a colourful frock and had discarded her usual dull headscarf to reveal a neatly combed brown bob. It struck me that Voula had pulled out all the stops in an effort to try and lure her husband home.

Snatches of their hushed conversation reached my ears, Voula begging her husband to return to the marital home, Kyriakos arguing that a return would be a threat to his sanity as he couldn't endure another day of living in such a toxic atmosphere. Voula appealed to her husband, pointing out that she was the one stuck alone with his mother, saying that although she had always been a dutiful *nyfi*, daughter-in-law, Kyriakos' mother treated her as nothing more than a drudge.

Before Kyriakos could respond, a short, stick-thin woman with a sour expression emerged from the kitchen, clad in rumpled black widow's weeds from head to toe. The fusty stench emanating from her musty clothing was unpleasantly overpowering.

"*Ti einai olos aftos o thoryvos?*" she screeched, demanding to know 'what's all this noise?' I considered her question a tad over the top considering that Kyriakos and his wife had spoken so quietly that I had struggled to eavesdrop.

Seemingly oblivious to my presence, the elderly woman fired off insults at the couple at such a rapid speed that it challenged my translating skills. The snippets I caught were along the lines of questioning Kyriakos' manhood for failing to cater to her every whim like a good son should, blaming him for the state of penury she had been in ever since he drove her husband away. In his defence, Kyriakos argued that he had been defending her honour when he thumped his cheating father, adding that he had always been a good son by providing for her when he toiled away at the post office before taking retirement. I couldn't fail to notice that his counter argument was delivered in a lacklustre way. No doubt he had faced down the same accusations so many times that he simply replied by rote.

In turn, his mother hurled some more insults his way, accusing Kyriakos of being a useless lump, a coward that had fled his home rather than facing up to his responsibilities, leaving her stuck in the house with his insipid wife. At this point Voula piped up; no longer the meek woman that I remembered from the shop, I could see the defiant fire in her eyes as she blamed her mother-in-law for driving Kyriakos away with her endless complaints, admonishing her for deliberately ruining their marriage.

Blatantly listening in on their argument, I could understand why Kyriakos had ended up so depressed that he felt the need to flee the house. Seemingly running out of steam, Kyriakos turned on his heel, announcing he was off to pack some clothes. Disappearing into another room, his absence drew the attention of the two women to me.

Curling her lip in contempt, Kyriakos' mother sneered, "*Ara eisai o Anglos pou grafei ta vromika vivlia."*

"Den eimai," I said, denying her ridiculous accusation that I was the English man that writes dirty books.

"O Victor douleve sto magazi," Voula said, telling the older woman that I used to work in the shop.

"Mia axiolypiti douleia gia enan enlika." Kyriakos' mother sneered that was a pathetic job for a grown man.

Refusing to rise to her bait, I chose to ignore her, a tactic I had belatedly adopted when dealing with the wart-faced old hag, Despina. As an aside, I had noticed that blanking Despina rather than reacting was guaranteed to make her blood boil, a reaction I considered a win; women like Despina hated it when the provocative gauntlet they threw down was simply trampled underfoot.

Telling Voula that I would wait outside, I stepped out to the porch area at the top of the stairs. I was surprised when Voula joined me, hesitantly looking me in the eyes and addressing me in tentative but more than competent English.

"I am sorry about the mother-in-law, Alexandra. Her tongue is sharp…she has lived the difficult life. She feel much the shame from her husband's mistake. She live it still as though it was yesterday."

"May I ask why she's dressed in widow's

weeds?" The question had been on the tip of my tongue since the old woman had emerged from the kitchen.

"She put on the black dress the moment that Takis was sent to prison and she never take it off again." I suppressed a snort at the thought of Alexandra wearing the same dull dress for decades; it would certainly account for the musty smell. "Her husband's actions influence her to this day. When I first to marry Kyriakos, she told me that my place was in the house. She told me that people would mistake me for a loose woman with no morals, like that Sofia who seduced Takis, if I went outside. From the day I move in, Alexandra never leave the house. She withdraw from society out of shame."

"And, I would hazard, holing up here turned her toxically acerbic. You must have the patience of a saint to put up with her," I observed, having formed my own impression that Alexandra was a bitter old shrew taking out her frustration on Kyriakos and Voula. I considered how much the vinegary old woman was losing out on by allowing her husband's dalliance to shape her life. She was missing out on the supportive friendships she could have formed with the likes of Kyria Maria, Lista and Dina, all much of an age.

"Can't you get her to move out?" I asked.

"It is Alexandra's house." Voula shrugged,

seemingly resigned to her intolerable situation.

"Have you never considered renovating the *apothiki* for her, or for you and Kyriakos? That way you could live separately and put some small distance between you."

"She would not like it."

"Do it anyway. Surely, it's better than having Kyriakos lodging with the Hancocks. My brother-in-law, Barry, and his partner, Vangelis, could fix the place up a treat. You're welcome to pop over and see what they did with my *apothiki*," I invited.

Sensing her reluctance to defy Alexandra's edict about gadding about outside the house, I encouraged her to defy her mother-in-law before Kyriakos decided to make his absence permanent. Moreover, I imagined another *apothiki* conversion would be a job that Barry would love to get his teeth into now they were almost done with Macey's place.

As Voula mulled my offer, Kyriakos joined us, toting a couple of bags he passed my way.

"Why not walk over there with us now," I urged Voula.

"Alexandra would not approve..." Voula hesitated, before filling her husband in on my suggestion.

"I cannot to believe I never to think of that," he groaned. Slipping an arm around his wife's waist, he pulled her close. "We could to have our own place, Voula. Think of that. I cannot to tolerate the much more of Edna and her cats."

Chapter 18

Some Poor Sap of a Chauffeur

It was the third day of Dot's stay in the Bucket household and, remarkably, it was going quite swimmingly. Although I'd had my reservations about offering the Bucket spare bedroom to Violet Burke's friend, Dot was proving to be far less of a nuisance as a guest than my mother would have inevitably been. Whenever she ventured out of her room, Dot made the effort to put some proper clothes on rather than slobbing around in her nightie or some ghastly candlewick number. She also displayed a cheery disposition and a willingness to get stuck into the housework.

BUCKET TO GREECE (VOL.15)

She didn't expect to be waited on hand and foot as other Bucket guests had done in the past: Spiros in particular sprang to mind, on both the entitled guest and slobbing front.

Over the course of the three days that she had been with us, I had barely had chance to vacate the shower before Dot dashed into the bathroom to give it a good bottoming, tackling the grout between the tiles with an old toothbrush and leaving the lav so gleaming that one could have eaten off it, not that I was so inclined. No sooner had we finished a meal than the plates were whisked away and washed by Dot's fair hand. I must say that I was most impressed by her dedication to sponge hygiene; it really was quite exemplary. Moreover, Dot ingratiated herself in Marigold's good books by fussing over her and telling her how lovely she looked in her posh Marks and Sparks' frocks, assuring Marigold that her arms didn't have the slightest wobble of bat wings. Dot even went so far as currying favour with Marigold by sucking up to her precious cats.

As soon as breakfast was out of the way, Dot hurried down to join Violet Burke on her cleaning round, sharing the workload as she'd promised, taking the strain from my mother's swollen feet. Peace was restored to the Bucket household when the two women were off cleaning.

V.D. BUCKET

After charring with Vi over at Sherry's place, Dot peppered her conversation with observations about Sherry's jolly hockey- sticks manner. I remained constantly amazed that my mother hadn't sacked Sherry as an employer; Vi never stopped mithering about how irritating she found the younger woman. When I raised the subject, pointing out that my mother could have the pick of any cleaning jobs in the village, she responded by saying, "Aye, but that Sherry might be all hot air and she never stops running her mouth, but someone has to keep an eye out for her. I don't want to see her falling for the charms of some other useless bugger like that mucky hippie what was free with his fists."

"Not to mention her bank balance," I added.

In truth, I suspected that despite Vi's low tolerance for Sherry, she felt a certain empathy for her, both women having been on the receiving end of a good clouting from some waste of a space bloke they'd had the misfortune to become romantically entangled with. Noticing that my mother never referred to my slacks as slacks, I asked Marigold to have a discreet word to see if my preferred trouser vocabulary brought back nasty memories of her second husband, Reginald Slack. Much as it would pain me to drop my slacks, I would hate to inadvertently rub salt in any possible painful memories that Violet Burke carted around in her head.

I was particularly relieved that Violet Burke hadn't demanded that I dedicate any free afternoons to chauffeuring her and Dot around in the Punto to see the local sights. Instead, my mother had roped some of the more gullible of the local villagers into providing free transport. I must admit it was quite a sight on the second afternoon of Dot's visit to see Moira Strange calling round to the *apothiki* to collect Violet and Dot in the sports car. The pair of them were sun-glassed and head-scarfed up to protect their hair from blowing in their faces, Dot squashed up next to Waffles in the miniscule luggage space behind the two seats. I did hope for Dot's sake that Waffles was going through a rare flatulence free spell. Whilst I'm sure Vi and Dot thought they resembled some glamorous Hollywood icons in their nifty headscarves, they bore more of a resemblance to Corrie's Hilda Ogden, with her trademark headscarf covering her rollers.

As Marigold and I had waved them off from the balcony, my wife had once again proved herself contrary, complaining that I wasn't whisking her off somewhere exciting too.

"But you said you couldn't bear to go out in the heat," I pointed out. "You could have always gone off with them for the afternoon."

"And exactly how do you imagine I could have squeezed myself into the Stranges' sports car, short of sitting on your mother's knee?" Marigold complained as she began her new daily ritual of toning her arms. Having coped well with a couple of tins of vine leaves, she had now progressed onto heavier items. Still improvising due to a lack of actual weights, Marigold had divided eight tins of Fray Bentos between two carrier bags, raising the bags above her heads. "Pass me another couple of pies, Victor. I think I can manage five in each hand."

As Marigold chucked a couple of extra pies in the bags, the bottom gave out on one of the carrier bags.

"Ouch," I cried out in pain as five tins of Fray Bentos rained down on my toes.

"Rather your toes than little Fluffs," Marigold said as the kitten darted skittishly out of the way.

Returning from a repping trip to the Caves of Diros on the first day of Dot's visit, I had been lost for words when Marigold told me that my mother had managed to persuade the oily Christos to take her and Dot out for the afternoon. Turning up to collect them, Christos had turned his greasy charm on my wife in the hope of persuading her to join the three of them down on the beach. Repulsing Christos' repulsive advances didn't go down too well with the have-a-go Greek Lothario who it seemed had only offered to take Vi and Dot out in the vain hope that Marigold would accompany them. Lumbered with Vi and Dot, Christos accused Violet Burke of misleading him by promising that Marigold would be coming along. Clearly my mother had used Marigold's name as tempting bait to snare herself and her sidekick a chauffeur driven pickup, Christos having borrowed his brother's wheels because he wouldn't have been able to fit all three women on the back of his motorbike.

On their return, Marigold had stern words with Violet Burke, accusing her of trying to pimp out her daughter-in-law.

"Aye, 'appen I should have left you out of it, lass," my mother apologised with surprising sincerity. "It was a right horrible sight, seeing that Christos strutting over the sand in his budgie smugglers. The way he was perving over all them women on the beach made me glad that Christos considered me and Dot a bit past it for his taste."

"Speak for yourself, Vi. You might be in your eighth decade but I'm still only forty-nine," Dot proclaimed. Clearly, she hadn't spent her time at the beach downing enough *ouzo* to loosen her tongue.

"I could have sworn she said she was sixty-four," Marigold hissed in my ear.

My mother surprised me by demonstrating how much of the local Greek vernacular she had picked up, telling me, "That Christos' *kamaki* technique could do with some work. Despite all his strutting, he didn't manage to reel in a single woman."

Enjoying a relaxing morning at home with Marigold, I had no idea what Vi and her friend had planned for this afternoon once they finished charring. *Avrio*, otherwise known as tomorrow, I was due to take the two women along with me whilst I repped on the lazy day cruise on Pegasus. Since I had surprisingly been spared their company on the two previous days, I had resigned myself to their presence on the pleasure boat, fully prepared for them to totally embarrass me in front of my tourist charges. My mother, at least, was incapable of going a full day without exhibiting some rather vulgar tendencies. I rather expected Dot might be in for a disappointment when she discovered that Pegasus wasn't actually the luxury yacht that Violet Burke kept banging on about. I had no idea if my mother had warned Dot to expect ardent advances from the owner of the yacht. Perchance if Dot took Wilf's ashes along, it may deter the good captain from too much drooling.

The peace of our morning elevenses was disturbed when Doreen flounced in to bend

BUCKET TO GREECE (VOL.15)

Marigold's ear about some nonsense. As Doreen came over all dramatic, I had a ringside seat at the kitchen table. From the way Doreen was carrying on, I surmised that she and Manolis weren't quite as loved up as they'd been, now that the first crush of infatuation was wearing off. Since Manolis had been dedicating more of his time to the newly opened *kafenio* than to the love of his life, Doreen had clearly taken the hump. She struck me as very needy on the attention front.

Rather naively, Manolis had suggested that Doreen could join him in his workplace and knock up a few snacks to serve with the drinks. Doreen's efforts in the *kafenio* kitchen were entirely predictable for anyone that had suffered the misfortune to be a regular at one of her expat dinner parties. It appeared that the blinkers had been removed from Manolis' eyes now that he'd actually tasted her cooking. By the time that Doreen arrived at the Bucket household, she was still in the grip of the huff she'd stalked out of the *kafenio* in.

"I can't believe the way my Manolis *mou* spoke to me," Doreen griped. Raising my eyebrows, I bit my tongue. There was no point further inflaming Doreen by pointing out that her Greek *mou* was superfluous to requirements since it duplicated her use of the word my. "Can you believe that he called me incompetent in the kitchen?"

Unable to hold my tongue any longer, I butted in before Marigold could comfort her friend. "I can. I've sat through more than one too many of your disastrous dinner parties."

"Victor, how can you be so insensitive? There's no excuse for Manolis speaking to Doreen like that," Marigold remonstrated.

"Just because your taste buds are dead from all those years of taste testing pet food…"

A withering look put me in my place before I could complete my sentence. Leaving Doreen to cry on Marigold's shoulder, I sensibly retired to my office with Fluffs. I could use the time by penning another paragraph of two of my moving to Greece saga.

Engrossed in grappling for just the right words, I lost track of time. It must have been just past noon when Marigold interrupted my writing to tell me that she and Doreen were going to join Vi and Dot for an afternoon out.

"Your mother has roped in some poor sap to chauffeur us around so we can enjoy a glass of wine with lunch out. It will do Doreen good. It may stop her dwelling on Manolis. He said some very thoughtless things…"

"There's no way to sugar coat an honest opinion of Doreen's cooking," I pointed out.

"Well, he was the one that asked her to lend a

hand in the kitchen...she thought it would be a good opportunity for them to spend some time together since he's been so wrapped up in his new venture. I said to her, 'Doreen,' I said, 'You want to be careful that he isn't taking advantage of your good nature by asking you to help out there. He could have paid someone to go in and cook if he's got it into his head to offer food...'"

"You've just given me an idea," I said.

"What? You think Doreen should ask Manolis to pay her?"

"Pay her to keep out of the kitchen, more like," I chortled. "If he's keen on offering food, Blerta has experience. She worked in a taverna kitchen in Albania before they moved here. I will put it to Manolis that he gives her a trial. She'd certainly be glad of some extra work."

"And if Manolis had some help, he may be able to take more time off to spend with Doreen...you are clever, darling."

"'Ere, Marigold, are you coming or not?" Violet Burke demanded, barging into my office. I was pleased to see that her ankles were well on their way to deflating, almost back to their normal bulge. "I don't want to keep that driver waiting or 'appen the dozy apeth will make some excuse to take off without us."

"What mug have you roped in to driving you

about today, Mother?"

"That drip, Norman…"

"How on earth did you persuade Norman to chauffeur you about for the afternoon?" I asked in amazement. Norman was not exactly on what one would call friendly terms with Violet Burke; in fact, he had openly admitted to me that he found my mother completely intimidating. Perchance she had petrified him into becoming a total pushover.

"'Appen the blithering idiot was taken in by Dot's charms."

"Well, that would be a first. Norman always strikes me as impervious to female charms. Don't tell me, Dot's gone and stuck a traffic cone on her head as a makeshift sunbonnet," I quipped.

"Dot has hidden charms, not to mention she's got a bit more nous about her than that scatter-brained Doreen."

"But Marigold has just said that she and Doreen are coming along with you…"

"Aye, well, Marigold insisted on Doreen coming too. She reckons Doreen needs jollying up. I could hardly argue with that wife of yours, not when she'd just offered to pay for a slap-up lunch."

"I am right here, Vi," Marigold reminded her whilst avoiding my eye. My wife was clearly caught on the hop by Vi letting on that she had plans to flash my plastic. "It won't kill Doreen and Norman to have to be civil to one another in the car…and it just might make Manolis jealous if he happens to see Doreen driving off with Norman…"

"Norman would need to take a bit of a detour to drive past the *kafenio*," I pointed out. "It's up a steep back street on the other side of the village."

"'Appen I'll tell Norman to swing by there. I'll come up with an excuse that I left something in the *kafenio* when I was cleaning earlier," Vi offered. "If I get Norman to blast the horn, that Manolis will have to sit up and take notice."

"It's not like you to matchmake, Vi," Marigold said.

"Don't go thinking that by buttering Marigold up, you can tuck into chips at lunchtime," I warned my mother.

"Perish the thought, lad. I'm that glad to have the use of my feet again that I'll willingly force another of them oily salads down. You know that I'm not one to complain about my aches and pains, but you've no clue how stoic I was when my feet and ankles blew up like that. I don't mind telling you, they give me a right old scare. Since I'm not ready for the knacker's yard just yet, I reckon it's time to mend my ways."

"We'll turn you Greek yet, Mother," I chuckled.

"I'm a bit long in the tooth for that lad, but 'appen there's something to that healthy Greek diet that you and Marigold are always bleating on about. Eight days it's been since I had so much of a sniff of a chip and I don't mind telling you, it's a bit of a novelty not having this tweed cutting my circulation off anymore."

Chapter 19

Prawn Saganaki

Since the ladies were lunching out, I decided to treat myself to a typical Greek lunch at home, one that would proudly grace the menu of many a taverna: *garides saganaki*, a colourful and tasty dish that can be prepared quickly, marrying prawns, tomato sauce and melted *feta*. Selecting George Gershwin's wonderful 'Porgy and Bess' to play in the background at a volume that would make Marigold tut, I donned my pinny in readiness for cooking. While the popular *saganaki* dish usually includes fresh shell-on-prawns, I improvised by utilising some frozen prawns from Lidl that I had defrosted earlier, thus allowing me to dispense with the messy business of peeling and deveining the crustaceans.

Singing, or rather, as Marigold prefers to put it, caterwauling along to 'Summertime', I prepared the sauce by sauteing a chopped onion, grated garlic and a chopped red chilli in a splash of extra virgin, before chucking some peeled and chopped tomatoes into the mix. Whilst the sauce simmered, I flash fried the prawns for just a few seconds before deglazing them with a dash of *ouzo*. Adding the sauce to the prawns, I crumbled some *feta* into the mix. Leaving the cheese to melt into the sauce, I poured myself a cold glass of sparkling mineral water with a slice of lemon before garnishing my wonderfully aromatic lunch with a sprinkling of freshly chopped parsley from Marigold's herb garden.

Sitting down to eat my lunch, I had a fixated audience of two; Clawsome and Catastrophe were glued to my dish, apparently tempted by the prawns. As the pair of them brushed themselves against my legs, meowing piteously, I decided to distract them from my own lunch by tempting them with an extra bowl of cat food.

"Do I have a treat for you two," I teased the cats, ripping into a sachet of a new brand of cat food that I had recently purchased from Lidl. Squeezing the contents into their bowl, I watched in amusement as the felines greedily hoovered up the copious amount of gravy. They didn't appear too impressed with the pellets of actual food swimming in the viscous liquid, noticeably eschewing the round brown lumps, though they could be leaving them for later. Apparently satiated, the cats lost interest in my prawns, preferring to stretch out in front of the open balcony doors rather than demanding a share of my food.

Enjoying my delicious meal, I decided to add the dish to my repertoire of Greek cuisine for the classes I run in the winter for culinary challenged expats. Realising their limitations, I decided it would be best to stick to frozen, ready-cleaned prawns. Expecting the likes of Sherry or Milton to successfully devein a prawn with a sharp knife might well cut the classes short by necessitating an emergency dash to the clinic for stitches.

Thinking of my classes, I made a mental note to try and sign John Macey up for them this coming winter, once he had installed himself in the village; most likely, a new expat in Meli could represent yet another regular addition to my classes. I realised there was a fair chance that Macey would declare that, in all modesty, he was already a master when it came to turning out Greek dishes. There again, if he did turn out to be inept in the kitchen, Marigold might not be too keen on having Macey cluttering up our space; for some inexplicable reason, he really seemed to rub Marigold up the wrong way.

Fortunately, my wife usually takes herself off to have her hair done in Athena's kitchen when my classes are in progress, saying there is no point in her learning how to prepare the dishes when I am such a natural in the kitchen. As an aside, she usually leaves me to don the Marigolds and get stuck into the scrubbing, staying out of my way until a good scouring had indelibly removed all traces of my cookery classes from the kitchen.

After polishing off my *garides saganaki*, I headed down to the garden, mindful of Guzim's insistence on the importance of keeping the chickens hydrated in the heat. Peering through the wire enclosing the chicken coop, I spotted Fix, Mythos and Dionysus, sprawled out on their sides. To my untrained eye, they appeared to be enjoying a spot of sunbathing; they certainly looked happy enough to me. Nevertheless, I couldn't shake off Guzim's warning that recumbent chucks were most decidedly depressed, even though I had taken his opinion with a pinch of salt.

As I filled up their water bowls from the hose, I heard my name being called. "Out here, Niko," I called back, surprised to see the taverna owner popping up in my garden during the afternoon.

"The Dina ask me to bring the home cook *horta* for the Violet Burke," Nikos said, proffering a large Tupperware box of boiled weeds. "She to tell me the Violet has to give up the fried potatoes and is determine to eat the healthy Greek food."

A look of scepticism was plastered on Nikos' handsome face as he spoke, hardly surprising since he was familiar with Violet Burke's disgusting preference for lard over olive oil.

"My mother certainly seems to be making an effort to change her ways, though I never thought that she would," I admitted. "I think her ankles were so abnormally swollen that they gave her quite the scare."

"The Dina was much upset to see the Violet to suffer."

"Well, I will make sure my mother chokes the *horta* down," I rather recklessly promised. "Whilst you're here, Niko, can I bend your ear about the chickens? Guzim is of the opinion that if the chickens are lying down, it is a sign that they are suffering from depression. What are your views on the matter?"

"The chicken have the good reason to be depress if they sense you are about to wring their neck. Until then, they live the life of Ripley…"

"Riley," I automatically corrected.

Ignoring my interruption, Nikos continued.

"How can the Greek chicken to be depress? They have the freedom outside and the nice hen house. They know when they are the well off, not crowded inside like the battery chicken who never to see the light of day. When our chicken to think of the battery farm, they know which side their bread is oiled."

"Buttered," I corrected, a tad gobsmacked by Nikos' logic. How on earth could our Meli chickens think themselves lucky compared to their battery farmed cousins when they knew nothing about them, living as they did in blissful ignorance of the appalling conditions involved in the murky environment of intensive poultry farming. Moreover, I questioned if chickens were even capable of thinking? I supposed it was possible; certainly, they appeared able to communicate with one another, their constant clucking and bokboking indicating they were inclined to be chatty. They were certainly intelligent creatures.

"It's not like you not to be in the fields at this time of day," I observed.

"I am taking the free afternoon to take the Dina down to the sea. She want to swim. Luckily, she is not the big girl blouse like you on the back of the *mothopodilato*."

Thrown for a moment by Nikos' bizarre adoption of one of Violet Burke's idioms, I replied,

BUCKET TO GREECE (VOL.15)

"The what? Oh, your moped. I do wish the pair of you would wear helmets. It's not only illegal but downright dangerous to take to the roads without protection."

"I never know anyone to love the rule more than you, Victor," Nikos chuckled as he departed, a broad grin on his face.

After replenishing the chickens' water bowls, I decided to make the most of my free time by indulging in a spot of reading; I don't mind admitting that I was gripped by the John Grisham that I had on the go, the paperback pressed on me by Gordon Strange who persuaded me I would love it despite my usual preference for a good hygiene tome. Since the light breeze drifting across the garden felt cooler than the hot air being circulated by the fans indoors, I popped inside to remove my button down and change out of my slacks into shorts. Grabbing a bottle of water, I headed back down to the garden. It was the perfect opportunity to grab some relaxing time in my deckchair.

As I devoured the gripping pages of the legal thriller, Grisham's tempting descriptions of food in Mississippi made me ponder creating some of the Southern dishes mentioned in his book for the imminent expat dinner party. As usual, Marigold had lumbered me with the responsibility of concocting some original foreign fare; I had dismissed her suggestion of sushi out of hand, regarding it as nothing more than a nasty bout of food poisoning waiting to happen.

Grisham's characters seemed to be forever stuffing their faces with Southern barbecue, collard greens, grits and chitterlings. If I did take the Southern cooking route, I would need to give the chitterlings, or chitlins as they are sometimes known, a miss, since they sounded disturbingly too reminiscent of the *kokoretsi* served on Greek Easter Sunday. Out of all of the Brits in the village, Barry was the only one that relished the spit roasted innards. Hominy grits, sounding like something that had been swept up from a gravel driveway, remained a mystery to me, along with Southern mush. Thinking that collard greens struck me as an American variation on *horta*, I toyed with the idea of boiling up a giant pan of weeds. If I chucked in some beetroot tops and a few rashers of bacon, I might be able to pass them off as authentic Southern fare. I would need to check that Doreen wouldn't be dragging her Greek-Texas beau along to the dinner party. It wouldn't do to be outed as cutting corners on the cooking front.

Alternatively, I considered breaking the strict rule decreeing that only foreign fare must be cooked up at the expat dinner parties: I could whip up a Greek feast and sneakily pass it off as Turkish.

BUCKET TO GREECE (VOL.15)

Despite the Greeks staunchly denying that Turkish food bore any resemblance to Greek, many of the dishes influenced each other and utilised similar ingredients. It would mean defiantly breaking the rules, which is not at all like me; I have never been one to knowingly flout a rule.

Still, it would spare me from having to get to grips with grits and mush if I created a Turkish *meze*, substituting the typical Greek *tzatziki* by giving it a twist, using grated carrots instead of cucumber to make a yoghurt and garlic dip. I could serve a Turkish main of a one-pot flavoursome dish of chicken pilaf. It would be a healthy dish for my mother to tuck into.

I must have drifted off to sleep in the deckchair. The next thing I knew, Marigold was rudely shaking me awake. Feeling a tad disorientated from my unintentional siesta in the sun, Marigold's words slowly began to sink in.

"Really, Victor. What on earth were you thinking, falling asleep in the sun? Just look at the state of your chest; it has a vivid sunburned imprint of your book. You'll be a laughing stock if you turn up on the beach looking like that."

Peering down, I noticed my torso was an angry red, the redness framing a white rectangle where my book had been resting.

"I'll just pop inside for the aloe vera. It should

calm it down nicely…" Marigold began.

"Sour milk. That's what you want to be rubbing on Victor's chest," my mother opined.

"If it's all the same to you, Mother, I'd rather not go round smelling like gone-off milk."

"Suit yourself, lad. It's typical of that wife of yours to go wasting her money on fancy lotions when a bog ordinary bottle of milk will get the job done," Vi said, sinking into the adjacent deckchair. I cringed as the fabric audibly strained against her bulk.

"It may have escaped your notice, Mother, but they don't sell bottles of milk in Greece. It's all cartons these days."

"I'll go up and fetch the aloe," Marigold trilled. "Ladies, do you fancy a cuppa out here?

"How about another glass of wine?" Doreen countered with a hiccup.

"I think you've had enough wine for now," Marigold responded.

"A cuppa will go down a treat, love. I'm that parched," Dot said gratefully.

"And make sure it's PG Tips, Marigold, none of that posh muck that Victor favours," Vi demanded.

"Victor, do sort out some more deckchairs for Doreen and Dot," Marigold called out as a parting shot. As she dashed upstairs to make a brew and grab the aloe vera, I was left alone with the trio of tipsy women.

Dragging some more deckchairs into the shade, I wondered how long I must suffer their company before politely making my excuses and leaving. The afternoon had overtones of turning into one of the boozy girls' nights In that my wife arranges.

"Nikos dropped some *horta* around that Dina cooked for you," I told my mother.

"I must be getting cracked in the head to even consider eating dandelions, but Dina swears by them," Vi said. "Her and Maria from next door are right agile on their feet and they swear it's all down to eating weeds, regular like. 'Appen it's worth trying if it stops my ankles from flaring up again. Anything's better than being forced into them hideous constriction stockings."

"Compression..." I corrected.

"'Appen I know better, lad. It was me that was constricted."

"Well, I'm glad to hear that you plan to tuck into some healthy *horta*. It's packed with antioxidants," I said.

"'Appen a good boiling will have killed the beggars off," Vi said, her grimace indicating she was confusing her vitamin packed antioxidants with some suspicious species of grub.

"I'll just pop up and give Marigold a hand," Doreen volunteered.

Watching Doreen tipsily trip across the garden, Vi said, "'Appen she's after persuading that wife of yours to open a bottle of wine. That Doreen never knows when to stick a cork in it."

"I have to say, I really like that Doreen," Dot piped up. "She's a bit of a hoot."

"She's right scatty. I reckon that blonde hair dye has gone to her head," my mother cackled. Adopting a serious expression, she added, "Dot's come to a decision."

"About what?" I enquired.

"About where to dispose of Wilf's ashes. She's going to bring him along on the yacht tomorrow and chuck him over the side in some scenic spot."

"Remind me not to buy any locally caught fish for the foreseeable," I quipped, wondering if eating fish that had swallowed human ashes counted as cannibalism. "Perhaps I could persuade the good *Kapetanios* to anchor up if anywhere in particular takes Dot's fancy."

"The pair of you are that lucky to have a good friend with a yacht at his disposal. It's right decent of him to invite us along," Dot enthused.

"It's more a case of him turning a blind eye whilst I sneak the pair of you on amidst the tourists that have forked out for the trip," I explained.

"Vasos would never begrudge us a free ride. I've been telling Dot what a smashing fella he is.

One of a kind…"

"That's certainly one way to describe him," I chortled.

"Fancy your friend having to take paying passengers on his yacht to make ends meet. I don't mind chipping in towards the petrol if he's that strapped for cash," Dot offered.

"I'm afraid that Vi has rather misrepresented the situation. Pegasus isn't a yacht. Vasos hires his boat out for tourist trips to the tour company I rep for."

"There's nowt wrong with biggin' the fella up. You have to admit that yacht has a nice ring to it," Dot said. "I have to say that your garden is right lovely, Vic. You must have them green fingers."

"I can't take all the credit," I said modestly. "The herb garden and the flowers are down to Marigold, and Guzim helps me a lot with the vegetables."

"The way the flowers are arranged by colour is like, what's the word, harmonious? Right soothing to the eye," Dot praised.

I had to admit that the three of us had done a marvellous job of transforming the overgrown wilderness into a beautiful Mediterranean garden. Marigold's floral displays were certainly at their finest during the summer. In homage to our adopted country, my wife had trained a blue and white floral display around the pergola, blue delphinium, hibiscus and hydrangeas making a stunning contrast to the white bougainvillea. She had continued the Greek themed motif by planting blue and white daisies around the base of the fruit trees.

"Well, it's right nice. It must be something, being able to pick your own fruit instead of buying it down the Co-op," Dot continued. "It's just a pity the garden's got that whiff of mucky chickens about it."

Recalling Guzim's advice about planting lavender around the coop, I mentally added another batch of plants to the ever-growing list of essentials we needed from the garden centre on our next trip to town.

"Will you be cooking one up this week, lad?" Dot asked.

"Cooking one of what up?"

"One of them chickens."

"Ooh, don't go saying that to my Victor. He's right sensitive about his two-legged pets...daft in the head, if you ask me..."

The rest of Vi's words were drowned out by a high-pitched scream emanating from the house.

"It sounds as though someone's murdering that wife of yours," Vi said, her chortle indicating the sound of murder being committed was a not an infrequent event.

"Murder," Dot squeaked, the colour draining from her face.

"That Marigold's a bit on the squeamish side," Vi told Dot. "What do you reckon it is this time, Victor? A spider or a lizard?"

"I suppose I'd better go and find out," I said, legging it towards the house as a second scream rang out. Since the second scream had a different timbre to Marigold's usual yelps, I surmised that my wife's sidekick had joined in the hysteria.

Bounding up the stairs, I burst into the kitchen, not too surprised to discover both Marigold and Doreen standing on chairs; in the throes of panic, the pair of them gulped for air.

"Do something, Victor," Marigold screeched. "The floor is alive."

"It's disgusting," Doreen cried.

Looking down, I had to admit that Doreen had a point. At first glance, I thought my eyes were playing tricks on me; it appeared that brown lumps of what I immediately deduced to be leftover cat food were moving across the floor on their own volition, at a rapid pace. Bending down for a closer look, I was fascinated to see that a colony of unnaturally large and shiny black ants had organised themselves into collective work groups, each individual group working in perfect harmony to bear the weight of an individual pellet of spurned food. Goodness only knows how many individual ants made up each rank but the way that they worked together so instinctively was nothing short of a miracle of nature, putting me in mind of a perfectly choreographed ballet.

"Don't just stand there gawping, Victor. Do something to get rid of them." As Marigold's strident demand brought me out of my trance, I noticed that the cat food bowl was almost invisible beneath a shifting mass of what must be thousands of ants. Whilst I had been mesmerised by the actions of the working groups transporting the pellets, the sight of a teeming mass of the things almost turned my stomach.

Grabbing the Marigolds, I slipped my hands inside before picking the bowl up and hurling it into the garden, shivering in disgust as the insects covered the yellow rubber gloves. With the Marigolds fast following the bowl into the garden, I batted the ants from my chest, prising loose the persistent ones that had gripped onto my chest hair. Sweeping up the moving pellets teaming with ants, I chucked the contents of the dustpan over the balcony onto the street.

Extending a hand to my wife, I assured her, "I think it's safe to come down now, darling."

"You missed one," she said, pointing to a large

ant still circling the kitchen floor, no doubt wondering where its colleagues had suddenly disappeared to.

"Don't worry. I'll give the floor a good zapping," I promised, grabbing a canister of fly killer from under the sink and spraying the kitchen liberally.

Marigold and Doreen stepped warily down from their chairs.

"What on earth was that? I've never seen anything like it indoors," Marigold asked.

"It appears that the ants were attracted by the leftover cat food," I explained.

"But I washed their bowls out this morning after they'd breakfasted," Marigold said in confusion.

"I may have been guilty of giving them a lunchtime snack," I admitted. "The cats didn't appear too keen on the actual food that was submerged in the gravy. I should have binned it rather than leaving it sitting around in the heat."

Grabbing a bottle of wine from the fridge, Marigold floored me with a withering look. "I'll leave you to make tea for your mother and Dot. Doreen and I need something a bit stronger after enduring that revolting display."

Chapter 20

Trifling with Cooking Sherry

Returning to the garden with the tea things, I couldn't fail to notice that the bottle of wine was already half empty, Doreen looking decidedly tipsy.

"I'll just pop inside to use the loo," Doreen hiccupped before making her way rather unsteadily across the garden.

With Doreen safely out of the way, I took the opportunity to ask how Norman had reacted to being roped into driving the four women down to the coast for lunch.

"Norman was a miserable so and so." An

exaggerated eye roll accompanied Marigold's words. "He did nothing but grumble about being dragged into playing chauffeur. I invited him to join us for lunch, but he refused. Can you believe, he said that he'd rather wait in the car eating a sandwich?"

"That does sound pathetically childish," I said.

"'Appen that Norman's not as daft as he looks," Vi opined. "I'd have rather got stuck into a nice Spam sarnie than lunching on nowt but chicken soup. Why them Greeks want to go sticking lemon in it..."

"*Avgolemono* is healthy," Marigold impatiently reminded her mother-in-law before lowering her voice to confide in me. "I think that Norman is perhaps regretting losing Doreen to another man..."

"I take it that refusing to budge from the car is a classic sign of jealousy," I interrupted, making no effort to conceal my sarcasm.

"Well, he probably finds it upsetting to hear Doreen talking about Manolis..."

"She certainly never shuts up about her favourite subject," I concurred.

"I do wish that Norman would make some effort to either win Doreen back or move on. It's most inconsiderate of him to keep messing up the seating plans at the expat dinners by turning up on his lonesome," Marigold said.

Since it seemed to me that Norman had demonstrated zero interest in rekindling his marriage, I didn't share my wife's optimism. I doubt even Marigold actually believed that Norman wanted Doreen back. Even if he did, there would be no prising Doreen away from her Manolis *mou*; she was much too loved up.

My thoughts were disturbed by yet another scream emanating from the house.

"Really, Victor. I thought you'd zapped the last of the ants…" Marigold began, her words cut short by the sight of Doreen dashing across the garden towards us, her face as white as a sheet.

"Doreen, are you okay?" Marigold rushed towards her friend. Taking her arm, she led Doreen back to the deckchairs.

"We've been burgled…" Doreen cried, clearly shaken out of the less than sober state she'd been in just minutes earlier.

"We've been burgled," Marigold parroted in shock.

"Norman just telephoned. When he got home, he found the place had been ransacked." Marigold visibly exhaled in relief; it was clear that her first reaction had been to presume it was the Bucket house that had been burgled. "I must get over there at once," Doreen gasped.

"Victor will drive you." Offering up my services, Marigold's tone brooked no argument as she guided Doreen towards the Punto.

As the three of us piled into the car for the two-minute drive, Doreen's initial shock gave way to anger and she started insulting her estranged husband, piling the blame on him for presumably leaving the house unsecured whilst they were out for the afternoon.

"Are you sure that Norman said your house had been burgled?" I quizzed Doreen. "Meli has always been a crime free zone. I've never heard of any instances of burglary in the village before."

"Victor, you don't suppose that Norman just said it as a ploy to get Doreen over there?" Marigold mused.

Parking the Punto, I snorted, "It would hardly be the most romantic play."

"Well, Norman isn't exactly known for romantic gestures," Marigold hissed.

An ashen-faced Norman rushed out to the car. "I'm glad that you're here, Victor. Can you telephone the police?"

"You mean you haven't already called them?" I asked in bewilderment.

"I tried. I called that 112 number but I couldn't make sense of anything they said. It was all in Greek."

"That's hardly surprising since it is the number for the Greek emergency services. How many times have I told you how important it is to get to grips with some basic Greek? You can't expect me to come running every time that you have an emergency where an understanding of the language is vital," I chided.

I experienced a sinking sensation at the prospect of having being unwillingly roped in to deal with the matter on Norman's behalf. Not only did I still find it an invariably convoluted task to communicate in Greek via the telephone, I had no wish to have any dealings with the police. I'd had quite enough of all that palaver when I'd been arrested for opening the local shop on a Sunday, leading to my being carted off to the police station like a common criminal. I occasionally still wake in a sweat, suffering disturbing dreams about my time in the cell and my worries that I am about to be summarily deported from my beloved Greece for daring to break the law, albeit it unwittingly.

Walking into the house, there was no immediate evidence of the place having been ransacked as Doreen had claimed. Sticking my head around the kitchen door, it appeared to be in its usual state of disarray, Norman no doubt having blithely left his patisserie mess for Blerta to clean up the next day. Stepping into the living room, I noticed that the expensive television was still in its usual place. Moreover, Norman's computer took pride of place on the table under the window, the screen saver set to a garish image of a strawberry gateau.

"Are you sure you've been burgled, Norman? Nothing appears out of place and it doesn't appear that a thief has made off with your most valuable items," I said.

"I didn't notice anything amiss at first when I got back," Norman replied. "It was only when I went in the spare bedroom that I realised the place had been broken into. The window in there is smashed. I'm wondering if I disturbed the burglar when I got back... if he or they took off when they heard me return, it could account for only the bedrooms having been ravaged..."

"Ravaged," Doreen repeated, dashing into the master bedroom, the three of us close on her heels.

"Oh, my," Marigold gasped, taking in the state of the room.

The dresser drawers, yanked open, spilled their contents onto the floor into an untidy heap, indicating someone had indeed been rummaging around furiously.

"My jewellery," Doreen cried, thrusting the wardrobe door open. Feeling along the top shelf, she sighed in relief as she pulled down an old shoe box. Yanking the lid off, she pulled out a wooden jewellery box. "It's still here. Thank goodness, I hid it well away."

"Perhaps they were after drugs," I suggested. "One reads of such things."

"I don't think druggies would break in to steal laxatives or Imodium." Despite Norman's words, he rushed into the bathroom, the rest of us following in hot pursuit. The doors of the bathroom cabinet had been left wide open, the contents spilling into the washbasin. "Nothing appears to be missing. Oh, wait, I don't see the Grecian 2000 or my Old Spice aftershave."

"There's a clue there," I quipped. "We need to be on the lookout for a burglar stinking of Old Spice."

Flooring me with a blistering glare, Doreen shook her head incredulously. "Where have all the towels gone?"

"The spare bedroom got the worst of it," Norman declared as we followed him in there to assess the damage.

The window was indeed broken, indicating the point of entry. Amidst shards of shattered glass, the odd traffic cone littered the floor. "Most of my cones are gone," Norman gulped.

"Who in their right mind would steal traffic cones?" I pondered aloud.

"Someone who appreciated their intrinsic beauty," Norman said. "I have, or did have, quite an extensive collection."

"And you're always bleating on about it," Doreen reprimanded. "Perhaps someone overheard you and didn't realise your cones are nothing more than a pile of worthless junk."

Wondering if perchance I had naively overlooked any value in a collection of traffic cones, I left the three of them to squabble whilst I headed to Norman's computer to Google the potential value of a traffic cone collection. To my utter disbelief, I discovered Norman wasn't the only person obsessed with building up a collection of traffic cones. My search revealed an entry in the Guinness Book of Records showing that a certain David Morgan in the UK held the record for the largest collection. The entry, dated from the year 2000, showed he had almost one hundred and forty different traffic cones. My search also confirmed my suspicion that a collection of witches' hats held little monetary value, even the most unusual cones costing less than a fiver.

Returning to the spare bedroom, I asked Norman how many cones comprised his collection.

"I had eighty-seven," Norman said, despondently adding, "Most of them are gone. There's only this handful left."

"Ah, so nowhere close to the number that David Morgan chap has accumulated."

"There's no need to rub it in," Norman said peevishly.

"At least they didn't get your special Christmas cone," Doreen comforted him. It seemed that knowing her precious jewellery had been spared from the thieves, Doreen could afford to spare some sympathy for Norman's traumatic loss.

"It's chipped." Norman's tone was desolate as he picked up the giant traffic cone, still in its traditional red stocking cap. "They must have slung it down with some force to knock a piece out it."

"Oh, for goodness' sake. Did it not occur to you to give the thing a good washing down after Christmas? It's still got fondant icing caked on," I carped. "I'm surprised that ants haven't taken over your spare bedroom."

"You're a fine one to talk, Victor Bucket," Doreen huffed. "It was your super hygienic kitchen that was overrun by those disgusting ants."

Ignoring Doreen's dig, I posited a suggestion. "Is it really worth calling the police since nothing of value appears to have been stolen?"

"Are you out of your mind, Victor?" Marigold demanded. "It's likely down to a fluke of luck that Norman's return alerted the thieves before they could get their hands on anything valuable. We must absolutely call the police. We can't risk burglars being on the loose in Meli. There's no telling which house they will target next."

Conceding my wife made a good point, I took a deep breath before reluctantly placing a call to the very same police station that I had been carted off to in my blood splattered pinny. Unfamiliar with the Greek for burglarised since it was not a word that I had ever envisaged needing in our crime free village, I stuttered something ungrammatical about thieves in Meli, saying they had broken a window to get in.

"*Kleftes sto Meli. Espasan to parathyro gia na boun mesa.*"

For some inexplicable reason, the policeman on the other end of the line struggled to understand my admittedly abysmal telephone Greek.

"*Ti?*" reverberated from the receiver.

"*Milas Anglika?*" I hissed quietly, hoping the others wouldn't overhear me when I asked the policeman if he spoke English. I supposed that it hardly mattered if the others did hear my question since only Marigold was capable of understanding the simple question I had asked in Greek. With a firm *ochi* resounding in my ear, I continued in garbled Greek, attempting to give the policeman concise directions to Norman's house. After several minutes of going around in circles, the policeman snapped that I should find a Greek speaking person to telephone the police station to explain properly.

"They're on their way," I told the others before wandering outdoors to telephone Spiros from my mobile. Summarising events for the undertaker, I thanked him profusely when he told me that he would contact the police with directions to Norman's house and then be straight over. Spiros' willingness to jump into the fray made me feel a little ashamed that I had been reluctant to rush to Norman's aid, my Greek friend never expressing any annoyance when I dragged him into any expat dramas on a regular basis.

Unsurprisingly, Spiros turned up in the hearse well before the police car arrived. I guessed the police would take at least thirty minutes to reach the village; that was rather optimistically presuming they would burn rubber and not spare the emergency siren.

"Never we to have the thief to bungle in the Meli," Spiros declared.

"Burgle," I automatically corrected.

"That too. Never," Spiros insisted, his furrowed eyebrows indicating he was obviously unnerved by this unusual event.

"I imagine that the agricultural policeman used to act as a deterrent against thieves," I posited.

"We not have one for decades. The people in

Meli not to steal from their neighbour..."

"Perhaps it was an outsider," I suggested. "Some random opportunist that just happened to be passing through the village."

"It is not good". Spiros' sombre expression outdid the serious face he adopted when attending to funerals. "Show me where they to break the window."

Leading Spiros through to the spare bedroom, I caught Doreen tampering with the crime scene by sweeping up broken glass from the window.

"Doreen. Drop the broom," I shouted. "You could be destroying vital evidence." Biting my tongue, I resisted the temptation to polish my sentence off with one of Violet Burke's dozy mares.

"Oh, I never thought," Doreen stuttered.

"You never do," Norman chimed in. "The police will probably want to fingerprint those pieces of glass."

"Perhaps you should concentrate on checking if anything else is missing. You only really gave the place a cursory glance," Marigold suggested. Grabbing a notebook, she offered to make a list of the missing items to present to the police.

"They've got away with at least eighty of my traffic cones," Norman volunteered.

"And all the towels are missing from the bathroom, even the ones that needed washing,"

Doreen contributed. Visibly paling, she added in a whisper, "Oh, my goodness. The cat. Has anyone seen Tickles?"

"Ah, you're thinking catnappers." My little quip went down like a lead balloon, earning me a glare from Marigold as she joined Doreen in hunting down the elusive feline.

Returning to the living room, Norman announced that the drinks cabinet had been cleaned out. "I thought you'd knocked the booze on the head," I said.

"Yes, but we keep some bottles in so we can offer any guests a drink. Drat, they've made off with my cooking sherry too. I got it in for a trifle. I thought I'd try to give Marigold's humble dessert an exotic twist."

"There's nothing humble about one of Marigold's trifles. They are widely regarded as a work of art," I said in defence of my wife's custardy pudding.

"What's that about my trifle?" Marigold asked, reappearing with Doreen who was clutching a reluctant cat to her bosom.

"The thieves have made off with Norman's sherry," I said. "Imagine the nerve of trifling with cooking sherry."

"I'll add it to the list," Marigold offered with a deadpan expression.

"Where was the cat?" I asked.

"Tickles was flaked out on the patio. I think he must have slept through everything," Doreen said.

"That's a pity. It might have been able to offer a description of the thieves to the police."

"Your humour is in very poor taste, Victor. I hardly think that a burglary is a laughing matter," Marigold remonstrated. "Who knows which one of us could be targeted next."

As I dwelled on that sobering thought, the police finally put in an appearance, their serious expressions stretched to the limit when Spiros revealed that Norman's *konoi kykloforias* had been stolen. Personally, I considered that traffic cones sounded more important in Greek. After ascertaining from Spiros that Marigold and I were surplus to requirements, they gave the pair of us our marching orders. I presumed they didn't want our extra DNA contaminating the scene.

"I'd been practising my alibi in Greek," I complained as we drove back home in the Punto.

"The rest of us could alibi one another but you should think yourself lucky that the police didn't question you," Marigold scoffed. "After all, you've been alone in the village all afternoon."

"Where I was planning the great heist of Norman's traffic cones from the comfort of my deckchair," I joshed.

Chapter 21

Newly Laid Fruit

Wandering through to the kitchen, my hair still damp from the shower, I anticipated the aromatic pleasure of the first freshly brewed coffee of the day. I almost jumped out of my skin to discover Dot lurking next to the kettle, dunking a teabag; I hadn't expected our houseguest to be out of her bed so early.

"Shall I do you a cuppa, lad?" Dot offered.

"I'm more of a coffee person at this time of day," I replied, declining the offer of PG Tips. "I like to enjoy my first coffee out on the balcony, in peace…"

BUCKET TO GREECE (VOL.15)

"Well, I'll join you then. 'Appen it'll be a nice change for you to have a bit of company," Dot said, clearly clueless to the meaning of peace.

"That will be nice," I fibbed half-heartedly. In truth, Dot struck me as such a kind-hearted soul that I could stomach her company without complaining. She was, after all, only with us for a week.

"Vi mentioned that Marigold likes a bit of a lie in, leaving you to fend for your own coffee."

"I'm more than capable of spooning some freshly ground beans into the cafetiere." Noticing that Dot was already done up in some kind of nautically striped tent paired with matching plimsolls, I observed, "You're up and about early."

"Aye, well, that's force of habit. Our Kevin can't even manage to brew his own instant. You know how young fellas are when it comes to grappling with challenging things like washing machines and kettles. I like to make sure I send our Kevin off to work with a decent brekkie inside him and a nice packed lunch. I hope he's coping all right without me. I worry he's likely to be nowt but skin and bones by the time I get home."

Dot's words put me in mind of an overindulgent mother sending her son off to infant school. It wouldn't surprise me if she announced that she still walked Kevin to the bus stop on a daily basis.

"Perhaps if he moves that Tiffany Billings in with you, she'll be able to see to Kevin's breakfast," I posited.

"I'll have my work cut out breaking that Tiffany out of her bad habits and no mistake. I bet her idea of a decent brekkie for that little tyke, Tyrone, is a pot noodle and a bag of crisps, washed down with a can of summat fizzy."

"I ran into Tiffany and Tyrone on my last trip back to England. It was the first time I'd ever seen anyone still in their pyjamas pushing a trolley round Tesco." I grimaced at the recollection.

"Well, there'll be none of that going on under my watch. I keep a respectable house. I'll not have that Tiffany showing me up; I'll have to learn her," Dot assured me. "I can't say I'm that thrilled that my Kevin got himself mixed up with that Billings' lot but I'll try to make the best of it. I have to say that forty-nine is a bit on the young side for me to be a granny though."

I choked back my laughter at Dot's words. It seemed that every time she was sober, she reeled her age back from sixty-four to forty-nine as though it was entirely plausible that could pass for under fifty.

As I carried our drinks out to the balcony, Dot offered, "Shall I take a cuppa through to Marigold?"

BUCKET TO GREECE (VOL.15)

"It's a kind gesture but she'll still be sleeping," I said.

"Aye, 'appen all that beauty sleep she packs in has worked wonders. She looks a decade younger than you even though Vi says the pair of you have nowt in it, age wise." I wasn't quite sure how to interpret Dot's meaning; did she mean that Marigold only looked fifty, or, perish the thought, that I was looking a bit past it? Best not to press the point: I may not like what I heard.

As Dot took a seat on the balcony, Fluffs appeared, rubbing itself against our house guest's legs. Scooping the kitten up, Dot went unusually quiet, totally transfixed by the magnificence of the sky as the grainy darkness transformed into an artist's palette of breathtaking colours. The clouds emerging at first twilight glowed pink against a background of blue as though illuminated from below.

"People tend to rave about the sunsets in Greece but in my mind, there's nothing like the first light at dawn," I mused.

Absentmindedly stroking Fluffs' fur, Dot basked in the beauty of the landscape at first light. The sea still a misty blip on the horizon, the village began to take shape in front of our eyes, the trees and vegetation gradually taking form as they emerged from the darkness. The heady silence which pervades the village first thing served to magnify the chirpy sounds of birds tweeting as they woke and the delightful tinkling of goats' bells in the distance.

"I wish I could bottle this and take it back to Warrington," Dot said with a hearty sign. "It makes a right nice change from the buses whizzing by and the din that the binmen make."

"Apparently the binmen are known as waste managers these days," I said, recalling my recent encounter with my childhood nemesis, Derek Little, and his deluded insistence on attempting to compare his job on the bins as equivalent to my illustrious career as a public health inspector.

"I can't keep up with all them changes, lad. 'Appen if they hadn't shut the chippy down when they did, me and Vi would have been renamed something right daft like fish frying operatives..."

"Or specialist handlers of haddock." I couldn't resist joining in.

"How about a cod and chips consultant?"

"Or purveyors of plaice and peas?"

Once our laughter had abated, Dot said, "You know, when Violet first told me that she was flitting over here to a strange foreign place, I thought she'd turned right daft in the head. Now that I've seen it for myself, I have to say that this Greece has got some right good things going for it... mind you, this heat's a bugger and all this quiet wouldn't half get on my nerves."

"Enjoy the quiet while you can, Dot," I advised. "You likely won't get much of it once that little nipper, Tyrone, moves in with you."

"Aye, that's true," Dot said with a resigned smile. "There'll be no peace at mine once Tyrone's around…and double that once that Kimberly pops out the new sprog. But that's what it's all about, lad. Having family around. That's why Violet made the move over here. Despite all her misgivings about the foreign food and that strange language that Greek lot speak, not to mention having no Tesco or a decent chippy on the doorstep, Vi felt the pull of family."

"Well, we're glad that she made the move." In spite of Violet Burke's tendency to oftentimes be a public embarrassment, on balance I felt genuinely glad to have her living under my feet.

"Marigold will need to be getting a wriggle on for our day out if she wants to tart herself up right nice for that yacht. I know how long it takes to get a face full of slap on to look halfway decent," Dot said. Her words drew my attention to her excessive use of blue eye shadow. I imagined that it wouldn't be long until she'd sweated it off in the heat. "I'm that looking forward to going on that yacht."

"It's not actually a yacht…" I reminded her.

"And Violet reckons that her mate...what's his name again? I can't get my brain around all these strange sounding foreign names."

"*Kapetanios* Vasos..."

"Aye, that's it. Vi reckons this Vasos fella is up on some right nice bits of seawater where I can sprinkle my Wilf."

"Marigold won't actually be joining us today. She has other plans," I told Dot. I didn't bother elaborating since the excuse I had made on Marigold's behalf was a complete fabrication. Marigold wasn't too keen on the very early starts that a day out on Pegasus necessitated. Also, she had expressed her opinion that the boat would be crowded to the gills in August with hot and sweaty tourist bodies that she had no desire to suffer rubbing up against.

"It will be just you and my mother."

"That's a right shame..."

I leapt up in surprise when Dot's words were interrupted by someone hammering on the front door. Wondering aloud who in their right mind would visit at such an early hour, I flung the door open.

"Good morning, Mother. It's not like you to bother knocking," I said in greeting.

"It didn't seem right to just barge in, lad, not with all this talk about burglars in the village. I might have given you a horrible fright if I'd just walked in. I didn't want to risk having you lamp me over the head if you mistook me for one of them thieves that's on the prowl."

"What are you doing here at this early hour? We have at least an hour and a half before we need to leave for Pegasus." I noticed that like Dot, Violet Burke was already dressed for the boat trip. Sporting a knee-length purple tent that concealed her recent weight loss, I couldn't help thinking that her compression stockings looked like a pair of knee socks. The bulging beach bag slung over one shoulder indicated she was set for the day.

"I thought I'd come up here and treat Dot to a nice cooked brekkie; she's been a right star helping me out on the charring front…"

"No doubt that's just an excuse to get your gob around a slice of bacon…"

"It is not," Vi declared in a decidedly affronted manner. "I'll make do with a bowl of porridge if you've got any oats in, even though it'll likely be that bland without a good dollop of Tate & Lyle."

"You can substitute the golden syrup with local Greek honey," I suggested.

"Aye, 'appen." My mother looked less than thrilled at the prospect.

"That scented honey is that moreish I could eat my own body weight in the stuff," Dot enthused.

"But anyhow," Vi continued. "Dot's on her hols and deserves a bit of a treat. I thought a nice fry up would fit the bill."

"You know how Marigold detests the lingering smell of fried food in our kitchen," I argued, determined to keep Violet Burke away from the temptations of the frying pan. "Why don't you go and join Dot out on the balcony? I'll bring you a cuppa and then knock up a nice healthy Greek breakfast for the three of us. I'll just pop down to the garden and collect some newly laid eggs and fruit…"

"I never knew fruit was newly laid, lad," Vi said with a wink.

Having collected the fresh ingredients for breakfast from the garden, I filled a plate with the early grapes from my Panos inspired grapevine, thinking they would make a perfect topping for the Greek yoghurt and honey I was spooning into bowls. I had passed on the fresh figs since the presence of a fresh fig never failed to set my mother off on a long-winded diatribe about her bowels; I really couldn't stomach the topic over breakfast. Scrambling half-a-dozen eggs with some freshly chopped chives courtesy of Marigold's herb garden, I piled them onto three toasted slices of Dina's delicious home-made bread produced in her outside bread oven, before calling the ladies in to breakfast in the kitchen.

"Eh, lass, we're in luck this morning." Vi gave Dot a firm nudge with her elbow as she spoke. Dot impressed me with her quick reaction, narrowly avoiding spilling her eggs down the front of her nautical tent thing. "Victor has spared us them fig things. I reckon he must have twigged that they go right through you; that's a right risky business when there's only one poky lav on that yacht."

"Really, Mother. Must we suffer your toilet references over breakfast?"

"It's not all gold-plated taps then, like they have in them luxury yachts on the telly?" Dot piped up.

"How many more times?" I said in exasperation. "Vasos' boat isn't a yacht."

"Well, it's like a yacht," my mother argued.

"In what possible way is his leaky old tub like a yacht?" I demanded.

"Well, it floats and it's got a captain…"

Having barely made inroads into my eggs, I was forced to abandon my breakfast to answer the ringing phone.

"Kalimera, beautiful towel," a familiar voice boomed down the receiver, Vasos' voice so loud that Vi was able to announce the name of the caller to her friend.

"That's my old mucker, Vasos, on the phone now."

"Victor, i thalassa einai poly taragmeni gia to taxidi me to ploio simera. Tha prepei na akyroso," Vasos yelled.

"What's he saying?" Vi demanded.

"He said that the sea is too rough for the boat trip today. He's going to have to cancel."

The two women groaned in disappointment. Telling me he was in urgent need of the toilet, Vasos abruptly terminated the call.

"I was right looking forward to it," Dot grumbled.

"Vasos wouldn't cancel unless the sea is dangerously rough. It wouldn't do to have all the tourists throwing up," I told her.

My conviction was borne out of experiencing one particular trip on Pegasus the previous summer when the sea had taken an exceptionally rough turn on the return journey from the Caves of Diros. I had spent hours dodging passengers drenched from the rough sea spray as they hurled over the side of the boat. Poor Sami had been tasked with the thankless job of mopping up vomit; I could only imagine the complaints he would have voiced if he hadn't been mute. The only good takeaway from that trip was the surprising revelation that I had developed an exceptionally solid pair of sea legs, not in the least affected by the turbulence of the sea.

Her tone oozing disappointment, Vi said, "I

was right looking forward to you meeting Vasos, Dot. I reckon the pair of you would have got on like a house on fire."

"Well, I promised you ladies a day out to remember, so, a day out you shall have," I rashly promised, following up with a muttered, "Just not on a yacht."

"What have you got in mind, Son?"

"How about I take you both out for a slap-up lunch at Takis' place on the coast," I suggested, referencing the taverna that Takis had recently taken over after I had given the kitchen a clean bill of health in my professional capacity, albeit retired, as a public health inspector.

"You mean that young fella that fancies doing Sunday roasts over the winter," Vi checked.

"Yes, indeed, that's the chap," I confirmed. "We could spend some time on the beach or have a mosey around the shops. Whatever tickles your fancy."

"Well, I'd set my mind on scattering Wilf today. I had to psyche myself up for it like. I've been carrying his ashes around for so long that it will feel right strange to be stuck with nowt but an empty urn," Dot said dolefully.

"I'm sure we can find a suitably scenic spot down on the coast," I said, recklessly disregarding any previous worries I'd had about Wilf's ashes potentially contaminating the fish or blowing into a tourist's cocktail.

"Well, if Vasos isn't taking the yacht out, 'appen he could drive down and join us," Vi suggested.

Considering her proposition, I reflected, in for a penny, in for a pound. Since Dot and Vi were sure to embarrass me anyway, I thought I may as well go the whole hog and invite the equally embarrassing *Kapetanios* to round up the numbers.

"I'll give Vasos a call back and invite him to join us for lunch," I agreed. Since Marigold wouldn't need to forsake her lie in to join us, I hoped to persuade her to come along too.

"That'll be right grand, lad," Vi enthused. "Seeing as we don't need to be making an early start after all, me and Dot might as well pop downstairs and put our feet up with a marathon Corrie watching session."

"Eh, that sounds like a grand plan," Dot agreed. "I'll just get these dishes done first."

"You'll do no such thing, Dot," I insisted. Considering the two women had accepted the disappointment of the cancelled Pegasus trip with such grace, the least I could do was pamper them by taking care of the mucky dishes.

Chapter 22

An Emergency Meeting

Marigold was still enjoying her lie in when Spiros made an early morning telephone call to the Bucket household. Dispensing with the usual pleasantries, he told me to get myself over to the *kafenio* pronto.

"What on earth is so urgent?" I asked the undertaker.

"I tell to you when you get here," Spiros replied enigmatically.

"At least give me a clue," I badgered.

"We are to hold the important village meeting. You must to tell the other English to come too. Tell to them, it is the emergency."

"Marigold's still in bed…"

"Only the English men," Spiros stressed, his tone suggesting his point ought to have been patently obvious.

"Ah, yes of course," I said, realising that although women were an integral part of the village, they weren't yet welcome in the *kafenio*. Intrigued by the urgency in Spiros' tone, I promised, "I'll see who I can quickly round up."

Calling Barry's mobile, I was greeted with a curt, "Not now, Victor. I'm balancing on the scaffolding. Whatever it is will have to wait."

Before I could remind him of the importance of donning a hard hat when scaling heights, Barry hung up on me, leaving me to worry that he was failing to take the necessary safety precautions. I decided if the meeting didn't run on for too long, I would head over to our renovation project afterwards and have stern words with my brother-in-law. If it hadn't been a joint venture with my investment riding on it, I would be tempted to dob Barry in to the health and safety lot to ensure he mended his reckless ways. As it was, I would simply have to resort to threatening to dob him in to his sister; although a grown man, Barry was known to cower if Marigold got one of her strops on. Cynthia was far too young to be a widow if

BUCKET TO GREECE (VOL.15)

Barry's irresponsible disregard of scaffolding safety resulted in him falling from a great height and landing on his thick head.

I fared no better with Norman since the local bore adamantly refused to leave the house in case the thieves returned to make off with his remaining traffic cones.

"There's only a piece of flimsy cardboard taped over the broken window to keep the thieving rascals at bay. I don't suppose you fancy popping over to ring a Greek glazier?"

"Try Barry," I suggested. "Give him a call and remind him to don his hard hat. And do try to learn a bit of Greek, Norman. I can't be expected to hold your hand every time your lack of the language lets you down."

Luckily, Gordon Strange demonstrated a much more willing attitude. Not only did he immediately agree to join me, he promised to pick me up from my doorstep momentarily in his flashy red sports car. Picking up the phone to call Milton, I thought better of it; the local purveyor of porn would be about as much use as a chocolate teapot in an emergency.

Roaring to a stop outside the *apothiki*, Gordon Strange greeted me. "You'll have to squeeze in next to Waffles. For some reason, he's refused to go behind the seats ever since Moira drove your mother and her friend about the other day."

"How odd." Reluctantly sidling in next to the glossy canine, I almost gagged at the overwhelming aroma of cheap perfume.

"Why on earth does Waffles smell like a tart's boudoir?"

"Moira went a bit over the top at the grooming parlour. Poor Waffles has been particularly flatulent all week. Moira thought the extra lotions and potions might help to cover the stench. She didn't like to accuse your mother outright but she thought that Violet may have sneaked Waffles some forbidden food when they were lunching out the other day."

"Forbidden food?"

"Gigantes plaki."

"Surely even Violet Burke wouldn't be dense enough to feed giant Greek beans to a flatulent dog," I snorted, edging away from Waffles' slobbering tongue as he moved in to give me a good licking; ever since our first meeting when I had fed the dog stale oregano crisps, the curly-haired creature practically frothed at the mouth with fondness whenever he encountered me.

Absorbing Gordon's words about my mother feeding forbidden food to the mutt, I considered that despite Violet Burke's addiction to green pulses in the form of mushy peas, she had a noticeable tendency to swerve actual beans. Whether broad or French runners, through to the popular large white Greek beans that are a distant cousin of the French variety, my mother has no time for the things.

I must say that Gordon's driving left something to be desired. I attributed his reckless need to speed through the village to some latent conviction that flashy sports cars had no business adhering to the speed limit. As Gordon swerved the car into the hedgerow to avoid a random stray, the pair of us came perilously close to being clocked on our heads by a low-lying olive tree branch. Gripping the dashboard, my knuckles turned white. I wished that I'd had the foresight to borrow Violet Burke's cycling helmet before imprudently accepting a lift from Gordon Strange. There were definite advantages to having a lid on the Punto.

The car certainly attracted envious stares from the old codgers in the *kafenio* as Gordon squealed to a stop outside our destination. Making my way inside, I was too distracted by wiping the dog drool from my cheek with my pocket handkerchief to warn Gordon not to let Waffles leap onto one of the newly painted chairs. I imagined the Stranges would have the devil of a job removing the inevitable blue streaks from the dog's curly coat. Goodness only knows where Christos had got his hands on a job lot of such slow drying paint.

Spiros was in the midst of a group of Greek men huddled around a table, deep in conversation; the group comprising Nikos, Giannis, Papas Andreas, Dimitris, Christos, Apostolos, Kyriakos, and a couple of old fellows that I couldn't really count as acquaintances since we were only on nodding terms. It appeared that the *kafenio* had acted as a magnet for the older men that weren't regular taverna customers. I presumed they must be early risers who eschewed late nights.

I noticed that Apostolos appeared a tad disengaged, his wistful glances towards the old barber's chair in the corner indicating it was the focus of his attention. I hoped he wasn't feeling in a scissor snapping mood; no matter how persistently he pestered me with offers of giving me my first haircut on the house, I had no intention of being on the receiving end of one of his infamous lopsided necklines. I do, after all, have standards to maintain when it comes to personal grooming.

Raising his eyebrows, Gordon shot a meaningful look my way as Manolis slapped a tray of glasses and a bottle of *raki* down on the table before joining the huddle. Since Gordon hadn't as yet tried his hand at olive picking, he was unaccustomed to the local habit of downing a shot of *ouzo* or *raki* first thing in the morning.

BUCKET TO GREECE (VOL.15)

Spiros gestured for us to join them, saying he would begin the meeting as soon as Kyrios Stavropoulos deigned to put in an appearance. I was quite impressed to see that Spiros had managed to round up so many locals on such short notice, particularly as such emergency meetings were unprecedented in my experience. It struck me that Spiros might be angling for the non-existent, lofty position of village president, inspired by my talk of meeting with the village president, Babis, at the home of Bill, Spiros' oldest friend, on our second honeymoon.

Dimitris volunteered the information that Kyrios Stavropoulos wouldn't be able to make it.

"But he comes here for the coffee every morning," Christos griped.

"I saw him in the shop earlier. Tina was haranguing him about his disloyalty in coming to the *kafenio* for his coffee. She only let up when he promised to drink his coffee outside the shop today," Dimitris said.

"That Communist traitor," Christos blasted, clearly annoyed that Tina had managed to lure back her regular customer.

I must say I took a great deal of personal pride in the way Dimitris' English language skills had come along in such leaps and bounds; I found the way in which haranguing just rolled off his tongue particularly impressive. If one overlooked his predilection to put an unnecessary Greek stress on each English syllable, his quick mastery of the language was almost flawless. Clearly, of the two of us, I was the superior teacher. Despite Dimitris' regular doorstep tutelage, no one could accuse me of mastering Greek to a flawless degree.

"We begin then," Spiros declared, banging his fists on the table to call the group to order.

Whilst the ensuing dialogue took place in an odd mix of Greek and English, I will favour English in this recounting of the meeting.

"Yesterday..." Spiros began, his dramatic pause signifying the portentousness of the words he was about to deliver. "Yesterday, the unthinkable to happen. The thief break into the house of the English man that is married to the Manolis' lover..."

"The Manolis have the lover..." Kyriakos exclaimed in surprise. I was taken aback by his obvious incredulity at this news. I would have thought that Doreen carrying on with Manolis would be a regular topic of gossip in the Hancock household.

"Or thieves. There may have been more than one of the bounders," Gordon interjected, the news of the burglary already common knowledge in the village.

"What did they steal?" Giannis asked.

"They made off with Norman's collection of traffic cones," I revealed. There was a collective gasp as I furnished this detail; although Norman was not personally known by most of the local Greeks due to his failure to make any effort to integrate into the community, the villagers had formed their own impression that Norman must be cracked in the head due to his infamously bizarre predilection for collecting traffic cones. Admittedly, I may have been the one responsible for spreading the word about his peculiar habit.

"I hear the thief to take the towel and the alcohol," Papas Andreas remarked. His words were met with another collective gasp, the men clearly shocked that the sanctity of a Meli home had been violated.

"I call the meeting because the burgle has to happen again. Last the night, when the Mathias was in the taverna, his house was broken too," Spiros said. It was obvious by the shocked reaction of the gathered group that this latest burglary was news to most of us.

"I was to lock up for the night when the Mathias come back in the terrible state," Nikos said. "He was the shaking and much the angry. The stupid thief had broken the kitchen window to get inside. This make the Mathias the furious because the door was not locked."

"There has never been the need for locked doors in Meli," Dimitris remarked.

"I'm not surprised that Mathias was angry that his window broken for no good reason. I'm sure that people will start to be more cautious about locking their doors after this," I said. I considered it particularly heinous of the thief to target the home of a vulnerable old pensioner.

"No one ever had the need to lock the door in Meli," Nikos declared, reiterating Dimitris' words. "The thief must be the outsider."

"Everyone must to start to lock the door and window when they to go out, to be the precaution," Spiros decreed.

"Surely not the balcony doors. We need to leave them open to get a through-draught at this time of year," I argued. I couldn't imagine a thief would be brazen enough to prop a ladder up on the street to access my balcony. "Anyway, it appears that the thief's modus operandi is to smash a window to get inside, whether the door is locked or not."

"Better to lock the house tight until the police to catch the thief," Spiros argued.

"How likely is that?" I asked. "They never caught up with Frenk when he put Tarek in hospital after attacking him with his *Rugovo* dance sword. Attempted murder is a more serious crime than burglary."

"The Albanian only try to murder the other Albanian," Nikos said dismissively.

"And they deport the Tarek for being the illegal." Dimitris' words reminded me that the police had summarily punished the victim whilst his attacker got off Scot-free by dint of disappearing.

As I reflected on this, one of the elderly gents stood up and stretched before heading over to the camp bed. Without so much as removing his shoes, he adopted a horizontal position; within less than a minute was happily snoring. None of the Greeks paid the slightest attention, though I noticed Gordon Strange hiding a chuckle.

The meeting was interrupted by the unexpected arrival of Kyrios Stavropoulos. "I manage to get away when the Tina to serve the customer," he boasted.

A round of "Bravo" followed, the *kafenio* men clearly impressed that the communistic pensioner had got one over on the woman in the shop. Each of them had felt the lash of Tina's tongue as she'd berated them for taking their morning coffee in the new establishment rather than outside the shop. Spiros quickly brought the late arrival up to date on the latest burglary.

"What did the thief steal from the Mathias?" Papas Andreas enquired, his brow furrowed in concentration beneath his cylindrical hat.

"They to steal the pension money from the tin in the kitchen..." Nikos said.

"And the blanket from the bed," Spiros added.

"The bottle of shop bought *ouzo* and *Metaxa* was missing," Nikos said.

"Leaving us to calculate that the thief isn't a teetotaller," I deduced. Recalling that the thief had made off with Norman's booze along with all of Doreen's towels, I asked, "Did the thief steal any of Mathias' towels?"

Shrugging his shoulders, Nikos looked over at Spiros. Neither of them had ascertained if towels should be added to the laundry list of stolen items.

"I call this meeting to plan what we must to do," Spiros said. "We must to be the extra virulent..."

"Vigilant," I corrected.

"And keep watch for the thief," Spiros added.

"Or thieves," Gordon piped up.

"So far the burglar or burglars have targeted houses when the owners weren't at home," I pointed out. "Both Doreen and Norman were out when the thieves broke in and Mathias was in the taverna when his house was robbed. One could conclude that the thieves were casing the joint, waiting until the property was empty before breaking in."

"It could to be the flute…" Spiros suggested.

"A fluke," I corrected.

"I think the big worry is that the thief could to target the house of the woman who to live alone," Spiros said. "The thief could to break in when the woman has no the company…"

"Then why did you make a point of making this meeting men only?" Gordon asked Spiros.

"I not to want to upset the woman with this matter…it is up to us the men to protect and watch out for the woman," Spiros declared. "We must to worry about the woman alone, the Litsa and the Kyria Kompogiannopoulou. Kyriako, now that you to live with the old English man that write the dirty book, your the wife and the mother are alone without the man to protect."

Having now had the displeasure of meeting Kyriakos' mother, I considered she would be more than a match for any burglar.

"And there is your mother, too, Victor," Spiros continued. "The Violet Burke to live alone…"

"Seriously, Spiros. I can't imagine any burglars being rash enough to risk an encounter with my mother. But Sherry lives alone and could be an easy target. It's general knowledge that she's worth a bob or two."

"And Tina. She is the alone above the shop," Papas Andreas said.

"Your mother is often alone, Andrea, when you are out conducting church business," I reminded the Papas. Andreas looked suitably worried at the thought.

"I have to go back to England tomorrow, so Moira will be alone," Gordon added. "It's a relief to know that she'll have Waffles with her."

"What use is the dog? It is more likely to lick the burgle than to protect the woman," Spiros spluttered.

"I think the police should to investigate the outsider," Apostolos piped up, causing Gordon Strange to shuffle uncomfortably in his seat before the barber elaborated. "The thief to steal the alcohol. It is well known that Victor's Albanian is the common drunk."

"And he is the outsider..." Dimitris added.

"And very shifty," Apostolos threw out.

"Hold on there," I interjected, feeling the need to leap to my gardener's defence without bothering to add my usual disclaimer that Guzim wasn't my Albanian. "I have never had reason to question Guzim's honesty and his days of drunken shenanigans are long behind him. He's been as sober as a judge since the birth of Fatos, working industriously to provide for his growing family."

Admittedly I laid it on a bit thick but Guzim had demonstrated his loyalty time after time. The least I could do was have his back when groundless suspicions were voiced simply because he hailed from Albania.

"I don't trust him," Kyrios Stavropoulos opined. "He come from the Communist Albania but he is not the good Communist."

"Why on earth should he be? Communism fell in Albania back in 1990," I pointed out.

"He is the outsider," Kyrios Stavropoulos reiterated.

"Well, I for one, have no reason to doubt his honesty. He's lived in the shed next door for years," Papas Andreas said solemnly.

"Why are you defending him?" Kyrios Stavropoulos demanded. "The Guzim is not the good Orthodox Church goer."

"Neither are you," the cleric countered, winning that round. "But I do have the thought on who the burgle is," Papas Andreas announced in a ponderous tone. Everyone fell silent, waiting for him to enlighten us. "The Albanian cleaner, the Agnesa, had been inside both of the homes that were burgle. It is the big worry because I let her to clean for my mother."

"Whilst not wanting to jump to a hasty conclusion, Doreen did mention that she had noticed things missing after Agnesa had been in to clean," I said.

"But she and the Drin to leave the village when I to catch the drunk Drin in the hearse," Spiros reminded us.

"Thus, making her less likely to fall under suspicion if she returned to Meli to break into the houses she was familiar with," Gordon suggested.

"I will to telephone the police with the Agnesa name," Spiros said. Clearly sold on the suspicion, he whipped out his mobile. "In the meantime, everyone must to be the virulent, lock the door and look out for the woman alone."

With the meeting adjourned, I declined Gordon's offer of a lift home in the sports car, assuring him that I needed the exercise. With a spot going spare in the flashy car, Papas Andreas practically threw himself in the passenger seat. I found the sight of the cleric clinging onto his conical hat as the car sped off, Waffles perched on his knee, most amusing.

Chapter 23

Skulking Around

Taking my leave from the *kafenio*, Manolis sprinted after me.

"Victor, I have the proposition for you. Doreen tells me you used to cook at the taverna…"

Predicting where this was going, I interrupted Manolis, deliberately downplaying my stint as a chef. "Truth be told, I was little more than a kitchen skivvy, just lending a hand when Dina, and then Nikos, were incapacitated."

"But Doreen tells me you teach cooking classes…me and Christos want you to cook at the *kafenio*. Many of the regulars are demanding food…"

"So, you expect me to cook at the *kafenio* after putting in a full day's repping?" My question oozed sarcasm.

"Yes." Clearly my sarcasm went over his head.

Eager to nip this in the bud, I claimed it would

be disloyal to Nikos and Dina if I cooked in a rival establishment. In reality, I knew that Nikos wouldn't care less, never bothering to worry his head about any competition in the village.

"But many the customer want food," Manolis reiterated.

"Perhaps you could learn to cook by attending my cookery classes this coming winter," I suggested, extending an invitation to Manolis whilst pointedly excluding his brother. The last thing I wanted was to give houseroom to the oily Christos and have him attempting to play footsie with Marigold under my kitchen table. "Anyway, you shouldn't be serving any food until you have the toilet situation sorted out. Your failure to provide suitable sanitation for your customers breaches all health and safety regulations. I couldn't possibly condone such flagrant defiance of the law."

Manolis' blank expression demonstrated that he was not particularly well up on the issue of government decreed hygiene edicts. No doubt such rulings hadn't been in existence when the *kafenio* was first established many decades ago.

"Actually, once you've sorted out the toilet, if you are still set on offering food, I do have an idea," I said.

"You will stop repping to cook…"

BUCKET TO GREECE (VOL.15)

"No, absolutely not." Even if the brothers offered to pay me double my repping rate, nothing could entice me to spend my days working alongside the oily Christos. I wouldn't put it past him to scuttle off to attempt to seduce my wife whilst I was up to my elbows preparing Greek salad. "But I know someone who has experience working in a taverna kitchen... do you know Blerta?"

"Blerta?"

"Tonibler's mother..."

"The mother of the British prime minister used to work in a Greek kitchen. I never heard that."

"Not Tony Blair's mother. Tonibler's mother. You must have seen the young boy with the spectacles and the oversized school uniform... would you like me to have a word with his mother, Blerta? She's an excellent cook. In fact, you've sampled her cooking already."

Since Manolis looked totally blank, I jogged his memory.

"At Sherry's expat dinner party. The only reason that Sherry's food was in any way edible was because she paid Blerta to rustle up the meal."

"The cheese dip and the baked lamb with yoghurt...it was very good. And you say this Blerta person cooked it? I think you have that wrong. Sherry told us that she cooked it."

"She was fibbing. Sherry kept Blerta hidden away in the kitchen and shamelessly passed the cooking off as her own. Between you and me, Sherry's as useless in the kitchen as Doreen…"

"Doreen is the wonderful cook." Although Manolis automatically sprang to his girlfriend's defence, his words held little conviction. "It is just that the *kafenio* regulars want the Greek food, not the English food that Doreen is used to making."

"Have you ever actually tasted Doreen's cooking? I would best describe it as a cross between soggy cardboard and charcoal."

"She made some snacks for the *kafenio*…" Manolis' curdled expression indicated he had sampled the snacks and found them lacking. Clearly his loyalty was torn between defending Doreen and admitting to himself that she was a complete disaster on the culinary front. Presumably he was unaware that Doreen had shared his less than glowing reaction to her cooking with Marigold, oblivious that she had been sobbing on Marigold's shoulder after he had accused her of being incompetent in the kitchen.

"I have not tasted one of Doreen's homemade meals because her husband has banned me from the house." Manolis was obviously reaching, realising that the snacks she had knocked up for the *kafenio* had just been a taster of the unpalatable food that

BUCKET TO GREECE (VOL.15)

Doreen slopped up.

"Well, Norman has done you a favour. Anyway, would you like me to mention it to Blerta? She has a few cleaning and ironing jobs in the village but perhaps you could come to some arrangement."

"Yes, speak to her, Victor."

I intended to propose to Blerta that she spend an hour or so in the *kafenio* each morning preparing a traditional one-pot Greek meal which the brothers could then heat up in the microwave to serve to their customers for lunch, the midday meal typically served any time during the afternoon. That way, Blerta wouldn't lose out on the income from her cleaning and ironing jobs. I knew that my mother was beginning to depend on Blerta to fill in any gaps in her own busy charring schedule.

"Of course, you will need to get the place up to code before taking someone on to cook," I stressed. "You must get the toilet sorted out first, and you'll need to install a separate wash basin in the *kafenio* kitchen for hand washing."

"But we have a perfectly good sink," Manolis declared. "Why should we waste money on another one?"

"To comply with health and safety regulations. Perhaps you would like to borrow some literature on the subject since you haven't bothered to familiarise yourself with any of the legal requirements. The books I have make for fascinating reading..."

"Doreen told me you are obsessed with the hygiene."

"I just like to keep up to date with any new developments the Food Standards Agency have introduced since I retired," I said. "If you take my professional advice, Manoli, you should close the *kafenio* down temporarily until the place is compliant with all the health and safety edicts. I wouldn't like to be in your shoes if a public health inspector decides to drop in..."

"But Nikos tells me in all the years the taverna has been open, he has never had a visit from the health inspector," Manolis protested.

"Well, on your head be it. But just remember that I warned you."

Flapping his hands as though batting my professional concerns away, Manolis said, "I would like to meet this Blerta."

"When I see her, I will ask her to pop over to the *kafenio*," I promised. "But you'll have to tell your brother to keep his hands, not to mention his smutty suggestions, to himself. Blerta is a happily married woman."

Taking my leave, I set off in the direction of the old ruin we had purchased. Since Barry had been balancing on the scaffolding earlier, he had missed the meeting. I needed to bring him up to date on the worrying spate of burglaries in the village whilst checking on the work in progress. Since my brother-in-law had allocated his two weeks of annual leave to getting on with the renovation whilst Vangelis was away, I was keen to see the latest changes. Naturally, as a co-owner of the property, I had put in my share of the graft. Over the course of the last several months, Guzim and I had toiled and sweated, hacking away at the overgrown garden, turning it into a tranquil green space. Although we had hacked away at the prickly pear plants since they posed a prickly danger to any potential tourists, we had left the naked men orchids to flourish.

Spotting a removal van outside John Macey's newly refurbished house, I presumed that Macey was finally moving in. Changing my course, I opted to take a circuitous route rather than risk being dragged into hauling boxes. Recalling the human chain of village men that had formed to assist with moving the Bucket belongings when we moved into our village home, I felt just a tad guilty for leaving Macey to struggle alone. However, time was too short for me to lend a hand. I needed to catch up with Barry before whisking my mother and Dot out for lunch with Vasos.

The sight of Panos' tractor approaching brought a smile to my face. Automatically preparing to enter into some cheery banter with the welly wearing farmer, I stopped short, remembering that Panos was no longer with us and the tractor was being steered by his granddaughter, Yiota. The loud throaty ticking of the tractor engine drowned out our mutual calls of greeting. Settling for exchanging a wave with the young woman, I was impressed with how quickly she had mastered the unwieldy vehicle.

As I strolled up the leafy lane leading to the ruin, the melodious tinkle of goats' bells competed with the ceaseless song of the cicadas in a charming countryside serenade. Skirting close to the hedgerows and leafy trees, I took advantage of the shade from the shadows they cast across my path. Although the day was set to turn into another scorcher, there was a gentle mountain breeze that I welcomed.

Passing the colourful bee boxes that Giannis was tending in his fields, another friendly wave was exchanged. Recalling how Dot raved over our local honey, I made a mental note to gift her a jar of Giannis' finest thyme honey, *thymarisio meli*, to take home to Warrington. There was no doubt in my mind that Dot's presence had been a good influence on my mother. I believed that the way Dot continually nagged her friend to take heed and follow doctor's orders had been instrumental in Violet Burke finally eschewing her lifelong addiction to chips. Not as much as a single fried potato had passed my mother's lips since she had been reunited with her old friend.

The peace of the morning was disturbed by raucous shouting emanating from the direction of our ruin. Quickening my pace, I practically jogged the rest of the way, hoping I wouldn't run into trouble on site. Turning into the property boundary, I recognised Barry's voice raised in anger just before I almost collided with a scrawny looking fellow clad in scruffy workman's attire; kicking at stones as he skulked away, he kept his head down. Drawing level with me, he looked up, a scowl plastered across his surly, weatherworn face as he spat on the ground contemptuously.

If my eyes didn't deceive me, it was Drin, the drunken oaf husband of the entitled-to-towels Agnesa. The last time I had caught sight of the inebriated Albanian, he was being floored by a thump to the face from his wife. A shudder of revulsion ran down my spine as I hurried past the coarse looking man, seeking the protection of numbers offered by the company of my brother-in-law and Blat.

Sighing with relief to see Barry and Blat on firm

ground rather than out of my reach up the scaffolding, I called out, "Barry, what on earth was that drunkard, Drin, doing here? He looked beyond furtive."

"I caught him lurking. When I asked him what he wanted, he said he was looking for labouring work," Barry revealed. "I didn't know who he was until Blat filled me in…"

"Drin has the very bad reputation in the Albanian community," Blat added.

"Blat reckons he's a bit of a tea leaf by all accounts," Barry added.

Noticing Blat looked a tad confused by Barry's use of the colloquial phrase, I duly translated, "A tea leaf is slang for a thief."

"And then, of course, I placed him as the fella I'd heard bad things about from your mother," Barry said.

"From the battle of the chars?" I posited.

"That's right. Violet had him dead to rights by the sound of it. She's a grand judge of character is Vi, I'll say that for her. Drin didn't half turn nasty when I told him we didn't need another labourer. He started shouting the odds, so I told him to sling his hook."

"Do you think he was genuinely after work here, or just casing the joint?"

"What? You've lost me, Victor."

"Looking around to see if there was anything worth nicking…"

"Stealing," Barry duly translated for Blat's benefit. I reflected Blat was certainly getting a crash course in English slang. It was doubtful that his British hero, Tony Blair, ever came out with such jargon. "I'm not with you."

"That's because you missed the meeting that Spiros called this morning. There was another burglary last night," I said.

"On top of the one at Norman's place?"

"That's right. Some shady crook broke into Mathias' house whilst he was in the taverna," I said. "Since the Albanian char, Agnesa, had cleaned for both Norman and Mathias, Papas Andreas posited the theory that she had something to do with it. Seeing Drin up here made me wonder if Agnesa had been passing on information to her husband about any valuables that she'd spotted in the houses she cleaned."

"But the thief made off with Norman's worthless traffic cones," Barry argued. "They can hardly be considered valuable items worth stealing."

"But that pair of ignoramuses wouldn't know they were worthless. They may have presumed Norman's collection was worth a few bob," I argued.

"You've got a point there," Barry conceded. "And the way that Drin fella was skulking, it set off alarm bells that he was up to no good. It was only when I confronted him, demanding to know what his game was, that he claimed he was after work."

"I tell Mr Barry that the Drin have the reputation of the workshy," Blat added.

"I'd better make sure that all the building materials are locked up securely when we finish for the day," Barry said pensively.

"It doesn't even make sense for Drin to be here in the village, unless he did indeed have a dodgy motive. He doesn't live up this way anymore," I said. "It's a bit of a stretch to suppose Drin would come all the way up to Meli looking for work when he and Agnesa are based down on the coast now. There's plenty of labouring jobs down there with all the new builds going up, if he was actually inclined to do an honest day's work."

"Well, I doubt Drin will show his face here again," Barry said with relief. "We made it clear he wasn't welcome."

Since Barry and Blat appeared to be taking a break, I filled Blat in on Manolis needing someone to cook for the *kafenio*. Blat perked up at the news, saying that it sounded right up Blerta's street. He said he would ask his wife to pop round to have a word with Manolis.

"Just make sure she doesn't get involved until Barry has installed a working toilet," I advised. "I'd hate to see Blerta compromised by the way Manolis and Christos operate outside the edicts of the Foods Standard Agency.

"Tonibler can to teach his mama much about the bacteria," Blat said.

"If Victor has his way, your boy will be an expert on hygiene rules before long," Barry chortled.

"And Mr Victor's rules are the best because they are the rules he enforced in the great Great Britain," Blat said proudly.

"Any word yet from Tony Blair on your moving to England?"

"Not a word," Blat said, his heartfelt sigh indicating he still chased the dream of moving to his hero's homeland. "I must write to him again. Perhaps he was too busy with the great general election he won this year to answer my other letters."

"He's sure to have more time to deal with his mail now that he's only got to concentrate on running the country," I quipped.

Surveying the property, I was amazed by the changes the two of them had worked. The pointing had been completed several weeks back, the scaffolding remaining in place whilst Barry installed the new windows and wooden shutters. The exterior, now hardly recognisable from its original state of decrepitude, boasted a much-needed facelift, the new windows and pale blue shutters presenting a welcoming façade.

Barry and I had butted heads over the renovation of late. Barry had been of the opinion that we should concentrate on just one of the two potential apartments so that we could begin to derive an income from letting it out as soon as, whilst work continued on the other one. I had argued that we should wait until both apartments were fully finished and all the building debris cleared away, since any tourists that holidayed in the first completed apartment wouldn't want to stay in the middle of a building site. Because Barry is a builder, he tends not to notice the general mess that the renovation work creates and is immune to the less than dulcet tones of a cement mixer and builders' hammering.

Since my opinion that no one wanted to holiday on a building site had the support of both Marigold and Cynthia, I won that round. I recalled that Cynthia had told Barry that any tourists we attracted would likely post negative reviews on Trip Advisor if they had to pick their way through builder' rubble and endure the din of any work in progress. In turn, Barry had scoffed, saying he doubted that the Trip Advisor site would take off. It was Marigold who finally talked Barry around, being able to twist her little brother around her little finger. He agreed that he would crack on and complete both apartments before we started advertising them as holiday lets.

"We're just about to take the scaffolding down," Barry said. "Do you fancy giving us a hand, Victor?"

"I'm a bit short of time, actually. I'm taking my mother and Dot out for lunch with Captain Vasos." I was certainly relieved that I had a convenient excuse for not getting stuck into dismantling the scaffolding.

"I was joking, Victor. Do you really think I'd let you loose on the scaffolding?" Barry joshed.

Chapter 24

A Proper Greek Octopus

With the news that *Kapetanios* Vasos would be joining Dot, Vi and myself for lunch at Takis' taverna down on the coast, Marigold decided to throw on a strappy sun frock and come along too; after all, the good captain could be guaranteed to provide free entertainment.

It was the first time we had visited the taverna together since Takis officially took over from the sparring couple, Vasilis and Angeliki. Since Takis was a trained chef, we were keen to see what new culinary twists he had added to the menu. At the very least, I felt certain that the bechamel topping on the *moussaka* would be free of clumps of mascara now that the kitchen was an Angeliki free zone.

"No sign of my old mucker, Captain Vasos," Vi grumbled, peering around. Grabbing an outside table in the shade of a mulberry tree, directly opposite the pebble beach, she said, "He won't be able to miss us here."

"I can tell that you're in your element here, darling, now that the place has received your official health inspector's seal of approval," Marigold cooed. Turning to Dot, my wife added, "I've lost count of the number of times I've had to restrain Victor from trying to sneak off and snoop in a taverna kitchen. He's never lost the thrill of uncovering some gross hygiene violation."

"There's nowt wrong with being fussy when it comes to cleanliness," Vi piped up in my defence.

"I must say that I have every confidence that the kitchen here does indeed meet my exacting standards," I concurred, certain that by now Takis would have banned the resident tabby from prowling around in the kitchen and cleaned the blood off the ceiling.

"That takes a load off my mind, lad," Vi concurred, sharing my exacting standards when it came to a pristine kitchen.

"I do love the new touches that Takis has added to the place," Marigold raved, pointing out the ceramic planters filled with vibrant orange sunflowers and the delightful addition of large pots of fragrant basil. Fanning herself with a menu, Marigold suggested that I try to persuade Takis to invest in some outdoor water-spraying fans to alleviate the heat.

"You can use your own powers of persuasion," I said, gesturing towards Takis who was making his way towards us. As I stood up to greet the new owner, he enveloped me in an enthusiastic bear-hug. Turning to my companions, Takis deposited double kisses on the ladies' cheeks, following the gesture with well-versed lines of flattery on their appearance. As he showered my wife with the most effusive compliments, Marigold basked in the younger man's extravagant flattery. Even Violet Burke demonstrated she wasn't immune to Takis' charm when he commented favourably on her recent weight loss; it really is amazing what a difference a week without stuffing her face with chips and Fray Bentos had made.

My mother demanded to know when Takis planned to start serving up the British Sunday dinners we had discussed previously, saying she could murder a nice roast dinner with all the trimmings right now.

"After the summer is end. Now there are many the Athenians holidaying and they want the good traditional Greek food…"

Takis stopped abruptly mid-sentence, seemingly fascinated by the oversized and most decidedly tacky orange fibreglass urn that Dot whipped out of her handbag and plonked down on the centre of the table.

"Why you bring the plastic pineapple to the lunch?" Takis asked, his expression contorted in confusion.

"That's not a pineapple. That's my Wilf. And I'll have you know that I didn't have him shoved in a plastic urn, that's proper fibreglass, it is. I chose it deliberate like; I didn't want my Wilf spilling out everywhere if I dropped him."

"Wilf?" Takis prompted.

"My dead husband."

"You marry the short-arse?" Takis' confusion noticeably grew. As an aside, so did mine: I supposed he must have been swamped with English tourists to have picked up such short-arse slang.

"How you manage to shove the husband body in something so small?"

"Dot had her husband cremated. The urn contains his ashes," I explained, realising the idea of cremation was most likely a decidedly foreign concept to the Greek man since cremation was illegal in Greece.

Clearly unable to grasp the concept of taking an urn full of human ashes out for lunch, Takis grabbed a chair from a nearby table and joined us, asking Dot why she wanted to cart an urn around.

"It's not too dissimilar a practice to the Greek way of storing human bones in a metal box in an ossuary," I said.

"They put human bones in a box," Dot spluttered. "That sounds downright macabre."

"After seven years in a Greek grave, the dead are exhumed," I explained.

"It's a right carry on," Vi opined. "They dig up the dead over here and wash the bones in wine..."

"Do they get a non-alcoholic scrub down if they were tee-total?" Dot queried.

"Wild horses won't drag me to the graveyard when it's time to dig up Panos. I reckon it's downright nasty. Let sleeping dogs lie is what I say," Vi said, absentmindedly twisting the emerald engagement ring on her finger.

"I recollect Spiros telling me that when they dug up Litsa's father, it was a terribly messy business as the corpse hadn't finished decomposing," I said, cringing as I recalled the undertaker's vivid description. "Spiros told me that Papas Andreas came over all official, claiming the body hadn't decomposed quickly enough because Litsa and Mathias hadn't prayed with sufficient devotion. Litsa was apparently most put out to have her devotion questioned because she's such a regular churchgoer."

"I can't understand why cremation is banned in Greece," Marigold said. "Remember when we had Aunty Beryl done, Victor? They did such a lovely job."

"The Orthodox Church will not to sanction the cremation," Takis explained. "We orthodox consider the body to be the temple of the God. We believe that a body reduced to ashes will not be resurrected."

"My Wilf was C of E, not that he was religious like," Dot said.

"Church of England," I translated for Takis' benefit.

"I rather think that banning the option of cremation is a bit of a money-making racket for the church," I dared to suggest. "The church must make a tidy profit out of renting graves and then charging extra for exhumations, not to mention the cost of hiring a space in the ossuary for storing the box of bones."

"Aye, lad, I reckon you've got a point," Vi agreed. "Folks over here don't just take the box home and stick it on the mantlepiece like Dot did with Wilf."

"There is some the troublemaker who fight

against the burial tradition and want to make the cremation legal," Takis told us. "Since the late nineties, the Greek Cremation Society make much the noise. They fight to change the law, but I think they do nothing more than blow in the wind. The church will never to relent. Myself, I spit on the idea of cremation for the Greek because it is the communist practice."

"Well, my Wilf was no communist," Dot argued.

"The church isn't alone in being against cremation," I said. "Spiros is dead set against the idea too."

"Well, he would be; the fella's an undertaker. 'Appen it would lose him some custom," Vi said.

"Can we please change the subject. It's just too morbid for a lunchtime conversation," Marigold pleaded, sending a withering look at the gaudy urn containing Wilf's ashes. Although she was far too polite to say anything to Dot about it, Marigold detested Dot's habit of slapping Wilf down on the table at every mealtime. Personally, I considered it very unsavoury to have his ashes so close to our food. I very much hoped that this would be Wilf's last meal with us, so to speak. Dot had set her heart on finding a scenic spot to scatter him after lunch.

"Shall we order now or should we wait until the good captain turns up?" I asked, not voicing the thought that if Vasos had been hitting the morning *ouzo*, he might be in no fit state to manage the drive.

"Now, I reckon," my mother decided. "I hope you lot can do without chips. I don't want you sticking a plate of temptation under my nose."

"The chips are excellent," Takis volunteered without a hint of modesty.

"The doctor has put my mother on a strict diet. Chips are banned," I told Takis.

"I think you're doing marvellously, Vi. I never thought you'd stick to a diet," Marigold said. "The least we can do to support you is to avoid anything fried."

"Mrs Burke, you want I bring you the nice chicken *souvlaki*? It not make you fat. I bring with rice, yes?"

"Aye, lad. That sounds a sight tastier than one of them oily Greek salads."

"Well, I want summat that's proper Greek," Dot declared, revealing an adventurous side. "Summat I wouldn't be able to get at home."

"I can to recommend the octopus in vinegar," Takis said.

"A proper Greek octopus. I've never run into one of them at Tesco or down the Co-op. I'll give it a go, lad," Dot decided.

"I'll have the same please, Taki," I said.

"And I'll go with the *moussaka*," Marigold

added.

Ordering half-a-kilo of white wine for the ladies, I told Takis that I would stick to water. With our orders completed, Takis went off to the kitchen to work his culinary magic, sending a waiter over with the wine.

"Ooh, you'll make us feel bad, lad, what with us having wine and you on nowt stronger than water," Dot fussed.

"I'm driving, Dot. But you needn't feel bad on my behalf. I will jazz up the water with some ice and a slice," I said, before requesting the waiter bring me, *"Mia feta lemoni gia to nero mou parakalo."*

"Ooh, you don't want to go bunging *feta* cheese in your drink, lad. It'll curdle right nasty," Dot opined, having picked up on the word *feta*.

"*Feta* is Greek for a slice," I informed her.

"I could have sworn it was that salty white cheese…"

"The word has more than one meaning," Marigold said with an indulgent smile, still happily glowing from being the recipient of Takis' flattery. My lovely wife is such a pushover when it comes to attention from younger men.

Sipping my water, I drank in the beautiful sight across from the taverna, the deep blue colour of the sea contrasting perfectly with the white edged waves lapping gently against the pebble shore.

BUCKET TO GREECE (VOL.15)

Gazing into the distance, I tuned out of the conversation between the ladies until a sharp nudge in the ribs from Violet Burke brought me out of my reverie.

"It's not like you, not to go and have some hissy fit over long distance," she said.

"What? I've no idea what you were talking about," I admitted.

"You could feign a bit of interest, lad. Dot was saying how Marigold went and encouraged her to use your telephone to call Warrington to check up on her Kevin."

"Marigold…"

Before I could have words with my wife, Dot interrupted. "I was that worried about our Kevin. The soppy lummox hasn't got a clue how to so much as spread his margarine on his toast. Anyhow, he swears he's managing all right with a pot noodle for his brekky and chippy suppers."

"So, he's mastered the art of boiling a kettle and operating a toaster," I chortled.

"Ooh, I don't know about the toaster." Dot's forehead creased with worry as she tried to work out if managing a toaster was beyond her son's skill set. "'Appen I'd better ring again later…I don't want him blowing himself up if he shoves his butter knife in to dislodge a burnt crust."

"He'll be right, lass. He won't want to be

dunking toast in his pot noodle. I'm right glad that my Victor wasn't brought up so helpless that he'd starve without Marigold to look after his needs," Vi said proudly. I marvelled at her change of stance; she usually complained that Marigold was a lazy mare for leaving me to do most of the cooking, even though I insisted I enjoyed it.

"Aye, you did a right good job with your Victor," Dot agreed.

Violet Burke avoided her friend's eye. Considering my mother had nothing to do with how well I'd been raised, she was a tad reticent to accept the credit.

"Our Kevin said there's no doubt about it, he's definitely gone and got that Chardonnay Billings up the duff. She went and did one of them home pregnancy tests. Our Kevin said she had to wee on a stick."

"With the way that Chardonnay Billings spreads it about, you want to be getting your Kevin to do one of them DNA tests," Vi advised. Catching my eye, Marigold almost choked on her wine. No doubt she recalled how she'd urged me to take a DNA test to establish that Violet Burke was indeed my mother and not a pretender to the title.

"That would be stirring the pot and chucking the cat among the pigeons," Dot said, doubling up on her idioms. "Our Kevin has only gone and done the decent thing and proposed to the lass."

"He's opening himself up to a lifetime of grief, saddling himself with a Billings." Vi's pronunciation of the word Billings was laden with so much contempt that she made it sound like a dirty word.

"Well, he won't be saddled. Can you believe, the cheeky mare only went and turned him down?"

"No! She never did? That Chardonnay Billings must need her head examining to turn down your Kevin." Vi protested so loudly that the other customers swivelled round in their seats to see what all the commotion was about. I can always rely on Violet Burke to embarrass me in public.

"Chardonnay reckons if they ever get hitched, she wants a right big do, not some hasty shotgun wedding," Dot explained.

Reflecting on my admittedly narrow dealings with the Billings' clan, I supposed a big do would involve a large and unruly gathering of shell-suited chavs, knocking back lager and chain smoking. No doubt the celebration would culminate in chucking slices of wedding cake at each other and some kind of thuggish brawl.

"Chardonnay told our Kevin that she reckons it would be a bit vulgar to get wed with the bump showing," Dot said. The notion that a young woman that freely wheeled her trolley around Tesco in her pyjamas even knew the meaning of vulgar, astounded me. "What do you reckon about getting wed with a bump on display, Marigold?"

Pursing her lips, Marigold feigned selective deafness. I couldn't blame her since we'd had something of a shotgun wedding ourselves, Marigold pregnant with Benjamin when we tied the knot.

"Marigold was up the spout with Benjamin when she married Victor," Violet Burke blurted out. Intercepting a glacial glare from her daughter-in-law, she observed, "Cor, if looks could kill."

Changing the subject, Marigold pondered, "I wonder what's holding Vasos up?"

Fortunately, the arrival of our food put an end to the tension. As expected, Takis had added his own unique touch to the dishes, garnishing the *chtapodi se xydi*, octopus in vinegar, with fresh caper leaves, and adding a dash of sweet paprika to the *kotopoulo souvlaki* marinade. Marigold's *moussaka* was served with a small side salad of cherry tomatoes and basil leaves, artfully displayed. Takis had restrained from messing around with the traditional *moussaka* recipe in case his Athenian customers took umbrage at his adding a novel twist to the national dish.

Tucking into my octopus, deliciously tender from the marinade of vinegar and olive oil, I brought the others up to date on the work coming along at the ruin that we planned to rent out.

"Barry dedicated his two-week annual break to cracking on with the job whilst Vangelis is away. With Blat helping, the pair of them have made marvellous progress and are about to start plastering the interior walls…"

"Barry does know not to plaster over some of the original stonework?" Marigold questioned.

"Of course. You'll be able to sort out the colour schemes and go shopping for the kitchenettes soon. Barry wants to get them in once the floor tiles are down."

"Fabulous." Marigold's excitement at the prospect of a pro-longed shopping spree was palpable. "Doreen and I can make a day out of it."

"Just remember not to get carried away, darling. We have a budget to stick to," I warned. I didn't mention I intended to police said budget rigorously.

"This octopus is a bit of all right," Dot said insincerely. Pushing her plate of half-eaten food to one side, she lit a cigarette before offering titbits of octopus to the taverna cat.

"You must want your head examining, eating that octopus," Vi scoffed.

"You know that I'm partial to a bit of fish with lashings of vinegar," Dot retorted.

"Technically, octopus isn't classified as fish. It's

a mollusc," I schooled Dot.

"But it comes out of the sea," Dot pointed out, blowing smoke over the table.

"So do mucky flip flops that wash up on the beach but you wouldn't go serving them up with chips," Vi countered.

As the two of them launched into a list of the most bizarre items likely to wash up on a beach, my thoughts reverted back to the demands I would face as the part-owner of a holiday rental. Realising that my mother was in increasingly popular demand as a char, I decided to broach the subject of her cleaning the apartments once they were rented out to holidaymakers. I wanted to ensure she would leave room in her busy work schedule to prioritise dashing in with her scrubbing brush and bleach, between tourists.

"I'd feel much better if I knew you were committed to taking on the extra job," I explained. "With your exacting standards, I know the apartments will always be well sterilised and presented in pristine condition."

"You're getting a bit ahead of yourself, lad," Violet Burke scoffed. "I can't be committing to scrubbing floors when you haven't even got the tiles down yet. Course if you went for a nice bit of shag-pile instead of tiles, I'd only have to push a Hoover around."

"Thinking ahead, I am simply trying to ascertain if you will be able to juggle your busy schedule to make the rental properties a priority once the first bookings come in, Mother."

"There's only so many hours in a day, lad. 'Appen that wife of yours could muck in and get her hands dirty for once…"

Marigold contented herself with rolling her eyes whilst Vi spoke about her as if she wasn't there. From the very moment the subject of purchasing and renovating the ruin to rent out had been mooted, Marigold had been adamant in insisting her contribution would be limited to design and décor. She had made it perfectly clear that she wouldn't be getting hands-on with any of the donkey work. The very idea of handling some stranger's soiled bed sheets or soggy towels made her squeamish.

"Mother, if we are going to make a success of renting the place out as a holiday lets, it's important that we maintain the very highest standards. No one does a more thorough job than you," I wheedled. Admittedly, I was going out of my way to butter up Violet Burke by implying that her standards were far superior to Marigold's lax ways, rather than admit that my wife had flatly refused to have anything to do with changing the beds or getting stuck in with the cleaning. "We could well have guests both departing and arriving on the same day. I need to be confident that any changeover days are run like a well-oiled machine, which I know they will be in your capable hands."

"If it's that important to you, lad, I'll take the job on," Vi agreed. 'Appen Blerta can give me a hand if you have a big tourist rush on."

"Violet was telling me about how you plan to rent out apartments," Dot said. "'Appen if I start saving up, I could bring our Kevin and Chardonnay over to stay for their honeymoon. 'Appen the prospect of a free holiday abroad might convince that Chardonnay to wed our Kevin after all."

"Are you cracked in the head? Why do you want to encourage your Kevin to go marrying a Billings?" Vi asked.

"She's having my grandchild," Dot reminded her. "Anyhow, if Chardonnay takes our Kevin's name, at least the sprog won't come out as a Billings."

"And you'd come out here with them, like?" Vi asked.

"Well, you went on that second honeymoon with your Victor and Marigold," Dot replied. "And 'appen Kevin and Chardonnay will be needing someone to keep an eye on that little tyke, Tyrone."

I cringed inwardly at Dot's suggestion. When I had stayed at Violet Burke's Warrington council flat, I had suffered the misfortune of witnessing the up-close shenanigans of the matriarch of the Billings clan, Edna, otherwise known as haddock on Friday. I could just imagine how Chardonnay Billings would trash Marigold's immaculately chosen décor, leaving a tide of ring marks from lager cans and a selection of prominent cigarette burns in her wake. Still, there was no point dwelling on it since it was all moot at this point. There would be no honeymoon if a DNA test indicated Dot's son hadn't spawned the Billings' bump. Even with a positive result, Kevin would still need to persuade Chardonnay to tie the knot.

"So, what's all this I was hearing about the village men meeting over at the *kafenio*?" Vi demanded.

"Ah, yes, I was going to mention that. Spiros called an emergency meeting of the villagers to discuss the sudden spate of burglaries in Meli."

"I'd hardly call the theft of Norman's traffic cones a spate," Marigold said.

"Unfortunately, there has been a new development. Someone broke into Mathias' house last night whilst he was in the taverna."

"Oh, how dreadful." Marigold visibly paled. "Why didn't you tell me about the meeting? I would have come along with you."

"You were still sleeping..."

"Don't you mean Marigold was the wrong sex to go getting an invite? I have it on good authority that only the blokes in the village were welcome at the meeting," Vi said.

"Is that true, Victor? That's completely sexist," Marigold said, her tone bristling with outrage. "Surely if there are burglars on the loose in the village, they could potentially target anyone in Meli."

"I'm afraid it was Spiros' call. He didn't want to go upsetting you women unnecessarily…"

"What tosh. 'Appen us women should have been told so we can arm ourselves. I'll have to find a likely weapon in case some fella breaks into my place. 'Appen he could be overcome with lust at the sight of a red-blooded woman…"

"Fortunately, I think we can rule Milton out as the likely culprit," I chortled, confident that Milton was the only chap likely to be deluded enough to be overcome with lust at the sight of Violet Burke and her swollen ankles.

"This is no laughing matter, Victor," Marigold chided. "The idea of burglars in Meli gives me the shivers."

"A good clout on the head with my chip pan should see off any nasty toerag that breaks in. 'Appen you should give it back, Victor. It's not much use as a weapon when it's gathering dust in your kitchen."

"Nice try, Mother, but you're not getting the chip pan back for the foreseeable," I said.

"Vi's not the only one in need of a weapon. Any one of us could be targeted next. I'm very disappointed in Spiros' decision to exclude women from his meeting." Her face etched with worry, Marigold chewed nervously on her lower lip. "Is there any news about the police investigation?"

"Well, Papas Andreas presented a theory that Spiros promised to pass onto the police," I said. "It turns out that the Albanian woman, Agnesa, had been employed as a cleaner in both of the burgled homes. Andreas thought she could have taken the jobs in order to case the joints."

"Case the joints," Vi sneered. "You sound like an extra in a low budget B movie."

"Since Spiros mastered the English language through watching American movies with subtitles, he understood the phrase perfectly. I doubt he'd have made head or tail of taking a shufti," I pointed out. "Now, as I was saying, Andreas very much regrets having Agnesa in to do for his mother…"

Dot butted in before I could complete my sentence. "So, are these Greek priests allowed to be police snitches? Doesn't it break the rules of the confessional?"

"I would imagine that as a man of God, Papas

Andreas' first responsibility is to his parishioners. Naturally he will want to ensure they are not the victims of crime; if doing so means snitching on Agnesa, so be it," I replied.

"I know that Doreen had no time for Agnesa. Things were forever going missing when Agnesa had been in to clean up after Norman," Marigold added. "Victor, do you really think the Albanian char could be the thief?"

"Well, as you know, I never took to the woman. She had a chip on her shoulder the size of Albania. Quite frankly, I was glad to see the back of her. I worried she would be a bad influence on Guzim if she stuck around; he already feels entitled to the cast-off contents of my wardrobe without getting any ludicrous ideas about making off with our bedding."

"Aye, but do you reckon she's the thief, lad?" my mother pressed.

"Let me give Spiros a quick call and see how the police reacted to Andreas' theory. I expect they felt obliged to at least check Agnesa out since the suspicion was voiced by two such respected members of the village; the priest and the undertaker."

Pulling out my mobile, I excused myself and wandered across to the pebble beach, placing my call in the shade of one of the tamarisk trees lining the beach. After exchanging the usual pleasantries, Spiros reported that the police had indeed taken the suspicions about Agnesa seriously. Planning to interrogate her, the police wasted no time in turning up at the popular coastal taverna where she was employed to wash up. However, it transpired that Agnesa had a cast iron alibi: plenty of witnesses were willing to vouch that she had been skivvying in the kitchen at the time when the two burglaries took place.

"What about her husband, Drin?" I asked Spiros. "Perhaps Agnesa had been casing the joints for him."

"I say the same thing to the police but they say they cannot to go around arresting the Drin on the hunch. There is no the evidence and no one to say they to see the Drin in the Meli." There was no point mentioning that I'd seen Drin in Meli that very morning since his appearance didn't coincide with the time the burglaries had taken place. "We must to continue to be the virulent until the thief is caught."

"Vigilant," I corrected, the word drowned out by the sound of an exhaust backfiring.

Terminating the call, my attention focused on the scruffy old banger with a dented bonnet clunking towards the taverna in a filthy cloud of belched exhaust fumes. The familiar refrain of the

Eurovision classic 'Die for You' blasted at some illegal decibel level, the lyrics completely butchered by the tone-deaf, sing-along driver. It appeared that *Kapetanios* Vasos was sober enough to drive after all.

Chapter 25

Gone with the Urn

Although the driver's door of the scruffy old banger wasn't in my line of vision, I guessed it must be even more mangled and dented than the bonnet as I watched Captain Vasos attempt to exit the vehicle through the driver's side window. With his torso firmly wedged, he struggled to extricate himself from the frame before finally shuffling across to hurl himself out of the passenger door. Since his noisy arrival inevitably attracted the eyebrow raised attention of all the diners in Takis' taverna, I chose to temporarily distance myself from any association with the tatty old car and its embarrassing driver.

Lingering behind the tamarisk tree as Vasos alighted and bounded into the taverna, I reflected that it was moments like this when an addiction to nicotine would have come in handy; a cigarette offering a valid excuse to absent myself.

Even though the beach road created some distance between us, I could still hear Vasos' bombastic greeting as he honed in on Violet Burke. Sweeping my mother off her feet and whirling her around in an enthusiastic embrace, no mean feat considering that she not only towered above him but weighed substantially more, Vasos bellowed his way through his gamut of English words that were utterly nonsensical when blasted out of context: "Beautiful towel…" "I love you…" "Bentos Fray…" "Mucky Trifle…"

Realising Marigold could well be squirming in embarrassment, I reluctantly strolled over to join them. Spotting my approach, Vasos jumped up from his seat next to Violet Burke, yelling "Victor, I love you." His words prompted Dot to hiss to Vi, "Is he one of them gays?"

"Course he's not," Vi retorted before surprising us all by throwing some Greek words together in an ungrammatical fashion to introduce the good Captain to her friend. "*O Dot einai filos mou apo Anglika chippy.*"

BUCKET TO GREECE (VOL.15)

Vasos beamed with delight as Vi introduced Dot as her boyfriend from 'English chippy'. It amused me to note that whilst my Greek friends had an almost universal tendency to chuck superfluous articles into their English sentences, Vi favoured neglecting them completely when she tried out her Greek. Likewise, she stubbornly refused to omit the final S from Greek names when addressing someone directly by name, accusing me of being pedantic to the point of pettiness each time I reminded her to try and stick to the convention.

"*Ennoei ti fili tis apo to magazi me psaria kai patates stin Anglia,*" I interjected, telling Vasos, 'She means her friend from the fish and chip shop in England.'

The pungent aroma seeping from Vasos' sweat stiffened tee-shirt wafted across the table, making me glad that I'd finished my octopus before he joined us. I watched in fascination as the sweat dripping from Vasos' head added a damp patch to his tee-shirt. Scratching around in his armpits in a leisurely fashion, Vasos shouted, "*Victor, dose mou o spotted dick.*"

I presumed that his request that I pass him a spotted dick was just more of his usual nonsense, until Violet Burke piped up with a translation.

"He wants you to pass him a napkin. The daft bugger only went and remembered all that gibberish I taught him in that posh place by the marina. You remember that place where that snooty cow from the book club tried to get us thrown out?"

"Smug Bessie," I confirmed.

"Sex on the beach," Vasos yelled, making me wonder if he had been able to follow Vi's sentence. He had, after all, plied my mother with sex on the beach cocktails in the posh place by the marina. Perchance the old sea dog understood more English than he let on.

"I don't mind if I do," Vi said with a wink.

"Do what, Vi?" Marigold asked in confusion.

"Knock back a sex on the beach or two. What do you say? Are you up for a sneaky cocktail, Dot?"

Please not, I thought to myself, not keen on the prospect of being lumbered with two inebriated pensioners for the rest of the afternoon.

Accepting a paper napkin, Vasos mopped up the sweat from his brow before tossing the now scrumpled and soggy serviette in the breadbasket. I shuddered at his total disregard for contaminating the remaining bread in the basket with his sweat.

Beaming with delight when he spotted the overflowing ashtray in front of Dot and surmising that she was a fellow smoker, Vasos pulled a battered packet of Marlboro out of his shorts. Slipping two cigarettes in his mouth, he lit them both, passing one to Dot. If Vasos had hoped to emulate Paul Henreid's romantic gesture in lighting Bette Davies' cigarette in 'Now Voyageur', he fell miserably short, Dot retrieving the scrumpled napkin from the breadbasket to wipe down the soggy tip of her fag.

Arching his back, Vasos made a song and dance of rubbing it vigorously. Having witnessed him managing to get Violet Burke's considerable bulk practically airborne, I wasn't surprised if his back was giving him gip.

"*Koimithika sto katastroma tou skafous,*" he said, telling us he'd slept on the boat deck, before bizarrely adding, to the great amusement of the other patrons who were blatantly hanging on his every word, that his back could do with a suet dumpling. "*Tha barousa na kano me suet dumpling.*"

"Get him a cushion, Victor," Violet Burke barked. "Fancy him remembering that I taught him a suet dumpling was English for a cushion. He's a right quick learner as well as being a handsome yacht owner."

My mother's comment about Vasos being handsome prompted me to wonder when she'd last had her eyes tested. I supposed one of my filial duties would be accompanying my mother to an eye doctor. It would likely be a time-consuming business. There was no just popping into Specsavers here in Greece; instead, an *ofthalmaitros* conducted an eye test before writing a prescription to take to a shop that sold spectacles. More often than not, there would be a lengthy wait whilst the lenses were delivered from Athens to go in the chosen frames.

Takis wandered over to greet the new arrival, taking Vasos' order for *briam*, a rich medley of roasted Greek vegetables, with a side of chips and *ouzo*. Marigold failed to control her laughter when Vasos, pointing at the fibreglass urn, requested that Takis cut him a piece of the pineapple. *"Boreis na mou kopseis ligo apo afton ton anana."* Confusing fibreglass for fresh fruit made me wonder if Vasos was also in need of an eye test.

I was greatly relieved that Takis was still hovering and thus able to explain that the pineapple was actually an urn containing Dot's late husband's ashes. It would have taxed me to the limit if I had been forced to offer an explanation in faltering Greek. Takis and Vasos engaged in a spirited Greek dialogue about the merits of cremation versus burial, Vasos opining that as an old sea hand, he hoped that when his time was up, someone would chuck him overboard to feed the fish.

"Taki, can you tell Vasos that Dot was hoping to scatter Wilf's ashes in the sea. Perhaps he knows a suitable spot, close to shore, if Dot paddles out," I said.

BUCKET TO GREECE (VOL.15)

As Takis duly posed the question in Greek, Vasos made a grab for the urn, shaking it vigorously.

"Here, don't go shaking my Wilf like that," Dot objected, grabbing the urn back. "He won't know whether he's coming or going."

"Beautiful towel. *Kalo ton filo mou me ti varka*," Vasos replied, saying he would call his friend with a boat. Standing up, he groped around in the pockets of his shorts. Coming up short, he bellowed, *"Pou einai to kinito mou?"* asking where his mobile was.

"To afises sto aftokinito?" I said, asking if he'd left it in his car.

"Isos." Vasos replied 'probably', leaning over the table and planting a smacker on my forehead before loping back to the car. Grabbing a fresh napkin, I gave my forehead a vigorous wipe, wishing I'd had the foresight to bring a bottle of hand sanitiser along.

I was relieved that Vasos' mobile was in the car since it spared us from his making the call from the table; I do abhor the ill-mannered practice of conducting a telephone call amidst company. Alas, my relief was short lived when Vasos returned to our little gathering before placing the call on his now retrieved mobile. Hollering at a volume that sent the taverna cat running for cover with an octopus tentacle grasped between its teeth, Vasos gesticulated wildly as though the person on the other end of the phone was right in front of him. All the while, smoke drifted across the table from the cigarette clamped between his fingers

Despite my knack of usually being able to understand the *Kapetanios* on the telephone, he rabbited away at such a great speed that I was at a bit of a loss when it came to translating, only able to pick out random words: boat, sea, dead, and friend, amongst them. I realised that despite his appalling lack of manners in making his call from the table, Vasos must go out of his way to make a concerted effort to slow down his speech whenever we communicate by phone. It really was thoughtful of him.

"He telephone the friend who is fishing nearby. He tell him to bring the boat so the Dot can go out to sea to throw the ashes," Takis informed us before legging it back to the kitchen to check if he had the necessary alcohol to throw a couple of sex on the beach cocktails together.

Finishing his call, Vasos boomed, "*O Adonis tha einai edo me to varka tou se dekapente lepta.*"

"He says Adonis will be here in his boat in fifteen minutes," I duly translated.

"Has he got one of them yachts too?" Vi asked.

"*Ti eidous varka?*" I said, asking Vasos what

BUCKET TO GREECE (VOL.15)

kind of boat.

"*To psarokaiko*," Vasos replied.

"A fishing boat," I translated.

"Will it hold all five of us," Dot asked.

"*Tha mas choresai kai tous pente?*" I repeated Dot's question in Greek.

Shrugging, Vasos said, "*Tha doume,*" meaning we'll see.

Takis returned bearing alcoholic drinks for Dot and my mother. "Two the screwdriver," he announced, apologising for lacking some of the necessary ingredients for the requested sex on the beach.

Despite Violet Burke's remarkable resolve in resisting the temptation of chips for the best part of a week, she came close to falling off the wagon when the waiter delivered Vasos' *briam* and chips. It was only Marigold's quick reaction in smacking Vi's hand away, that kept my mother on the straight and narrow.

"Here, Victor. What's the Greek word for a screwdriver?" Vi asked.

"*Katsarida,*" I replied.

"*Theleis katsarida?*" Vi asked Vasos if he wanted a screwdriver.

Marigold doubled over in laughter, unable to speak.

"What's so funny?" I snapped, having a feeling

I may have made myself the butt of a joke.

"*Ochi, einai frikti,*" Vasos said in disgust.

"Did he just say they're horrible?" Vi asked. "It's not like Vasos to go turning booze down..."

"He didn't turn down a drink," Marigold interrupted, having finally got her fit of the giggles under control. "You asked Vasos if he wanted a cockroach."

"Never. I only repeated what Victor said," Vi protested.

"Victor confused his cockroaches with his screwdrivers," Marigold said. "The Greek word for a screwdriver is *katsavidi*."

"*Vasos, theleis katsavidi?*" Vi asked, waving her screwdriver under his nose.

"*Nai, pes ston Taki na valei ena ouzo.*" Vasos replied in the affirmative, saying, 'Tell Takis to put an ouzo in it.'

"*Den nomizo oti prepei na anakateveis ouzo kai votka,*" I said, telling Vasos that I didn't think he should mix *ouzo* and vodka.

Five minutes later, a small fishing boat drifted close to the shore and Vasos announced, 'Adonis is here.' "*O Antonis einai edo.*"

The five of us duly trooped across the beach. Cradling the urn closely to her bosom, Dot addressed the ashes of her late husband, Wilf, through the fibreglass. "I'm going to find you a nice bit of sea to spend the rest of your days in. You'll get plenty of peace and quiet in the water. I remember how you never could abide noise, Wilf, so it should suit you right nicely."

"Here, I recognise that fella in the boat. He's the chap I was dancing with at Marigold's vow renewal do." Vi's voice was giddy with excitement.

"Let's hope his feet have recovered from the experience," I quipped.

"How many of us can he take in his boat?" Vi asked. "I don't fancy it capsizing under our weight."

"*Posa atoma sti varka*?" I asked Vasos how many people could go in the boat.

"*Kanenas.*" Vasos' reply of 'none' confused me. Surely his friend didn't expect Dot to hand over Wilf's ashes for Adonis to dispose of, excluding her from the moment.

Vasos patiently explained to me in laboriously slow Greek, that as a professional fisherman, Adonis wasn't allowed to take anyone in his boat. Any breach of the law risked exposing Adonis to an eye-watering fine. However, if we all kept a beady eye out for the sea police turning up, Adonis was prepared to risk taking Dot in his boat as long as she kept her head well down.

As I translated this for the benefit of Dot and Vi,

both women expressed their thanks for Adonis' kind gesture.

"You'll be all right on your own, lass?" Vi checked.

"I'll be all right, Vi. I've got my Wilf with me," Dot assured her.

"Well, you have until you go and scatter him," Vi reminded her.

"But Wilf will be a sight happier in the Greek sea than he would be being carted round in my handbag. He was forever complaining about the amount of junk I lugged about in my bag."

Yelling for Adonis to bring the boat a bit closer to shore, Vasos picked Dot up and threw her over his shoulder in a fireman's lift, paddling out until he was level with the boat where he handed Dot over to Adonis.

Vasos re-joined us on the pebble beach, the four of us enthusiastically waving them away until we lost sight of the boat as it skirted a bight in the coastline.

"I reckon Dot will be safe enough with that Adonis fella. He was a right proper gent at that vow renewal do; he didn't go in for any of that funny business. Still, 'appen we'd better wait here until they get back," Vi said, reminding us that Dot couldn't swim. "There's nowt of her. If a wave knocks her off her feet as she paddles back in, she could end up joining her Wilf."

Despite the sea being totally calm, we acceded to Vi's request, Vasos keeping his binoculars trained on the water on the off-chance that the sea police might turn up out of nowhere.

Chapter 26

Caught Red-Handed

After finally disposing of Wilf, Dot was a tad teary on the drive back to Meli. Between snuffles, she explained, "I'd got that used to carting Wilf around in my handbag, I feel a bit bereft now that he's gone."

"'Appen you should have had him buried, lass. You could have taken solace in visiting his grave."

"Aye, but Wilf was adamant that he didn't want to spend his final years in an underground coffin. He couldn't abide the thought of maggots and beetles feasting on his rotting flesh. 'Appen he'll be happy with that bit of sea as his final resting place; it was a right lovely spot, dead picturesque. My Wilf always had a hankering to holiday in Greece. He'd be right chuffed knowing he went and made it over here, in a manner of speaking."

"Aye, it'll be like he's on a permanent Greek holiday," Vi said.

Marigold whispered to me that she considered Dot was being very stoic in the circumstances. My wife had grown quite fond of Dot in the short time that she'd been with us.

"Did you find scattering Wilf's ashes a moving experience, Dot?" Marigold asked solicitously.

Dot's response completely floored us. "I couldn't bring myself to scatter him in the end…"

"You mean he's still in your handbag?" Vi blurted.

"No, he's in the water, all right. But I got to thinking how cold the sea might get at night, so, in the end, I chucked him over the side of the boat, urn and all. My Wilf never could abide taking a cold bath, the water had to be that steaming that he couldn't see to shave in the bathroom mirror."

"So, his ashes are still inside the urn?" I clarified.

"Aye, that's right. At least he won't end up as fish food. But, oh my, it was that lovely a spot where I dropped him in."

As we pulled up in Meli, Marigold asked if she could tempt anyone with a cuppa in the garden.

"Aye, lass. That would be right grand," Dot enthused.

"Victor, pop upstairs and put the kettle on," Marigold ordered.

"And don't be brewing any of that Greek muck with twigs in it, Son," my mother barked. "We'll be wanting proper PG Tips."

When I returned to the garden laden down with the tea tray, the ladies were comfortably settled in deckchairs, sunning themselves and laughing uproariously.

"Would you like to fill me in on the joke?" I asked, playing mother by pouring the tea.

"Marigold's come up with a right belting idea for this evening," Vi said. "Belting it is. I never knew the lass had it in her."

"Oh, yes." My words lacking any trace of enthusiasm, I sent a warning look in Marigold's direction. I had rather hoped that Dot would take herself off to the *apothiki* with Vi for the evening, leaving me to enjoy some alone time with my wife. Since I was rostered on the next morning to guide a coachload of tourists to Vathia, I needed an early night. Leading my charges around the village of old stone tower houses always equated to a long day. Since the Vathia trip inevitably attracted a couple of clued-up history buffs, I would need my wits about me, the tourists invariably bombarding me with hundreds of questions about the history of the area.

"I'm going to call the girls and see if they fancy joining us for one of my girls' nights in. I'm hoping to round up Doreen, Cynthia, Sherry and Moira," Marigold said, her eyes sparkling mischievously. "Vi, do you think I should include Edna? I know you're not keen."

"'Appen she's likely to be a damp squib like usual, but in the circumstances, the more the merrier. Give Sampaguita a bell too. I'm that fond of the lass," Vi said. "And don't forget to ask Yiota. She's sure to be up for it."

The last thing I wanted was a bevy of inebriated women littering my home. I decided I must intervene in a timely manner and attempt to scupper Marigold's plans before they took hold.

"Really, Marigold. I consider it a tad insensitive of you to be arranging a social gathering, considering that Dot has only just scattered Wilf, so to speak. I'm sure she just wants to relax quietly this evening without any fuss." Admittedly I was pulling a Guzim by attempting to pull on my wife's heartstrings.

"Nay, lad, it's just what the doctor ordered. It'll be right grand to see the looks on them fellas' faces," Dot chortled.

"Fellas? You're inviting men to your girls' night in? You might have consulted me first, Marigold," I complained, thinking her plans were beginning to resemble a party. Considering she had already lumbered me with cooking for the expat dinner party later this week, it really was most inconsiderate of my wife to be hosting an impromptu jamboree.

"If you'd let me finish before getting on your high horse," Marigold said in a sniffy tone. "I'm organising one of my girls' nights in, but we're going to go out for it."

"Isn't that a contradiction in terms?"

"While you were making the tea, we were talking about the way that the men in the village have shown their true colours of late; I never knew they could be such a sexist lot. For starters, the newly opened *kafenio* is going out of its way to discourage female customers. That's sexual discrimination."

"'Appen it's illegal," Vi butted in.

"And then there's the way that Spiros deliberately excluded all the women from the village meeting this morning as though we didn't have the right to be kept abreast about what's going on under our own noses. So, we've decided to gate-crash the *kafenio* this evening and show the men in this village that we've no intention of staying put indoors like meek little housewives," Marigold announced.

"No one in their right mind could ever accuse you ladies of being meek," I fired back.

"If I can round up enough of the girls, the men won't dare to challenge our presence in their precious male-only zone." Marigold's tone oozed self-righteous defiance.

"So, there's no question of your friends partying here," I confirmed.

"Of course not, darling. I thought that you'd appreciate some peace and quiet this evening since you have such an early start tomorrow. I know you need to be full of beans for your Vathia trip."

Really, Marigold could be the most thoughtful of wives at times. I counted my lucky stars yet again for our fortuitous meeting in the bucket aisle of B&Q all those years ago.

"You haven't included any of your Greek girl friends in your plans," I pointed out.

"Well, I would have but I don't want to have to spend the evening translating. My head is like a sieve after a couple of drinks and I forget all my Greek. Athena's away, Sofia's bladder rules her out since the place has no suitable toilet, and I very much doubt that Tina would be up for a night out in a rival establishment," Marigold said.

"We're going to get Yiota to come along and

she's Greek," Vi reminded me.

"And Yiota's English is so good that I won't be pressed to translate," Marigold said in relief.

"Marigold, do make sure you keep your distance from that oily, Christos," I advised. "Given the chance, he'll be all over you like a bad rash."

"Don't you worry, lad. I'll stick right by your Marigold. If that creep starts getting all mushy or trying anything on with the lass, he'll have me to answer to," Vi assured me. "I've heard tell that Christos has a weakness for redheads but he's never tried owt on with me."

"Perhaps his weakness doesn't extend to older woman," Marigold diplomatically suggested.

"I'll have you know I'm nowt but a spring chicken. I can still pass for the right side of sixty in the right light."

"That would be in the dark, then," I teased.

"Aye, appen." My mother nudged me indulgently in the ribs. "These pins of mine have gone and let me down now that they finish in swollen lumps. Back in the war, I was always known for my shapely pins."

"It's a pity we didn't persuade your old mucker, Vasos, to come back with us now that we're planning a wild night out," Dot said.

"Even in the dark, Vasos couldn't pass for one of the girls," I said, wondering just how wild of an evening they planned to make of it.

Downing her cuppa, Marigold announced she would head indoors to start phoning around the girls. Closing my eyes, I tuned out as Dot and Vi chatted between themselves, putting the world to rights. With the subtle scent of bougainvillea blooms pervading the garden and the sun warm on my face, I could feel myself dozing off to the soothing cluck of chickens, the clink of tea cups and inane snippets of chatter. Anyone would think that Vi and Dot were obsessed with that Billings' lot, 'Coronation Street', and the local paucity of a nice bit of deep-fried haddock served with proper mushy peas.

The next thing I knew, I was rudely awoken by a piercing scream, hotly followed by anguished cries for help. *"Voitheia. Voitheia."*

Leaping out of my deck chair, I realised the cries were emanating from the upstairs of Kyria Maria's house next door. The calls for help were quickly followed by the sound of Maria screeching, *"Stamata klefti,"* meaning 'Stop thief.'

From my vantage point, I had a bird's eye view as a blurry figure hurled himself out of Maria's upstairs bedroom window. My neighbour screeched, *"Stamata klefti,"* again, followed by, *"Min ton afiseis na xefygei,"* meaning 'Don't let him get away.'

Before I could even think of reacting, Guzim

sprinted past me and vaulted over the garden wall, throwing himself on the figure that had landed in Maria's garden, poised to escape. Struggling to hold onto the thief, Guzim made a grab for his legs, dragging him to the ground. The two men rolled around in Maria's vegetable patch as though engaged in a common brawl.

"Don't just stand there like a big girl's blouse, Victor. You need to get stuck in," Violet Burke yelled at me. "Get over the wall and give Guzim a hand to restrain that tea leaf. Guzim's too puny to keep the fella overpowered on his own."

"You expect me to scale that wall?" I retorted.

"Oh, for goodness' sake. Call yourself a man, lad. Hop to it. Me and Dot can give you a hand over," my mother instructed. Dragging me by the arm, she pulled me over to the wall where she and Dot bent over, putting their hands together to form a makeshift step.

"You'll do yourselves an injury," I tutted, grabbing and upending one of Marigold's large ceramic plant pots.

Reluctantly stepping onto the pot, I grasped the top of the wall and hoisted myself up. Holding on tight with my legs dangling a good inch above the ground, afforded me a bird's eye view of Guzim struggling to cling onto the thief's trousers as said thief desperately tried to escape Guzim's clutches.

"Now, just haul yourself over, lad," Vi barked.

"I could do myself an injury if I land…"

"Stop your mithering," Vi grumbled, giving me an almighty push from behind that resulted in my landing in an undignified heap in Kyria Maria's garden. "Now, get up and help Guzim to overpower the fella."

Spotting help was at hand in my person seemed to give Guzim a second wind. With the thief now upright and poised to leg it, Guzim yanked hard on the fellow's trousers, causing the miscreant to lose his footing. With the thief sprawled face down on the ground, I took the initiative and sat on him whilst Guzim tried to catch his breath. As the thief bucked beneath me in an effort to break free, Kyria Maria dashed into the garden and started laying into the intruder with a soup ladle, walloping him indiscriminately.

"*Tha xefygei. Katse pano tou, Maria,*" Violet Burke yelled over the wall. I was gobsmacked to say the least to hear my mother saying in Greek, 'He's going to get away. Sit on him, Maria."

Maria jumped to it, sitting on the fellow's legs; I doubted it would make much difference since Maria is so tiny that she probably weighs no more than a feather. The intruder continued to wriggle like a man possessed until Guzim, having recovered his breath, yanked the chap's head up by his hair and got a good look at his face.

"*Einai o Drin.*" In a shocked tone, Guzim announced it was Drin. Spitting in the intruder's face, Guzim denounced Drin as a dirty thief, "*Vromiko klefti.*"

"I heard screaming. What on earth's going on?" Marigold asked, panting from her dash down to the garden.

"Drin has been exposed as the thief," I said.

"Drin?" Frowning in concentration, Marigold tried to place the name.

"The drunkard, workshy lout that is married to the Albanian cleaning woman, Agnesa," I reminded my wife. "He broke into Maria's house and then tried to escape by jumping out of an upstairs window. Luckily, Guzim reacted at the speed of light and vaulted over the garden wall and caught Drin red-handed."

"Should I call the police?" Marigold called out.

"Call Spiros and Barry and tell them to get over here sharpish," I said, not at all confident that Marigold's Greek would be up to the job of communicating the urgency of the situation to the police over the phone.

"Here, Victor. Catch hold of this and tie the thieving toerag up until the police get here," Vi instructed, lobbing our washing line over the wall. "I'll come over and give you a hand to subdue him."

"You'll do no such thing," I responded. "You'll do yourself an injury climbing over the wall."

Whilst Kyria Maria and I continued to prevent Drin from escaping by sitting on him, Maria ranted that she had returned from picking *horta* in the fields to discover the thieving rascal rifling through her bedroom drawers. She told me that when she screamed in shock, Drin ran away like a coward and hurled himself out of the window. Maria was full of contempt for the intruder, asking how stupid he must be to smash a window to get in when she always left the door unlocked.

As Maria spoke, she gave Drin another few clouts with the soup ladle. Whilst I don't generally condone violence in any form, I can't say that I blamed her. The thieving Drin had proved himself to be a complete half-wit of a bungling burglar, going around the village unnecessarily breaking windows when two of his targets had left their doors unlocked. Moreover, he could have scared the life out of my elderly neighbour. Drin was lucky that Kyria Maria was made of stern stuff; she could well have dropped down dead from the shock of finding the Albanian oaf in her bedroom.

As Maria recounted her ordeal, Guzim gnawed through my washing line, no easy feat considering he is practically toothless. Using one half of the washing line, Guzim tied Drin's hands behind his back, using the other half to secure his legs.

"*Guzim, eisai iroas. An den eiches piasei ton klefti, tha eiche xefygei,*" Maria said.

"What's Maria saying?" Vi demanded.

"She said that Guzim is a hero. If he hadn't acted so quickly to catch hold of the thief, he'd have got away."

"*Den itan tipota,*" Guzim replied, modestly professing 'it was nothing.'

By the time the local police, summoned by Spiros, turned up, word of the thief being caught red-handed had spread around the village like wild fire. Maria's garden was crowded with locals hailing Guzim as a hero. Ironically, as the police hauled Drin to his feet to cart him off, it transpired that his jump from the upstairs balcony had resulted in a broken ankle; even if he had managed to make his escape, it was doubtful that he'd have managed to hobble very far.

I delighted in watching Apostolos, the local barber, eat humble pie, having insinuated only that morning that Guzim was the thief by dint of him being an outsider. The local men hoisted Guzim on their shoulders and carried him around on high. They applauded his quick action in hurling himself over the garden wall and tackling the burglar with no thought at all for his own safety. All the snide comments that the villagers had uttered over the years, pointedly excluding Guzim from being accepted as one of the locals and making him feel like an outsider, went out of the window with the realisation that Guzim had selflessly floored one of his Albanian compatriots in his determination to rush to Maria's aid.

"*Voitheia kai o Victor.*" Guzim modestly insisted that I had helped too.

"*Anoisies. O Drin tha itan me ton anemo an ochi i grigori apantisi sou,*" I replied,

"What did you say, Victor?" Vi demanded.

I told Guzim, "Nonsense. Drin would have been gone with the wind if not for his quick response."

"You're not wrong there, lad," Vi agreed. "Even Maria's tortoise could have made it over that wall quicker than you did."

Papas Andreas promised Guzim that he would not forget his bravery, whilst Kyria Maria told Guzim that she would knock up a batch of macaroni and meatballs for him. I had to laugh when my Albanian quietly confided to me that he'd rather have one of my tasty curries.

Chapter 27

Going Out for a Girls' Night In

Marigold had arranged for the 'girls' to all meet up at the Bucket house before heading over to the *kafenio* en masse, parroting the platitude about strength in numbers and correctly surmising that none of the women would feel comfortable entering the *kafenio* alone. Having persuaded my wife to herd her friends together in our garden rather than have them cluttering up the grand salon, Marigold allocated me the role of wine waiter, putting me in charge of pouring the plonk.

"Just offer them a glass of wine each before we

set off," Marigold directed. "We'll need a spot of Dutch courage to face down the men in their male-only territory. Although I very much doubt that they're going to extend a warm welcome, we're determined to hold our ground."

Even though Marigold had extended the invitation at short notice, there wasn't a single no-show, all of her friends turning up to support the cause as though they had belatedly discovered the women's lib movement. I hoped that they didn't get so carried away that they started burning their bras and cultivating armpit hair, or stopped shaving their legs. An unwanted image of Violet Burke's hairy legs flashed into my mind, reminding me that my mother had already dispensed with her razor.

Retrieving another couple of bottles of Lidl's finest wine from the fridge, I squared my shoulders and returned to the fray down below. I must admit to finding it a tad unnerving to be the only man amongst a group of hyped-up women; it rather put me in mind of entering a lion's den. Encouraged by Marigold and Violet Burke, the women were vehemently vocalising their disdain for the dyed-in-the-wool misogynists that populated the village.

"Present company excepted, darling," Marigold cooed as I refilled her glass. So much for her promise it would be just the one glass of wine before the off; the group was already on the verge of collective tipsiness.

Wandering over towards the chickens, I surveyed the sea of brightly clothed women from a safe distance. Flitting about the garden with the grace of a social butterfly, Marigold was the perfect hostess, dressed for the part in one of her posh Marks and Sparks' floral frocks. Although the fuchsia roses on her dress ought to have clashed with her Titian locks, Marigold carried off the look with chic panache. Honing in to lend Sherry an arm as her jolly-hockey-sticks pal tripped across the garden in unsuitable heels, Marigold saved her friend from coming a cropper and falling flat on her face when Sherry's heel caught in the hem of her flowing caftan.

Violet Burke and her sidekick, Dot, had pulled out all the stops for an evening out. In spite of the heat, they had dressed to the nines in some itchy looking tweed; their hair backcombed into immovable bird's nests, the slap on their faces applied with a trowel. They appeared to be under the delusion that gate-crashing the *kafenio* was akin to making a grand entrance to some kind of forbidden, even exotic, nightclub. Considering my mother slops her mop around in the *kafenio* on a daily basis, I found it hard to fathom she would think the place would morph into a sophisticated hive of excitement as soon as the sun went down.

BUCKET TO GREECE (VOL.15)

"Cooee, Victor. Cynthia needs a top up," Marigold trilled, beckoning me over to join them. I wasn't thrilled at the prospect of the group lingering to down more of my wine; the longer they hung about in my garden, the less time I would have to devote to my date with John Grisham. My plans for the evening involved nothing more taxing than finishing the gripping legal thriller. Nevertheless, I slapped a smile on my face and ambled over to the group huddled around my wife.

With a noticeable bounce to her glossy hair, Cynthia looked more relaxed than usual. Moira Strange had brought the primped and preened Goldendoodle along, the dog once again reeking of cheap perfume.

"Just in case all those men make us feel a bit uneasy, it will be comforting to know we have Waffles with us as a protective guard dog," Moira said.

"'Appen that horrible cat of Cynthia's would make for a better guard dog than that soppy mutt of yours," Vi opined, earning herself a haughty glare from my sister-in-law. "That cat's that vicious. It's always got something to hiss about."

"Oh, I know," Moira agreed, twisting the pearl earrings in her perfect lobes. "Waffles has been terrified of Cynthia's cat ever since Kouneli ambushed him at Doreen's dinner party. He comes over all flatulent with fright at just a whiff of Cynthia's cat."

"My Tickles hides under the bed if it spots Cynthia's cat. The dreadful creature tries to mate with my cat even though Tickles' is a tom." I tried not to stare as Doreen ran her fingers through her perm as she spoke, unwittingly exposing the bald spot that I was responsible for.

"Kouneli didn't earn its reputation as the village purrvert for nothing," I quipped.

"You're certainly fond of repeating that lame joke, Victor. How would you like it if I went round insulting your precious pets?" Cynthia demanded, pouting her lips.

"Feel free," I invited. "I'm used to it. Marigold never has a good word to say about my chickens."

"'Appen she would if you'd relent and let her bung one of them in the oven," Vi snorted.

"At least you don't have to contend with people wanting to cook your pet, Cynthia," I pointed out. "I imagine that vile cat of yours would be most unpalatable."

"You have the most warped sense of humour, Victor Bucket," Cynthia observed snappily. "I do hope you'll try to keep it under control when you babysit Anastasia. She's already beginning to come out with the strangest things. I don't think it's usual for a toddler to be able to name so many different types of bacteria. I'm certain she picked it up from you."

"There's nowt wrong with the bairn being up on her germs," Vi said in my defence.

"Oh, good grief. What on earth is Kyria Maria doing here?" Marigold asked in annoyance as our elderly neighbour put in an appearance, her customary black widow's weeds making her stand out like a sore thumb amongst the rainbow of colours the other women were modelling.

"I invited her to join you all," I admitted. "She had a dreadful shock this afternoon and I don't think it's hit her yet. I thought she'd appreciate the solidarity of some female company. After all, you've all spent the last half-hour banging on about the sisterhood."

"You might have consulted me first, Victor. I'll be stuck with translating for Maria all evening," Marigold grumbled.

"I think it's jolly thoughtful of you, Victor, to invite that poor old lady from next door. Such a horrid ordeal she went through," Sherry brayed, exposing her horsey teeth. "I couldn't begin to imagine the shock of coming home to discover a strange man in my bedroom."

"'Appen you'd think all your Sundays had come at once," Vi cackled. "Anyhow, Maria won't be any bother. She can stick close to me and Dot.

She's a darn sight more fun than that Edna. Speaking of Edna, it looks like Sampaguita and Yiota need rescuing from her. She's gone and attached herself like a leech," Vi said before linking her arm in Dot's and plodding off to greet our Greek neighbour.

Catching Sampaguita's eye, I spotted the polite smile frozen on her face. As I approached, I noticed her eyes were glazing over as Edna droned on, offering a descriptive account of her lodger's rash.

"I just need to borrow Sampaguita," I interrupted, taking the Filipino woman's arm and steering her away.

"Thank you for rescuing me, Victor," she said. "Edna never fails to patronise me by referring to me as foreign."

"I put it down to her colonial mindset and all those years the Hancocks' spent in Africa. How are you getting on with Haralambos?" I asked, recalling how Spiros had told me the gouty old fellow she cared for had been making her life a misery.

"I don't like to speak ill of the ill, but Haralambos is the nasty old man. Just this morning, he lost his temper and threw his chamber pot at his daughter, Ioanna. She has a terrible black eye."

"I really think you should consider jacking it in. He doesn't deserve your care," I said bluntly.

BUCKET TO GREECE (VOL.15)

"Spiros says the same but I cannot to leave Ioanna to cope on her own," Sampaguita insisted.

"I thought Spiros was going to have a word with Giannis and let him know how badly his grandfather is treating Ioanna," I said.

"Spiros had the funeral...when he found the time, he could not find Giannis."

"I saw him tending his bee boxes this morning."

Spotting Yiota approaching, we changed the subject. It would be most insensitive if we were the ones to enlighten her that her boyfriend's grandfather was treating Giannis' mother like a punch bag. Yiota was quietly fired up about all the girls descending on the *kafenio*. She had already fought to be treated to the same respect as the men, winning over their objections to her joining the volunteer fire brigade. She had then demonstrated her worth by becoming the hero of the hour when she was the one to rescue a donkey in the face of grave danger.

"Cooee, Victor," Marigold summoned me again. If she seriously expected me to uncork another bottle, I would make a point of serving warm plonk.

Joining my wife, she said, "Some of the girls are beginning to complain about the stench of your chickens so I think it's about time we made a move. Can you call everyone to attention, darling?"

"Couldn't you just have done that yourself," I replied peevishly. The irony of my wife jumping on the women's lib bandwagon and then expecting the man of the house to herd her female guests together, clearly eluded Marigold.

"I'll do it," Vi said. "Here, everyone get your backsides over here. Marigold has summat to say."

With everyone gathered together, Marigold launched into her spiel.

"Now, ladies, when we get to the *kafenio*, we must all stick together and not allow the men to intimidate us. We must refuse to budge, no matter how many dirty looks we're on the receiving end of from the regular male clientele."

Gauging the reaction of the group of women, almost to a tittle, most of them seemed determined to vent their annoyance that the *kafenio* brothers were less than welcoming to the fairer sex. Even Edna argued that it was wrong for the men to have a women-free zone to go to. I suspected her opinion was nothing more than a selfish worry that Milton may start frequenting the *kafenio* for morning coffee, unable to resist the temptation of watching Violet Burke slopping her mop around. By effectively being barred, Edna would be unable to keep an eye on the straying eyes of her husband.

"I don't think my Manolis *mou* is going to be happy when we all turn up," Doreen worried.

BUCKET TO GREECE (VOL.15)

Unconsciously rubbing her bald spot, she bleated, "I just hope he realises it was all Marigold's doing and I'm just going along to support my friend."

"Tell me you didn't go blabbing with that big mouth of yours to that boyfriend of yours," Vi snapped. "We're after putting the wind up them fellas by taking them by surprise."

"I didn't say a word. Marigold swore me to secrecy. But being deceitful and keeping things from my Manolis *mou* doesn't sit well with me."

"I thought you'd be used to a bit of deception seeing that you're playing around behind the back of that dopey husband of yours," Vi said.

"I am not playing around behind Norman's back. We are estranged, as well you know," Doreen retorted.

"I thought you'd be the first to appreciate a bit of female solidarity, Doreen," Marigold said. "You always say that you find it unnerving when you pop into the *kafenio* to see Manolis and you're the only woman in there."

"That's true. Some of the customers glare at me as though I've no business being there," Doreen admitted.

"*Boroume apla na pame?*" Kyria Maria piped up impatiently.

"What's she saying?" Sherry asked.

"She said, 'Can we just go?'" Marigold translated.

"Yes, indeed, let's get over there. Now, I do hope you all remembered to use the loo. Victor tells me that the one in the *kafenio* lacks running water."

"Not to mention a door," I muttered under my breath. Perish the thought that I would say it aloud and risk a mass stampede of women desperate to use the Bucket bathroom.

Chapter 28

The Public Health Inspector

I was so engrossed in my gripping legal thriller that I was tempted to ignore the telephone ringing, only the dogged persistence of the caller refusing to hang up persuading me to abandon my book.

"Victor, you'll never guess," Marigold trilled down the phone line. "This is going to make your year. I doubt you'll be able to contain your excitement..."

Clueless what Marigold was wittering on about, I interrupted her to express the hope that she hadn't been mixing her drinks.

"Victor, will you just listen for once? A public health inspector has just turned up in the *kafenio* and is preparing to inspect the place…"

The portentous impact of Marigold's words momentarily eluded me, since I was floored by the oddity of an inspection taking place during the evening. On reflection, I reasoned that dropping in at such an unexpected hour would give the health inspector the element of surprise.

"Are you listening, Victor? There's a health inspector here. I expected you to be whooping with excitement at the very least."

"Of course, I'm listening, you just took me completely by surprise. I was beginning to think public health inspectors didn't exist in Greece, or if they did, that they never ventured out to the sticks." As I spoke, I was gripped by a sudden rush of euphoric excitement. This could be my golden opportunity to witness a Greek public health inspector in action. Perchance, we could even compare notes and swap tales.

"You must come over at once, darling. I'm sure the pair of you will bond over tales of grubby kitchens and disgustingly curdled sauces contaminated with all manner of unspeakable things." It appeared from her words that Marigold must have been listening to me after all; she had some of my health inspecting jargon down pat.

BUCKET TO GREECE (VOL.15)

"I must say that I'm intrigued to see him in action," I enthused.

"So, you'll come over now. We're having a grand time winding the local men up and watching Manolis running around like a headless chicken. He's in a complete panic about the health inspector turning up on the one day your mother hasn't been in to clean…"

"Missing the odd slop with my mother's mop is the least of his worries," I said. "Christos and Manolis are flagrantly breaching any number of the Food Standard Agency's regulations by failing to install a toilet with running water and…"

"Are you coming over or not?" Marigold pressed impatiently, already familiar with my gripes about the brothers' lack of adherence to hygiene rules.

"I most certainly am," I promised. "I'll just grab my hairnet and my white coat."

No sooner had I hung up the telephone than it rang again.

"Victor, you must come to the *kafenio* at once. It is most urgent," the caller begged, the twang of a Texan accent identifying him as Manolis. "I need your help. A health inspector has just rolled up to conduct an inspection…"

"I already know," I told him.

"You already know," Manolis spluttered.

Anger reverberated in his tone when he continued speaking. "I knew that someone must have tipped him off but I never thought it would be you. I thought we were friends, Victor...how could you do this to me?"

"Don't start throwing unfounded accusations around, Manoli. I most certainly did not tip off any public health inspector; I wouldn't even have the first clue of how to get hold of one in Greece. The only reason that I know he's there is because Marigold just called to tell me."

"What? Oh, if I am wrong, I am sorry." The sound of Manolis slapping his head in frustration echoed down the phone line. Adopting a grovelling tone, Manolis changed his tune. "I am sorry that I unjustly accuse you, Victor. I should have to know you would not go behind my back and alert the authorities. We are brothers, after all..."

"Brothers..." I spluttered. I had only recently discovered three half-brothers crawling out of the woodwork, having been clueless to their existence for most of my life. The last thing I wanted was Manolis claiming to be another brother. I reserved that honorary title for my brother-in-law.

"Marigold and Doreen are the good friends. That makes us the brothers," Manolis insisted.

"It most certainly doesn't."

"But if I marry Doreen, she will want Marigold

to be her *koumbara*," Manolis said, referencing a role that was just a tad meatier than the run of the mill matron of honour. Although a *koumbara* did indeed fill that role, she was also expected to be the godmother of any future children the newlyweds may produce. Considering that Doreen was well past the age of popping out any offspring, I was more than happy to dismiss Manolis' brotherly claim out of hand.

"Doreen is still married to Norman," I reminded him.

Brushing aside Doreen's marital status, Manolis continued to grovel. "Victor, you must forgive my outburst. It must be Tina from the shop that tipped the health inspector off. The woman is consumed with anger about our opening a rival shop. Say you forgive me for thinking you could betray me. I am sorry."

"Apology accepted." Just because I responded graciously didn't mean I hadn't caught the hint of desperation in Manolis' voice. It was easy to surmise that he was after something and I had a pretty good idea what it was. Right on cue, Manolis launched into a plea.

"Please come over at once, Victor. You will know how to communicate properly with the health inspector. You can talk to him and explain that you and I have already discussed making the toilet and the unnecessary extra kitchen sink. You can tell him you know we have plans to put things right, hygiene wise…"

"Intending to fix your gross hygiene violations is not the same as actually doing it. If you recall, I advised you that you were operating on dodgy grounds by not providing a flushable toilet with a door for your customers. I warned you about ensuring there was adequate additional sanitation in the kitchen…"

"But you will know how to smooth things over. Please come, Victor, I beg you."

"I'm on my way," I told him, neglecting to mention I had no intention of interceding on his behalf in my professional capacity. I recalled that I had distinctly warned him that he was skating on thin ice by flagrantly breaching any number of hygiene edicts. Since he had chosen to chance it, he couldn't expect me to try and bail him out by sweet talking the civil servant currently prowling around his premises. Professional honour dictated that I was firmly on the side of the unknown health inspector.

Parking the Punto outside the *kafenio*, I adjusted my hairnet and smoothed my white coat. About to alight from the car, my mobile rang. I was certainly in popular demand this evening.

Wasting no time on pleasantries, Nikos explained

why he was calling. I could sense the urgency in the usually unflappable taverna owner's words. "Victor, I have just to hear that the public health inspector is in the village. He could to turn up here any the minute. I not to want any the trouble."

"He's at the *kafenio now*," I confirmed. It was no real surprise to hear that word of the inspector's presence in the village was already general knowledge. I was accustomed to the Greek practice of one business urgently alerting another whenever a tax inspector was on the prowl: it wasn't a leap to suppose the grapevine operated in the same way when a public health inspector arrived in town. It never ceased to amaze me that the only time I received a printed receipt for a coffee was when a tax inspector was known to be doing his rounds.

"You think he will to inspect the taverna?" Nikos asked.

"I suppose since he's already in the village, he may well make an impromptu visit to the taverna. I certainly always made a point of dropping in on a place unannounced if I happened to be inspecting other premises in the vicinity. One is always more likely to uncover something a business would prefer to sweep under the carpet if one drops in unexpectedly."

"You think I should to close the door now and turn out the light?" Nikos asked.

"I wouldn't," I advised. "If he's already aware that you are open, shutting up shop may well make him speculate that you have something to hide. It would certainly rouse my suspicions if I was in his shoes."

"Can you to tell the Violet Burke to come immediately to clean? Today of all the day, the Violet take the day off to go gadding out on a yacht." I couldn't help but chuckle at Nikos' adoption of gadding. There was no doubt that my mother's influence was rubbing off on his English vocabulary. "The Dina think this morning about cleaning but decide to leave it; she say, the Violet will come tomorrow. If the health inspector to find any the dirt, he will to close the taverna down. How will the villagers manage to eat if we to closed?"

To be fair to Nikos, ever since he had taken my mother on as a char, the taverna has been nothing short of exceptionally clean. Violet Burke has such exacting hygiene standards that once she committed to the job, she refused to allow Nikos and Dina to wallow in their usual spit and sawdust a day longer. I supposed it was sod's law that the health inspector may well spring a surprise visit on Nikos on the one day my mother had taken off. With Nikos and Dina's slapdash standards, it was easy to imagine the grease and grime piling up quickly during Violet Burke's absence.

Nikos let out an anguished gasp. "You must to tell the Violet to clean the outside bread oven too. If the inspector to close it, the village will have no bread."

"Well, they could always pick up a loaf at the village shop," I joshed. "Sorry, Niko, I was just being facetious. I will have a word with my mother now. She's in the *kafenio* with Marigold and a few of the girls. Knowing how fond she is of you and Dina, I think I can promise you that she'll come right over. In fact, you'll probably get two chars for the price of one since I'm sure that Dot will come along to lend a hand."

"Bless you, Victor." I visualised Nikos making the sign of the cross with his barbecue tongs.

"Look, Niko, I'll try my best to stall the health inspector and keep him talking until Violet and Dot can get your place gleaming like a new pin," I promised. The last thing I wanted was an over enthusiastic health inspector closing my favourite taverna down. I'd already promised Marigold that I would take her to the taverna for dinner when I got back from Vathia the next day. I would hate to disappoint her.

"You say the Violet Burke is in the *kafenio* now?"

"She is indeed," I confirmed.

"I come now on the *mothopodilato* to fetch the

Violet and Dot. There is no time to be waste," Nikos said.

"In the meantime, tell Dina to bung some bleach down the lav," I advised.

Entering the *kafenio*, I impatiently swatted an anxious Christos aside as I tried to locate my mother in the crowded room. Spotting her engaged in a stand-up row with the communistic pensioner, Kyrios Stavropoulos, I hurried to her side, amazed that two people could conduct an argument when neither one understood the other's language to any degree.

Taking my mother's arm, I led her outside, gesturing for Dot to join us. I explained that Nikos and Dina were very worried that the health inspector may drop in after inspecting the *kafenio* and perchance uncover some dirt since Vi hadn't been in to do her usual cleaning session that day.

"'Aye, appen they're right to be fussing. Much as I like the pair of them, neither of them are what you'd call up on their hygiene. Dina, bless her, she's not one for cleaning up after herself. Nikos thinks nowt about letting mucky grease pile up on his grill."

"Vi's always saying how she has to scrape manky dead flies up off Nikos' grill 'cos he never bothers to give the thing a proper scrubbing down," Dot added.

BUCKET TO GREECE (VOL.15)

"So, the two of you don't mind popping over there now? Nikos is on his way over to give you a ride."

Right on cue, Nikos raced up on his moped. Sensing Nikos' urgency to be off, Dot hopped right on but Violet Burke's skirt didn't have enough give to allow her to get her leg over, forcing her to wedge herself on in side-saddle style between Nikos and Dot. I reflected that despite the two women being a bit glammed up to be scrubbing the taverna, neither of them wasted a second getting all precious about it. I had to admire the pair of them for putting hygiene considerations before anything else.

Returning to the *kafenio*, I swerved joining the ladies or the grumpy old men who were glaring at them as though they were some alien species. On a mission to find the Greek public health inspector who was nowhere in sight, I buttonholed Christos to ask where I could find him. Instead of answering my question, Christos launched into a vociferous complaint about the *kafenio* being invaded by a bunch of stroppy foreign women demanding equal access to the newly opened local watering hole. Considering Christos thinks of himself as the local Lothario, I would have thought he'd have been in his element surrounded by a gaggle of tipsy women. With the local men threatening to boycott the place unless Christos threw the women out on the street, he was firmly stuck in the unenviable role of piggy-in-the-middle. At least he was too preoccupied to chat up my wife.

Interrupting Christos' complaints, I asked him again where I could find the public health inspector.

"Manolis show him the toilet," Christos said. Unlike his brother, he appeared breezily indifferent to the presence of the health inspector, the war between the sexes apparently of more concern.

Slipping through the *apothiki* into the courtyard, I spotted Manolis in the company of a white coated youngster who still looked wet behind the ears. Sighing in relief that I had turned up as promised, Manolis introduced me.

"Victor, this is the health inspector, Thanasis. He speaks perfect English so you will have no problem communicating. Thanasis, this is Victor Bucket. Before he retired to Greece, he was the most important health inspector in the whole of England." Manolis was certainly laying my credentials on with an exaggerated trowel. "I am lucky that Victor lives locally and has been able to share his wisdom about complying with hygiene regulations."

Clearly, Manolis was trying to butter up Thanasis by implying that he had actually taken a blind bit of notice of my recommendations.

Thanasis was clearly impressed to meet a

fellow public health inspector, albeit retired, especially when it transpired that I had spent more years on the job in my illustrious career than he'd been alive. Thanasis readily admitted that he was newly qualified; having been in the job for less than a year, he was still trying to find his feet. He explained that his remit was to visit outlying tavernas and restaurants that had somehow eluded inspections by dint of being off the beaten track. However, an anonymous tip off that a new *kafenio* had just opened that wasn't up to code with modern food standard regulations, had brought him to Meli. Since Thanasis was not only a bit green but demonstrably nervous, he welcomed me to tag along on his inspection. In turn, I was delighted to accept his invitation.

Taking Thanasis by the arm, Manolis tried to steer him back towards the *kafenio*. Resisting, Thanasis reminded Manolis that he had been just about to show him the toilet facilities before I arrived. Clearly, Manolis' cunning plan to distract the health inspector by introducing him to me hadn't worked. The young public health inspector was determined, come hell or high water, to cross the toilet off his inspection list.

Chapter 29

No Regrets

One look at the disgusting toilet was enough to convince the public health inspector to close down the *kafenio* immediately. Manolis' argument that Thanasis hadn't even looked in the very clean kitchen yet carried no weight, nor did his claim that the builder was booked to install a new toilet in the *apothiki*. As a last resort, Manolis offered the health inspector a sneaky brown envelope. I am proud to report that Thanasis displayed complete professionalism by rejecting the temptation of the bribe out of hand, before commencing a very thorough inspection of every last nook and cranny.

With every last customer summarily turfed out, Thanasis stuck a Notice of Closure on the door, telling the brothers he would return in one month to re-evaluate the situation. He assured them that if they successfully complied with fixing the long list of health and safety requirements that he had discovered they breached, he would be happy to give them the stamp of approval to re-open their business.

"I can't say you didn't warn us, Victor," Manolis dolefully admitted, resigning himself to the temporary closure.

Despite Thanasis decreeing the place must close, Manolis invited the two of us to take a seat and enjoy a coffee on the house. Since all the *brikis* had passed inspection with flying colours, we were happy to accept the offer. Over coffee and *ouzo*, Thanasis and I compared notes on the horrors of some of the grottiest establishments we had inspected, complete with whiffy chefs who failed to practise personal hygiene. Obviously, with my wealth of experience in the field, I had far more revolting stories to share. Thanasis promised to give me a call when he was next on a job in the area, saying he would value my expert opinion if I cared to tag along. I was already looking forward to the opportunity to snoop around some kitchens.

Leaving the Punto parked up at the *kafenio*, I decided to stroll back through the village, making my way home under the stars. Reflecting that although I still occasionally missed my illustrious career as a public health inspector, spending the evening swapping tales with Thanasis had brought home the forgotten tedium of certain aspects of the job. I certainly didn't miss the unpleasant drudge work of uncovering hidden hygiene horrors lurking in the dark recesses behind fridges and cookers, or the feeling of nausea that overcame me when I lifted the lids off pans of suspect sauces, unleashing indescribably noxious smells.

In retrospect, my career had involved a great deal of tedium that I had glamorised in my mind since giving it up, perchance because having a responsible job title carried more clout than that of a kitchen skivvy or humble rep. Looking back on the daily grind of work back in Manchester, I realised it wasn't a patch on retirement in my own little patch of Greek paradise.

As I approached the house, Marigold stepped out of the shadows to meet me, slipping her arm into mine.

"I was watching for you from the balcony? Did you have a fun time with the health inspector?"

Reflecting that I couldn't remember the last time I had enjoyed an evening quite so much, I decided to keep that to myself, simply sharing with Marigold that confabbing with the public health inspector had been an agreeable experience.

"I worried that you may come home full of regret...I did rather badger you into taking early retirement and moving out here," Marigold admitted.

"And I am glad that you did, darling. I have no regrets. I wouldn't trade the wonderful life we've made here together in Meli for anything."

"Not even for the chance of heading up the whole of the Foods Standards Agency," Marigold teased, her lilting laughter contagious.

"How do you fancy joining me for an early morning rendezvous tomorrow, Marigold? I'd love to share the splendour of a glorious Greek sunrise with you by my side.

"You'll have to settle for sharing it with Dot and your mother," Marigold chortled. "You must be out of your mind if you think I'm getting up before the crack of dawn."

A Note from Victor

I hope you enjoyed the latest volume of the Bucket saga.

All Amazon reviews gratefully received, even a word or two is most welcome

Please feel free to drop me a line if you would like information on the release date of future volumes in the *Bucket to Greece* series at
vdbucket@gmail.com
or via Vic Bucket on Facebook.

I am always delighted to hear from happy readers.

Printed in Great Britain
by Amazon